STORIES IN SCRIPTURE AND INSCRIPTIONS

Comparative Studies
on Narratives in
Northwest Semitic Inscriptions
and the Hebrew Bible

SIMON B. PARKER

New York   Oxford   •   Oxford University Press   1997

Oxford University Press

Oxford   New York

Athens   Auckland   Bangkok   Bogota   Bombay   Buenos Aires
Calcutta   Cape Town   Dar es Salaam   Delhi   Florence   Hong Kong
Istanbul   Karachi   Kuala Lumpur   Madras   Madrid   Melbourne
Mexico City   Nairobi   Paris   Singapore   Taipei   Tokyo   Toronto   Warsaw

and associated companies in
Berlin   Ibadan

Published by Oxford University Press, Inc.
198 Madison Avenue, New York, New York 10016

Oxford is a registered trademark of Oxford University Press

Library of Congress Cataloging-in-Publication Data
Parker, Simon B.
Stories in scripture and inscriptions : comparative studies on
narratives in Northwest Semitic inscriptions and the Hebrew Bible /
Simon B. Parker.
p.   cm.
Includes bibliographical references and indexes.
ISBN 0-19-511620-8
1. Narration in the Bible.   2. Bible. O.T.—Criticism,
interpretation, etc.   3. Inscriptions, Semitic.   4. Middle Eastern
literature—Relation to the Old Testament.   I. Title.
BS1171.2.P27   1997
221.6'6—dc21   96-52802

1 3 5 7 9 8 6 4 2

Printed in the United States of America
on acid-free paper

Acknowledgments

The story of the writing of this book has a setting in several institutions and includes several characters other than the author. I am grateful to Boston University for a semester's sabbatical leave that enabled me to write the bulk of this work and to Harvard University, whose Department of Near Eastern Languages and Civilizations granted me the status of visiting scholar during that time (and hence access to the Widener Library), as well as the opportunity to present versions of chapters 2 and 3 to a graduate seminar. The libraries of the Boston Theological Institute and of Brandeis University were additional valuable resources.

I am indebted to my graduate assistant Tim Koch, whose reading of several chapters from the stance of a critical, general reader exposed numerous infelicities of expression and organization; to my colleague Katheryn Pfisterer Darr for her characteristically meticulous editorial annotation of several chapters, which disposed of a large number of unnecessary words; to Edward L. Greenstein, who undertook to read the whole manuscript and made several corrections and suggestions. F. W. Dobbs-Allsop gave me the benefit of his written response to chapter 2.

Thanks to Bruce Zuckerman, I was able to study West Semitic Research's photographs of the Zakkur inscription. Ivan T. Kaufman kindly lent me his photographs of the Siloam inscription.

I should also like to express my gratitude to the editors of Oxford University

Press: to Cynthia Read, who so readily accepted the manuscript, and to Cynthia Garver, who so attentively saw it through production.

Finally, I wish to thank my wife, Sonia, for her continuing confidence and support, my brother, Martin, for staying away during the holidays when I was trying to finish the manuscript, and my sons, Jonathan and Jeremy, for their merciless questioning of whether I was doing any work at all.

Contents

Abbreviations

STORIES IN SCRIPTURE
AND INSCRIPTIONS

Introduction

Reading Biblical and Other Ancient Near Eastern Narratives

Approaches to Biblical Narratives

The study of biblical prose narrative has taken several quite distinct forms in recent decades. The dominant approach in the modern period has been historical. Interest in recovering Israel's and Judah's histories entails an analysis of biblical texts to determine their relation to the past of which they speak. Such analysis includes reconstruction of the literary past of the texts themselves—their origins, their transformation in different contexts over time, and their final adaptation to their various present biblical contexts.[1] This approach uses literary and historical questions and techniques to distinguish different stages in the composition of the text and to relate these stages to specific social and intellectual contexts. Some recent contributions to the ongoing historical enterprise have been increasingly skeptical about the possibility of reconstructing the literary history of biblical texts or the history of which the texts speak.[2] While all would probably agree that biblical narrative is a unique historical testimony to the intellectual and imaginative (and, less directly, social) world of its authors, the periods in which the authors lived and the narratives were composed remain in dispute. Where independent, contemporary documentation is lacking, there is no universally accepted criterion for deciding whether realistic narratives in the Bible are based on historical events or created out of the author's (or the community's) imagination.

During the last few decades, students of biblical narrative have increasingly availed themselves of literary criticism (as that term is understood by readers of

3

modern literatures) in their reading. Such readers use the questions and categories of literary criticism, from classical times to the twentieth century, to illumine the narrative techniques and effects of the texts. While historical study is diachronic, most of this new literary study has been synchronic. While historical critics interpret discrepancies, irregularities, and linguistic and stylistic shifts in the text as evidence of different origins, sources, or layers, many literary critics now interpret every element in the final, present form of the text as part of a single whole. Indeed, some literary critics take the whole biblical canon, the canonical Bible, as the interpretative context for their work, embracing literary criticism on the one hand and the Bible as a distinct corpus of literature on the other.[3] Taking biblical narrative as a whole, they attempt to describe its peculiar narrative assumptions and techniques—its poetics, its narratology.[4] Where historical criticism tends to focus on the relationship between text and the social context of its production, such literary criticism tends to focus on the internal relationships of the text.

Increasingly, however, some literary critics are turning their attention to another relationship, that between text and reader, and to the social context of the reader's "production of meaning." At its most extreme, such literary criticism treats biblical literature in even greater isolation from its cultural environment. The entire transaction takes place between the Bible and the modern reader. This approach puts the reader rather one-sidedly in control of the literature, conforming it to the categories and interests of current criticism without regard to the categories and interests of ancient literature. Rather than seeking to let the literature of ancient Israel address us on its own terms—however remote from ours, and however we may finally judge them—it too easily makes of biblical literature a reflection of our own concerns at the end of the twentieth century, whether secular or theological. But modern readers with no special expertise in criticism or history have recognized again and again that the response of ancient audiences to many features of the stories must have been different from ours. Narrative rhetoric, like any other rhetoric, is designed to create a certain impression on the hearer or reader, and that impression is lessened or confused by a reader's ignorance of the presuppositions of the texts. Some apprehension of the ancient cultural and social environment that the rhetoric presupposed and addressed—in which the composer made his or her choices—is essential for fulfilling the role of "implied reader" (that is, the reader the narrative envisages and whose competence it takes for granted), the first role that the would-be critic should perform in receiving any communication.[5]

In biblical studies, many representatives of each discipline—the historical and the literary—reject the other for largely similar reasons: its alleged lack of rigor and the transience of its results. Admittedly, there are serious limits to our ability both to appreciate ancient Israel's literature and to reconstruct its history. There are limits to our knowledge of the language of the texts, their literary styles and traditions, their social world, their mental world, and the real events and characters to which they may refer. Those who work with these ancient texts must live with uncertainty. Precisely for that reason, separation of the two disciplines is unfortunate. Adequate understanding, explanation, and assessment of ancient texts require attention to all dimensions of a narrative—literary and historical, internal and external, intellectual and social. The reconstruction of a text's prehistory requires attention to the synchronic condition of the text and its environment at any hypothesized stage of its production. By contrast, a "synchronic" reading, just as much as a diachronic reading, is a reading from a particular social and historical context that may also posit a particular social and historical context for the final stage of production of the text—whether a particular pericope or the whole Bible. However stable and fixed the final masoretic text, the production of it was and the reading of it always will be a social and diachronic activity.[6] Literary critics who know the social and intellectual world of ancient Israel and the nature of its text production appreciate the specific character of Israel's narrative texts better than those who read them only as parts of a finished book (collection of books)—on a par with, or in the context of, later literature. Historians who recognize the literary character of the written narratives gain access to ancient Israel's intellectual and social world in a way denied to those who read them naively as direct representations of past events or who dismiss them altogether as historical sources because they do not provide documentary evidence.[7] But as M. Bloch has written: "in the last analysis it is human consciousness which is the subject matter of history. The interrelations, confusions, and infections of human consciousness are, for history, reality itself" (1953, 151).

A third kind of investigation of biblical narrative emerged with the discovery of ancient Near Eastern literature. The recovery of numerous narratives of many different types from throughout the Near East over the last two centuries has encouraged comparative studies of these and biblical narratives. Such studies have usually addressed to some extent both historical and literary questions, attending to literary characteristics and qualities of each narrative and to its historical and social character as the product of a particular culture, time, and place. The best comparative studies of this kind recognize that narratives in ancient literature are produced not only out of a particular culture but also out of a larger narrative tradition, and that comparison with other similar narratives in that tradition— serving the same purpose, using the same structure, or referring to the same subject—reveals aspects of a text that might remain hidden or a matter of speculation in an analysis of one narrative alone. Comparative study may lessen the conjectural element in historical analysis by providing exemplars of hypothetical earlier versions of a story and lessen the subjective element in literary criticism by exposing what is traditional, conventional, or generic in a story.[8] While excessive concentration on similarities or differences among texts distorts any conclusions about their relationship, giving due weight to both contributes to the understanding and explanation both of the individual narrative and of the features it shares with others.

The essays in this book are examples of comparative study. They set narratives preserved in the Bible beside narratives preserved in inscriptions from Judah and its cultural milieu—Northwest-Semitic–speaking Syria-Palestine—and they address both literary and historical questions as a means of shedding fresh light on the character, function, and history of these ancient narratives. They attempt to engage the worlds the ancient texts create and also to probe the traditions they presuppose. While the focus is of necessity on the written texts, I seek to bring into peripheral view their social background: the speakers and hearers of these stories which were recorded in writing.

Biblical and Ancient Near Eastern Narratives

The last two decades have seen the publication of several books that attempt to describe the narrative techniques and qualities of biblical prose narrative (see n. 4). One aspect of this enterprise has been definition of the distinctiveness of that corpus by contrast with other ancient literatures. Thus Meir Sternberg has written that "the Bible's reality model and its compositional status are poles apart from the Homeric or Near Eastern" (1985, 88). Sternberg here has in mind particularly the place and function of omniscient narration. The omniscience of ancient Near Eastern narrators stands against the epistemological limitations of all their characters, both human and divine. The omniscience of the biblical narrators stands in the service of an omniscient character, Yahweh. For Sternberg, the major contrast between ancient Near Eastern (and Homeric) narrative and biblical narrative is a function of the contrast between monotheism and polytheism. He contrasts the biblical narrative corpus with the polytheistic narrative tradition of the ancient Near East and identifies biblical monotheism as a significant factor accounting for differences between the two. What is the value of these comparisons and this conclusion?

It is generally recognized in comparative studies that the less like the things being compared, the less valuable the comparison. Similarities will be too few and slight to allow significant generalizations, and differences will be too many and obvious to sharpen the definition of the individual entities being compared. Thus, for example, we would not expect a comparison of Homer and Hesiod with the narrative corpus of the New Testament—the Gospels and Acts of the Apostles—to reveal anything significant about the characteristics of New Testament narrative (or Homer or Hesiod).[9] For similar reasons, general comparison of biblical prose narrative with Mesopotamian (or Greek, etc.) poetic narrative is not particularly illuminating. Occasional individual features of biblical prose narratives may fruitfully be compared with some elements of the old mythic-epic tradition (see n. 10), but before comparing the two corpora as wholes we should consider whether they are really comparable. Two fundamental differences between the two corpora suggest that they are not.

First, the biblical narrative corpus is by definition part of that body of literature selected, compiled, and designated by Jewish religious leaders in Hellenistic and Roman times as the authoritative religious and national tradition. Biblical narrative as such is interpreted within the dominant monotheistic, didactic, historical framework of this collection, rather than in the contexts of the society, culture, and literary activity in which the narratives were first produced. Sternberg's book is an impressive example of such interpretation (1985). There is, however, no comparable ancient Near Eastern religious-national canon in the context of which ancient Near Eastern narratives are interpreted that might serve as the basis for comparison and contrast. Without such a canon, we can only compare unlike with unlike.

Second, even disregarding their secondary biblical context, Israelite prose narratives belong to genres quite different from that of ancient Near Eastern mythic-epic poetry (the primary narrative expression of polytheism which Sternberg has in view, along with Homer). To characterize the one by contrast with the other is analogous to characterizing the modern novel by contrast with the "Christian epics" of Dante or Milton. Admittedly, a few brief texts preserved in biblical prose narrative may be claimed to be in different ways an extension of the mythic-epic tradition,[10] and comparing these with that tradition sharpens our perception of their distinctiveness. But such specific comparisons make even clearer that a gross comparison of the two large corpora of narratives is a comparison of incomparables.

Thus, the comparison of most biblical narratives with ancient Near Eastern mythic-epic narratives appears to be a category mistake. Israel did not have mythic-epic literature, and no ancient Near Eastern society had a Bible. On the one hand, the cuneiform mythic-epic tradition is poetic in form and had its written foundations in the second millennium, with little original, creative work in the first millennium.[11] Israel's narrative literature, on the other hand, is a prose corpus composed entirely in the first millennium. In fact, virtually all surviving or recovered Northwest Semitic narrative literature of the first millennium from the Assyrian to the Persian periods is prose.

To say something precise about the distinctiveness of narratives preserved in the Bible vis-à-vis narratives of their ancient Near Eastern environment requires that we meet two conditions corresponding inversely to these two objections to the comparison by Sternberg and others. First, we must take biblical narratives not in their final, heteronomous, canonical context, but on their own terms as large-scale or small-scale literary creations. (Given the incorporation of shorter narratives into ever larger narrative compositions in the Bible, it is important to recognize in smaller-scale narrative units substantive links with the larger context and in larger-scale units the resistant integrity of component narratives.) Second, we must compare prose narratives with prose narratives and, within that comprehensive category, prose narratives with prose narratives from the same general period or cultural milieu, and of the same genre or type.

There are several prose narratives in Northwest Semitic inscriptions recovered from ancient Israel and its Syro-Palestinian environment and dating from the 250 years before the fall of Jerusalem (587 BCE). Several of these epigraphic narratives have significant features in common with narratives now incorporated in the Bible. A comparison of these biblical and extrabiblical materials may suggest and authorize some conclusions about relations between Israelite prose narratives preserved in the Bible and epigraphic prose narratives from Israel and its environment during the Assyrian period. The limited body of epigraphic evidence cannot be expected to permit significant generalizations about the uniqueness or origins of Israelite narrative, but it may eliminate some false generalizations and lead to some specific conclusions about particular types of narratives. Within the limits of the few types represented, such comparisons promise to cast some fresh light on parts of ancient Israel's narrative tradition.

Little detailed attention has been paid as yet to narratives in Northwest Semitic inscriptions. The inscriptions have been studied intensively, but much of that study, valuable and fruitful in various spheres, has neglected or ignored the narrative material qua narrative. One scholar who has considered these inscriptions in the context of a study of Israelite historiography is John Van Seters. In his monograph on ancient historiography, Van Seters concludes a review of the major memorial inscriptions of Iron Age Syria-Palestine by raising the question whether Israel or Judah may have had similar royal memorial inscriptions: "The general uniformity of these memorial texts in the Levant, especially in the ninth and eighth centuries B.C. from Karatepe in the north to Moab in the southeast, suggests that such texts were not unknown in Israel and Judah, even if none has yet been found" (1983, 195; the suggestion is repeated on p. 298). The alleged "general uniformity" of these texts, however, is more apparent than real. The few major memorial inscriptions from Syria-Palestine are, on closer inspection, surprisingly diverse in form, subject matter, and style (see chapters 4, 5, and 6 in this volume). But this is no argument against the possibility that the kings of Judah and Israel produced memorial inscriptions. Although no such inscriptions have been found in Israel or Judah, despite the extent of excavation in Israel,[12] the comparisons in chapters 4 and 5 suggest a more specific judgment on this question.

Van Seters goes further, suggesting on the basis of two stylistic features found both in the inscriptions and in the books of Kings that these "may in fact indicate that historical narrative in inscriptions influenced biblical historiographic prose in general" (1983, 300). The detailed comparative study of narratives in three major royal inscriptions with the most closely related biblical prose narratives (chapters 4, 5, and 6) should either support or weaken this hypothesis.

Oral Storytelling in Ancient Israel and Judah

While more written texts have been recovered from the territory of ancient Israel and Judah than from other Syro-Palestinian states of the Iron Age, the yield remains slight. Even after acknowledging the loss of writings on perishable materials such as papyrus and leather, it must be admitted that the paucity of writings on the cheapest, imperishable materials—stone and potsherds or ostraca—suggests very little writing activity for a population of a few hundred thousand over a period of four centuries (early tenth to early sixth centuries).[13] Inscriptions in Judah are negligible until the eighth and seventh centuries, after which they again disappear. Their significant rise in number during those two centuries correlates with other archaeological indicators of state development at that time, and their distribution suggests the correlation of literacy with close ties with and dependence on Jerusalem—confirmed by the absence of inscriptions after Jerusalem's destruction and the collapse of central organization in Judah.[14] Writing was thus almost certainly restricted to people in the service of the government and, judging by the content of the inscriptions, was used largely for official business.[15] The only substantial literary narrative recovered from these communities is the Balaam inscription from Tell Deir ʿAlla, east of the Jordan, which is both too damaged and too little understood to justify its inclusion in this volume.[16] Most written texts dated to the period of the kingdoms of Israel and Judah either served some immediate practical purpose, such as communication (witness the letters written on ostraca found at Lachish and Arad) or short-term record-keeping (such as the administrative notes written on ostraca found at Samaria), or more emblematic purposes (such as inscriptions on seals, which abound inside and outside Israel).[17]

If ancient Judah and Israel and the other small states of Syria-Palestine were oral societies in which only a very small minority of the population could write—and those probably all officials in the service of the royal government—virtually all "literature" must have been oral. (To avoid the oxymoron "oral literature" Jack Goody has proposed the term "standardized oral forms.") Although the surviving literature contains no reference to specialized storytellers in ancient Israel or its environment, there must have been numerous settings and occasions in these societies, like all others—including modern, highly literate societies[18]—in and on which people told stories: in nuclear and extended family settings; in respites during work in the fields, at court, at religious gatherings, and not least at the city gates, where so much social business was done. The evidence for oral story-telling is limited but suggestive. Israelite narrative literature depicts a variety of situations in which individuals tell stories for various purposes. To cite just a few examples: a follower of a miracle worker recites miracle stories to entertain the monarch at court (2 Kgs 8:4–5a); political figures recite fables to hostile political powers as instruments of persuasion (Jdg 9:6–21; 2 Kgs 14:7–12); in the trial of a prophet for announcing the destruction of the temple in Jerusalem, elders tell a story of the royal response to a similar prophecy in the past (Jer 26:17–19); a social group concocts a story to trick its neighbors into an alliance (Josh 9:9–13); and various individuals recite (true and false) petitionary narratives to win a par-ticular decision from the king or other person of influence (on which see chapter 2). Only the latter is attested epigraphically, but the others cannot be dismissed. Their narrative contexts require that they be realistic, so that, though the actual events may not have been historical, hearers of those larger narratives would find them credible.

One kind of story that must have been common in Israel's (and its neighbors') oral culture would have told of adventures in war—especially, perhaps, of memo-rable victories or escapes. Stories of actual events may have been recounted ini-tially in the first person by participants or survivors, or possibly in the third person by observers. In either case, hearers of stories that were particularly impres-sive or politically significant might then transmit them further in the third person.

But the retelling of stories involves their reinterpretation. In the long term, we have seen such reinterpretation in the retelling of biblical stories over two millen-nia. Many quite secular stories incorporated into the Bible have, because of that context and the cultural context of readers, been retold and interpreted in religious terms over the centuries. In recent times, by contrast, the religious literature of the Bible has been read and reinterpreted in secular terms. In prebiblical, Israelite times, too, shifts in social and historical context produced changes in the telling and interpretation of stories. As we know from ethnographic studies, versions vary with the occasion and teller, and with his or her purpose with respect to the specific audience.

In many settings, stories would have been told, not so much for an immediate practical end, but to express, reinforce, or deepen people's understanding of their experience.

> When one looks to the social practices by which social life is accomplished, one finds—with surprising frequency—people telling stories to each other, as a means of giving cognitive and emotional coherence to experience, constructing and negotiating social identity; investing the experiential landscape with moral significance in a way that can be brought to bear on human behavior; generating, interpreting, and transforming the work experience; and a host of other reasons. (Bauman 1986, 113, with bibliographical references)

Such oral stories may be quite sophisticated in their techniques: "everyday oral stories demonstrate the same complexities in manipulating point of view, identity of reference, and multiplicity of meaning which have hitherto been treated as special qualities of literary language" (Polanyi 1982, 155).[19]

Given the ubiquity of stories in any society, the question for a largely oral society is not: Does this written story go back to oral tradition? but rather: Why was this story put in writing? The second question may be difficult or impossible to answer, but the first must be judged nugatory. Since originality was not prized in these societies as it is in ours, writers of stories, even if not deliberately recording a story they had heard, would consciously or unconsciously build on and echo heard stories. The presumption must be in favor of oral antecedents, except where specific literary antecedents can be demonstrated (as most obviously in the case of stories in Kings retold by the Chronicler).[20]

Since storytelling was primarily an oral activity in these societies, the fixed, written material we now have before us is a by-product of an ongoing social process: the telling and retelling of stories. Further, in a largely oral society, the commitment of a story to writing does not end the ongoing retelling and adapting of that story to fresh circumstances and new audiences. Later oral versions may well contribute to the work of later scribes "copying" an earlier written version. Such additions from the oral tradition, as well as purely scribal variants, were part of the history of the biblical text during the centuries of freer written transmission before it was permanently fixed in its final form.[21] The text we have is thus at a considerable remove from its first written form and therefore far from being an immediate reflex of its original oral environment. All of the epigraphic narrative material, however, comes to us as the only written deposit of the narrative in question and as the product of the author during his or her lifetime.[22] Unlike biblical narratives, inscriptions are an immediate by-product of the oral culture in which they were produced. Careful analysis of these narratives may shed more direct light on this environment.

The Stories Treated in This Book

The following studies benefit from numerous philological and historical studies of the inscriptions but attempt to go beyond these in analysis of the inscriptions' literary characteristics and especially of their use of narrative. The main limitation of the inscriptions in this context is the number and scale of the narratives found in them. But the few that we have include not only minimal narrative (that is, a narrative consisting of two successive, connected events) and minimal story (consisting of two states of affairs separated and differentiated by an event)[23] but also more fully developed stories and, in one case, a chain of related stories. The briefer stories are best seen as examples of the reduction or précis of the told story, what Campbell has called "the reported story" (1989).[24]

In the Bible, by contrast, narratives abound, ranging from telescoped, reported stories to expansive, elaborated narratives. Although the Bible as such dates from the end of the pre-Christian era, the writing down of its narratives ranges in date from the second century BCE to several centuries earlier.[25] This book sets aside the final context of the canon[26] in order to read Israelite narratives in their earlier (prebiblical or precanonical) forms and environments without the superimposed, defining term "biblical." Most of the stories discussed in the following chapters are incorporated into the very long and complex narrative comprising several "books" known as the Deuteronomistic History, generally regarded as a product primarily of the sixth century, though with some older sources and later additions.[27] But texts with a history—all biblical texts and, as we shall see, some epigraphic texts—have varying social and cultural environments. My aim is to read narratives in the inscriptions and comparable narratives preserved in the Bible in ways that take account of their different contexts and histories, focusing on their written, literary character, but recognizing that they are originally the products of largely oral communities.

The next two chapters examine narratives in two Hebrew inscriptions: the petitionary narrative on an ostracon from Mesad Hashavyahu (late seventh century), which is contrasted with several petitionary narratives in Samuel and Kings; and the story of the completion of the Siloam tunnel—originally inscribed on the wall of the tunnel at the end of the eighth century—which is compared with three minimal accounts of the construction of the tunnel in Kings, Chronicles, and Sirach.

The subsequent three chapters investigate narratives in several royal inscriptions from Israel's closer and more remote neighbors. First, the stories of the military campaigns of King Mesha of Moab in the one extensive Moabite inscription (second half of the ninth century) are compared with accounts of similar campaigns in Kings and similar summaries of David's and Joshua's campaigns in (respectively) 2 Samuel and Joshua. Other campaign narratives from the contemporary Aramaic inscription from Tel Dan and the Aramaic treaty from Sefire (mid-eighth century) are also considered here. Next, a brief and a lengthier account of a particular diplomatic strategy from two inscriptions from Zinjirli (one Phoenician from the third quarter of the ninth century, and one Samalian from the third quarter of the eighth) are compared with two narratives from Kings and brief accounts of a similar strategy in Kings, Samuel, and Deuteronomy. Finally, a story of miraculous deliverance from a siege in the Aramaic inscription of Zak-kur of Hamath is compared with four stories of such deliverance from Kings.

The concluding chapter not only summarizes the fruits of the comparisons but also reviews what has been discovered of the narratives' social and historical contexts and explores the implications of the presence or absence of a divine role in the narratives. Through these studies, I hope to enable the narratives to speak across, instead of through, more than two millennia and to assist readers around the turn of another millennium to encounter at least a few of these narratives afresh.

Petitionary Narratives

Individual Israelites or Judeans, in difficulties that neither they nor their families could overcome, had recourse to other agents of relief. Normally, they would turn first to the town elders, heads of families of the *mishpāḥâ*.[1] In some circumstances, however, these were not satisfactory avenues for assistance. Perhaps the local authorities had acted unjustly, taking advantage of their position to exploit those with limited resources or influence, or favoring the party under whom the aggrieved had suffered. Perhaps the local authorities had officially ruled against the injured party. Under such circumstances, those who had been wronged addressed a petition to a higher authority. During the monarchies, the final such authority was the king (2 Sam 15:2–6 and other passages to be reviewed shortly). Servants of the king and inhabitants of the capital city probably brought their cases directly to the king. The appointment of regional judges and of a supreme court apart from the king appears as an innovation at the end of the monarchy (in Deut 16:18; 17:8–9).[2]

Often, the justice or legality of an action or legal decision was not at issue at all—the complainant was simply appealing for relief from adverse circumstances. In such cases, the petitioner may have addressed, not those responsible for the administration of justice, but anyone who, the petitioner believed, could help him or her.[3]

Two aspects of the petition had a crucial bearing on its success: the facts of the case and the rhetoric of their presentation. Unless the hearer was already familiar with the petitioner and his or her situation, an essential element of a petition was the petitioner's account of what had caused his or her current distress. The petitioner might add other elements: a reference to the availability of witnesses, a reminder of past good behavior, praise of the hearer's discernment, confidence in his ability to bring relief, a direct appeal for compassion, or indeed, in theory, anything that the petitioner calculated would have the desired effect. But the narrative presentation of the facts was the foundation of the petition—and might be so effective that further elaboration was unnecessary. In other words, the petitioner's chances of success depended significantly on his or her ability to construct a narrative that itself compelled the hearer to respond with a particular decision or action. At issue is the individual Israelite's ability to tell a story in such a way as to lead the hearer to a specific, desired response. Such stories are the subject of this chapter.

To begin this investigation with the petitionary narrative, then, is to start with the ordinary Israelite's storytelling ability. Storytelling ability refers here to the skill with which relevant events from an individual's experience are selected and ordered, speeches composed, character limned and responsibility assigned, words chosen and arranged, and the point of view and finally the judgment of the hearer affected. More imaginative creativity was required only in exceptional circumstances, to be discussed toward the end of the chapter.

Characteristically, the petitionary narrative is incomplete: it reaches a climax, which the addressee is expected to resolve by his action in the present. Its incompleteness as story is part of the rhetorical pressure the petitioner brings to bear on the addressee. Once the story has been resolved by the addressee's action in real time, it may be retold by the petitioner to others as a complete story, with the addressee of the petition, now in the third person, providing the resolution. Ultimately, if found to be of interest and value, it may be retold by others with the petitioner also in the third person.

Further, the petitionary narrative expresses the point of view of a particular party. The rhetoric of the petitionary narrative is designed to make his or her version of the story so compelling as to ensure a particular outcome. Where the distress arises from a dispute with another party, the rhetoric of the petitionary narrative attempts to convey equally the justice of the petitioner and the injustice of the injury suffered. But the narrative unintentionally implies that it may be told from another point of view: that of the other party.

Petitions were normally presented orally and so are inaccessible to the modern reader. In ancient Israel we have two different perspectives on the nature of the typical oral petitionary narrative. One derives from a written version of an actual petition, which we owe to the fact that the petitioner could not see the official in question and had to resort to dictating the petition to a scribe, in the expectation or hope that this written version would reach the official. This is a real petition, but the medium in which it appears—an inscription—is abnormal; the context in which it was used can only be inferred. The second perspective derives from several biblical narratives in which a petition is quoted. These are literary rather than actual petitions, but the narrative contexts present them as oral speeches and provide them with specific social settings. While these petitions reflect the artistry of the writers, part of that artistry is replication of the essential characteristics of an oral petition.

The preceding general characterization of the oral petitionary narrative derives from these two perspectives. It will, in turn, illumine our reading of each of the petitionary narratives reviewed in the rest of this chapter.

The Mesad Hashavyahu Inscription

In 1960, excavations were conducted at a small fortress, now called Mesad Hasha-vyahu, on the Judean coast halfway between Joppa and Ashdod. It was evidently a shortlived Judean outpost around 600 BCE (Wenning 1989, 169–96). In a guard-room of the fortress, excavators found a number of inscribed broken sherds that once constituted a single ostracon. This had been used in the later seventh century to write a fourteen-line message.[4]

> (1–2) Let my lord, the officer, hear the case of his servant.
> (2–6) Your servant was reaping, was your servant, in Hasar-ʾasam. Your servant reaped and measured and stored for days before stopping.
> (6–9) When your [se]rvant had measured his harvest and stored it for days, Ho-shaʿyahu ben Shobay came and took your servant's garment. When I had measured my harvest for days, he took your servant's garment.
> (10–12) And all my comrades will testify for me, those who were reaping with me in the heat of the sun, my comrades, will testify for me. Truly,[5] I am innocent of any of[fence.
> (12–14) Please restore][6] my garment. But if it is not[7] your duty to resto[re your servant's garment, then sho]w him mer[cy and resto]re your [ser]vant's [gar-ment] and do not ignore [[8]

The message is addressed to "my lord, the officer" by "his servant." It is evident from the contents of the inscription that the sender is a field-worker and that he is directing a petition to a local authority—presumably the officer in charge of the fortress. We must suppose that the peasant came to the fortress seeking the commander's intervention on his behalf but was denied access to him. Petitioners had to catch the official in question when they could, as is evident in several biblical examples (1 Kgs 20:38–39; 2 Kgs 5:26; 8:5). We owe the preservation of this petition to the unavailability of the commander of Mesad Hashavyahu. The worker's only means of communication with the authority was evidently in writing, and so he dictated the burden of his message to a scribe. Presumably a scribe was maintained at the entrance to the fortress to record deliveries, messages, and the like, as needed. (That an official scribe was involved is suggested both by the fluency of the writing and by the fact that the ostracon had been specially prepared for writing: the edges were chipped to produce straight sides.)

The message consists of four parts.[9] The first is an introductory appeal for a hearing: "Let my lord, the officer, hear the case of his servant" (ll. 1–2). (David used a similar formula in his appeal to Saul in 1 Sam 26:19: "Let my lord the king hear the words of his servant.") As noted by Naveh in the first edition of the inscription, this opening statement is marked off from the rest of the message by its third-person reference to the addressee (Naveh 1960). It is the one formal sentence in the whole text and was either provided by the scribe or included by the peasant because it was universally familiar as the opening formula used by an inferior in petitioning a superior. In any case, it functions like the abstract of a narrative, expressing the point of what follows, the purpose for which the narrative is told. The second part is the narrative itself (ll. 2–9). Third is a reference to the availability of witnesses (ll. 10–11) and the speaker's assertion of his innocence (ll. 11–12). This is the most forensic part of the petition. Witnesses and oaths of innocence are used in formal trials, and the peasant's reference to both here suggests his willingness to appear in a formal court.[10] Yet, he is not asking for such a trial.[11] As the text concludes with the spelling out of the petition proper, the direct appeal to the officer is for the return of the garment (ll. 12–end). Here, the desperation of the petitioner is clear. He concedes that the commander may not see himself as under any obligation to return the garment and so begs him to return it at least out of compassion (ll. 12–14). This last section—in effect, the climax of the petition—is more personal and emotional than the preceding. Although the document stands as our only written record of an actual petition, there is no reason to consider any of these elements atypical.

One stylistic feature dominates this inscription: repetition. Almost throughout, the speaker makes his statements twice, repeating the same thought in only slightly different words. Thus: "Your servant reaped and measured and stored for days before stopping. When your servant had measured his harvest and stored it for days" (ll. 4–7); and: "When your servant had measured his harvest and stored it for some days, Hosha'yahu ben Shobay came and took your servant's garment. When I had measured my harvest for days he took your servant's garment" (ll. 6–9). (In the last section of the inscription, the three-fold repetition of "return your servant's/my garment" depends heavily on restoration.) Sometimes the sentence boundaries are uncertain. In lines 10–11, "those who harvested with me in the heat of the sun" may be read with the preceding or following sentences (in apposition to "my fellow-workers" in each case). But in view of the repetitive style of this document, I am inclined to render these lines with one sentence: "All my fellow-workers will testify for me, those who harvested with me in the heat of the sun, my fellow-workers, they will testify for me" (similarly Smelik 1992b, 56). If this characterization of the style of the text is valid, the first statement of the narrative should probably be translated something like: "Your servant was harvesting, was your servant, in Hasar-'asam" (ll. 2–4).[12] It seems better to read each of these two passages as one sentence with pleonasm, rather than as two sentences.

This style is neither elegant nor economical. While the repetition serves in part to emphasize the facts of the case, as seen by the speaker, the clumsiness must reflect the manner of speech of the illiterate author (perhaps exaggerated by his agitation and anxiety under the circumstances), as he pours out his story to the scribe.[13] Inferior as it is in aesthetic qualities, it is a rare piece of evidence for the voice of a simple peasant—the only such voice we hear among the few passages of continuous prose recovered from ancient Israel. We owe its recording to the mechanical, literal way the scribe fulfilled his task, making no attempt to polish or refine the peasant's expression. Presumably he did not receive the kind of baksheesh that would have persuaded him to make the presentation as appealing and persuasive as possible.

We turn now to the peasant's narrative. It may be outlined as follows:

Orientation or exposition: I was reaping in Hasar-'asam, and reaped, measured and stored for some days (lines 2–6).
Complication: Hosha'yahu then came and took my garment (lines 6–9).

As noted, the story of the petitionary narrative is incomplete. But this document allows us to fill out the rest of the story for ourselves. Its climax is represented by the whole document as a performative utterance: the appeal to the official for redress. The content of the final appeal—return of the garment by the official—constitutes the desired resolution of the story. Thus we can predict the general form of the whole story, if it were recounted after a favorable judgment by the official.

In this particular narrative, as we have seen, the unsophisticated rhetoric of the field-worker is characterized by repetition of clauses, phrases, and individual words. He presents very few facts—he was doing his job and Hosha'yahu took his garment. The repeated references to his working seek to convince the implied hearer that he was fulfilling his obligations. But the lack of any explanation for Hosha'yahu's taking his garment leaves the reader uncertain about the legality of this act.[14] The one reference to stopping work in lines 5–6 perhaps explains Hosha'yahu's action. But the narrative presents the stopping as nothing in comparison to the ongoing work; if that is Hosha'yahu's reason, it is belittled and pushed aside. The narrative conceals, rather than discloses, what the reader needs to know. Possibly the peasant could take for granted that the commander of the fortress was already familiar with the general situation. If he could not, there is a vagueness in the account of the alleged wrong that invites rejection of the petition. (Compare the vagueness in the "soldier's" petitionary narrative—which was rejected—in 1 Kgs 20:39b-40a [discussed later in this chapter]). In comparison with the biblical examples to be reviewed, the modern reader must judge this a very inadequate petitionary narrative.[15]

Perhaps his awareness of the inadequacy of his narrative rhetoric leads the peasant finally to throw himself on the official's mercy (ll. 12–14). He has little sense of what the commander might consider relevant evidence, does not anticipate possible objections to the case he has made, and has little confidence in the effectiveness of his witnesses or his own assertion of innocence. Ultimately, he depends not on being able to present a compelling legal case—he perhaps knows how the stronger argument can be made to appear the weaker in a court of law, or may even fear that Hosha'yahu has the law on his side—but on the concluding appeal. In any case, he does not want a trial. He just wants his garment back.

As noted before, the efficacy of the petitionary narrative depends on its presentation of the right of the petitioner and the wrong of the injury suffered. But the peasant is unable to communicate either of these. If the commander heard his petition and bothered to inquire into the matter, the other party, Hosha'yahu, might have the opportunity to recount his version of the case. His narrative would focus on the same event but recount it from a different point of view—perhaps including additional information, perhaps elegantly worded—giving his reason why he "took" the petitioner's garment, but possibly also denying that "fact."

Petitionary Narratives in the Bible

The Mesad Hashavyahu inscription is an actual petition. Biblical petitions, by contrast, are the compositions of Israelite authors.[16] But whereas the inscription is preserved in a scribal record divorced from its original social context, the petitions in the Deuteronomistic History occur in narratives in which they are presented as oral speeches functioning in specific social contexts. Further, since all these petitions appear in literary contexts in which they have a larger narrative function, full appreciation of them demands attention to those present narrative contexts.

These biblical petitions have two other general characteristics which distinguish them from that of Mesad Hashavyahu. First, they include all the pertinent information and, except in one case, eliminate virtually everything except the narrative. Second, they are economical and effective. As used by biblical narrators, petitions depend almost exclusively on the narrative art of the petitioner—his or her rhetorical power as a storyteller.[17]

2 Kings 8:1–6

Before turning to the specific forms and uses of actual petitionary narratives in biblical literature, we may usefully compare and contrast with the Mesad Hashavyahu petition the account of a petition in 2 Kings 8:5–6. This account is complementary to the inscription: the inscription constitutes an actual petition, preserved in writing but lacking any context; 2 Kings 8 refers to a petition and provides the social context—the occasion, the parties, and the outcome—but does not quote the petition itself.

The king is listening to Gehazi's stories about Elisha, when, in the middle of the story about Elisha's revival of a woman's dead son, in comes the woman in question (*wehinnēh hā'iššâ* . . .), appealing (or petitioning, *ṣô'eqet*)[18] for (or concerning, *'al*) her house and land (cf. v. 3b: "she went off to appeal to the king for her house and land" *liṣ'ōq 'el-hammelek 'el-bêtâ we'el śādāh*). After Gehazi has identified her, "the king enquired of the woman and she gave him an account" *(wayyiš'al hammelek lā'iššâ wattĕsapper lô).*

Why is the petitionary narrative not quoted? The point of the story which this episode concludes is the coincidence of the woman's appearance with Gehazi's telling of her story. This brings together two distinct narrative lines: the woman's departure from Israel at Elisha's initiative, stay in Philistia, return, and setting out to appeal to the king for her estate (vv. 1–3) and Gehazi's response to the king's request for stories about Elisha's great deeds (vv. 4–5a). The force of the coincidence is noted both by the narrator ("and there was the woman . . . !" *wehinnēh* v. 5a) and by Gehazi (v. 5b). The woman's appearance authenticates Gehazi's story, and Gehazi's story disposes the king favorably toward the petitioner. Passing notice of the king's enquiry of her and of her account leads to the conclusion of the story, which spells out the king's generous disposition of the petition of this woman "whose son Elisha revived" (the story's refrain). For the biblical story, what is of interest is not the details of the woman's speech but the continuing reputation and influence of Elisha.

Nevertheless, several fairly standard features of the biblical use of the petitionary narrative appear here. First, the petitioner interrupts the official in the course of some other activity—precisely what the fieldworker failed to do. Second, the verb *ṣ'q* appears to be used of the action of appealing or petitioning. In such contexts, however, it may have the more narrow sense of "appeal for a hearing," referring, that is, to the opening statement or cry of the petitioner (it appears in only one of the three cases in which an opening appeal is quoted and in all three cases in which it is not). On the two occasions when the opening appeal is "Help (*hôšî'â*), oh king (my lord)!," the king replies: "What is the matter?" (2 Sam 14:5a; 2 Kgs 6:28; cf. 1 Kgs 1:16), inviting the petitioner to proceed. If *ṣ'q* does refer to such an appeal for a hearing, mention in 2 Kings 8:6 of the king's enquiry of the woman may refer to such a response. Third, the petitioner recounts or narrates her story. Here, where the story is not quoted, her speech is referred to by the verb *spr*, a word more suited to narration than a nonnarrative appeal.[19] The subject of the narrative has already been supplied in the earlier references to her appeal (vv. 3b and 5a), so its repetition here is unnecessary.

In other cases, the petitionary narrative is quoted because of its significance in the narrative context, expecially as an object of interpretation and a device for eliciting judgments. In what follows, the most interesting biblical examples are presented in order of increasing artistic complexity.

2 Kings 4:1–7

While most petitionary narratives preserved in the Bible are addressed to the king—he being the ultimate court—any individual in critical need might petition any appropriate official (as in the case of the field-worker) or, indeed, as the next passage shows, any person of power or influence.[20] The petition in 2 Kings 4:1–7 is addressed to a prophet. The petition itself is very abbreviated in favor of an extended account of the prophet's response (vv. 2–7). A certain woman appealed (*ṣā'ăqâ*) to Elisha. The quoted petition follows immediately, a narrative without any of the other components of the petition that we saw in that of the fieldworker. The narrative consists of three clauses, the first two constituting the orientation or exposition and the third the complication.

> Your servant, my husband, has died—and you know that your servant feared Yahweh—
> and the creditor has come to take my two children to be his servants.

The rhetoric of the exposition is significant. The dead man is identified first as "your servant" and only secondarily as "my husband," and the first term is used again in the one other reference to him (in the second clause), emphasizing the relationship between Elisha and the deceased. The second clause gives that relationship specific content: the introductory "you know that" insists that the addressee is a witness to the dead man's piety.[21] Thus, the rhetoric of the exposition asserts the addressee's familiarity with the merit of the deceased and implies his obligations toward his "servant's" widow. The merit of the needy party and the obligations of the addressee toward that party press the addressee toward a favorable judgment or action.

The petition is not for legal justice—the creditor is presumably acting within his rights. The process by which the man's family fell into debt and the legitimacy of the creditor's claims are therefore irrelevant. Consequently, the complication ignores developments leading up to the present crisis, concentrating exclusively on the latter.[22] That is all that Elisha (and the reader) needs to know. This account of the woman's desperate situation renders any additional appeal superfluous. By identifying the man in question, reminding Elisha of his obligations, and referring to the immediate crisis, the woman achieves her aim; with Elisha's reply, the narrator achieves his goal of exhibiting Elisha's care for the families of his prophetic followers, as well as his miraculous powers (so Würthwein 1984, 288). The petitionary narrative serves both the personal interests of the petitioner and the larger interests of the narrator.

1 Kings 3:16–27

In its present context, 1 Kings 3:16–27 demonstrates Solomon's wisdom, granted him by Yahweh in a dream (3:5–14), through a test, a seemingly unresolvable legal case.[23] The story and its main point are well known, but it will reward closer inspection in this context. Two women come before the king.[24] One speaks, beginning with a self-deprecating address: "(17) Forgive me, my lord"—in effect, an appeal for a hearing (cf. the opening words of the field-worker's petition.)[25] She then begins her narrative. The exposition or orientation describes the general situation: "I and this woman live in the same house.[26] I gave birth with her in the house. (18) Then on the third day after my giving birth, this woman also gave birth. We were together, with nobody else with us in the house, just the two of us in the house." Then comes the complication: "(19) Then this woman's son died during the night—she lay on him. (20) And so she got up in the middle of the night and took my son from beside me—your maidservant was asleep—and laid him beside her, and her dead son she laid beside me. (21) When I got up in the morning to feed my son, there was a dead child! But when I looked at it carefully in the morning light, it wasn't my son, whom I had born, at all!"[27] The narrative gives all and only the information necessary for the hearer to grasp the situation and appreciate the wrong the woman has suffered. The introduction and exposition depict the shared house, the births of the two babies. The absence of any others is emphasized in the verbless clauses of v. 18b, which draw attention to themselves by interrupting the narrative flow and separating the exposition of prior events from the critical events now demanding resolution. Since the women are prostitutes, it may be necessary to emphasize that, following the births of the two babies, there were no clients in the house. Verse 21a then describes what the speaker discovered in the morning—a dead child beside her. The final event is her recognition that this is not her child (v. 21b). This realization explains and justifies the allegations of vv. 19–20 (for the only witness to the actions recounted there was the actor, the other woman—who will deny them!) The only explanation for what she finds in the morning is that the other woman has put the dead child there and taken her live child. The recounting of the reconstructed events in chronological order is an appropriate rhetorical strategy for a petitionary narrative. To begin the complication with the discovery of the dead child and then to spell out what are in fact inferences concerning what had happened in the night would weaken the case; the initial surprise and mystery of discovering the dead child and the subsequent unraveling of what must have happened would cultivate the hearer's and reader's intellectual curiosity, rather than emotional sympathy.

Apart from the opening address, the petition consists entirely of a narrative. Corresponding to the field-worker's reference to witnesses is the statement that no one else was present; that is, there were no witnesses. This absence of witnesses explains why the woman must bring her case to the king. Perhaps his wisdom and judgment will not have to rely on witnesses (cf. Prov 25:2; 16:10). For the narrator, by contrast, the lack of witnesses closes the circle, ensuring that the king is faced exclusively with two conflicting testimonies and that readers will conclude that the only judgment they could give is *non liquet*.

This petition also lacks a final appeal. But like that of the woman who appealed to Elisha, it has no need of one. The narrative has stated the case clearly and fully. All the relevant facts have been presented. It requires only the implied resolution that the woman hopes Solomon will provide: the restoration of her baby to her. (In fact this is never reported but only anticipated in Solomon's final command in v. 27; the narrator's interest lies not in the ultimate fate of the two women, but in Solomon's judgment.)

Rhetorically, a recital of the bare facts shifts in v. 21 to the speaker's point of view at a particular time and place (on waking in bed in the morning): "There was a dead child!" *(wĕhinnēh mēt)*. The phraseology suggests the impressions and feelings of the speaker at this discovery. But a second discovery comes on top of that one, a discovery that is delayed by the intervening examination—"I looked carefully at it in the morning light"—and is expressed also from the woman's point of view: "It wasn't my son at all!" *(wĕhinnēh* again). The deep personal feelings involved are now expressed more directly by the additional clause, "(my son) to whom I had given birth."

The rhetoric of the petition is apparent even in the preceding factual statements. Parallelism between the beginning of v. 20 ("She got up during the night") and the beginning of v. 21 ("I got up in the morning") sharpens the contrast between the practice of deceit during the night and the discovery of deceit in the morning and thus between the other woman as devious offender and the speaker as innocent victim. Again, the contrast is made more telling and the betrayal more shocking by the emphasis on the commonality and parallelism of the shared lives of the two women in vv. 17–18.

Even the apparently objective, factual petitionary narrative is told from one very interested point of view and is designed to persuade the hearer of the rightness of that point of view. Since, in this case, the other interested party arrived with the petitioner, her point of view can now be stated. The narrator has the other woman respond immediately: "No! My son is the living one and your son is the dead one!" Given our knowledge of the first woman's story, this assertion implies a rather different story, namely, that when the first woman woke in the morning and discovered that her baby had died in the night, she invented her story in hopes of getting the other woman's child.

The second woman addresses not the king, but her accuser. The first woman responds in kind: "No, your son is the dead one and my son is the living one!"[28] For the moment, the king is ignored as the two women shout at each other. At this point, the narrator concludes the presentation of the case with: "And so they argued before the king"—at once projecting a continuing futile argument and reminding us that this is a royal audience.

This is the only case in the Bible in which both petitioner and adversary come before the king at the same time. This unique conjunction serves one purpose of the story: to lay before the king two alternative accounts, neither of which can be confirmed or proved false. The narrator now introduces the first words of the king, who registers this dilemma by reiterating the concluding claim of each woman: "One says 'This is my son, the living one, and the dead one is your son!' and the other says: 'No—the dead one is your son and the living one is my son!' " Repeated emphasis on the unresolvable deadlock is necessary for the reader, whose sympathy has been engaged by the first speaker.

Since there are no witnesses and no guarantee of who is telling the truth, it is impossible for the king to judge whether (1) the first woman's story is true, or (2) she has invented it because what happened during the night was the death of *her* child. At this point, Solomon and the reader are equally informed and equally at a loss. The plot seems to have reached an impasse. But now Solomon draws ahead. In a famous example of lateral thinking, Solomon orders that the live baby be cut in two and that half be given to each woman. We learn only of the command, which looks like a kind of resolution of the dilemma, but not of his plan, in which the order is only a device for revealing a different kind of information that will enable him to render the perfect judgment. Precisely because the order itself is a kind of resolution, we may not be inclined to look beyond or behind it for this underlying motive. At this point, then, we are really in the dark and will be enlightened only at the narrator's pleasure as the plan begins to work.

On hearing the king's order, "the woman whose son was the live one, because her feelings for her son were so strong, said: 'Forgive me, lord—give her the live child, and don't, whatever you do, put it to death!' while the other was saying:[29] 'It shall not be mine or yours, cut it in two!' " The speeches of both women are "innocent": the first because the true mother is speaking from her heart; the second because the other woman recognizes only the objective justice of Solomon's order, not the strategy lying behind it. But the reader is no longer innocent. The relative and causal clauses preceding the first speech explain to the reader both that woman's speech and Solomon's subsequent judgment. The location of these two clauses prevents readers from interpreting the speeches for themselves and so anticipating—and sharing in—Solomon's judgment. Thus readers neither share the plan as Solomon conceives it nor interpret the new evidence for themselves as it is heard. With these two clauses, "the woman whose son was the live one, because her feelings for her son were so strong," the narrator discloses to the reader what Solomon had planned to elicit and the significance of the following speech, and so reserves for the king the wisdom of his action and his judgment, while preserving both the reader's admiration for him and dependence on the narrator. The different responses of the two women constitute the resolution of the plot. Following this revelation, the final denouement of the story is a foregone conclusion: Solomon cancels his first command and orders the live baby given to the one revealed as his mother.[30]

What is the particular function of the petitionary narrative in this larger story? Clearly, it is important for the story that the king (and the reader) cannot decide between the two versions of events—that recounted in the petitionary narrative and that implied in the other woman's denial of it. As Sternberg has emphasized, we are never told which of the two women was the mother of the live baby; and the story, through the counterclaims of v. 22 and Solomon's assessment of the case in v. 23, denies that the testimony of either woman is superior to that of the other. Sternberg concludes that the reader remains ignorant (1985, 166–69).[31] But this is to read the case as a judge, not as the reader of a story.[32]

Certainly we, as readers, are to recognize the judicial *non liquet*. But recognizing the judicial role in the story is only part of our role as readers. Pace Sternberg, the biblical narrator's presentation of the two women's stories is also designed to engage the readers' sympathy for the first woman. First, generic expectations dispose us in this direction. In all biblical petitionary narratives, the reader's sympathies or interests are engaged on the side of the petitioner rather than the party against whom the petition is lodged. Second, the first woman tells a full, clear, unadorned tale. Nothing in the wording of her speech suggests deception or trickery. Third, the second woman says nothing to appeal to our sympathies as readers. There is no second narrative to counterbalance the first one. Admittedly, in the masoretic text, the first woman then resorts to the same level of argument, as the narrator equalizes the two claims before the judge. But the reader, while recognizing the impenetrability of the case facing the judge, is already disposed to believe the speaker of the petitionary narrative and so to conclude that she speaks first when the baby is threatened with the sword. The narrator uses the technique of the petitionary narrative—the rhetoric of persuasion by facts—in telling his tale, precisely in order to win the reader's sympathy for the first woman. Were this not his intention, he could have spelled out the other woman's narrative version of events as well. Either course would have equalized the women's impact on the reader. Had he chosen the other woman as the primary petitioner—recounting that her housemate awoke in the morning to find her baby dead beside her; claimed that she, the speaker, had exchanged babies during the night; and was now demanding that the speaker give her the live baby—he could have won our sympathy for her.

The narrator chose to quote fully the petition of the one woman, and the effect of that choice is to dispose the reader in her favor. But since neither of these women is of any narrative importance outside this story, why should the narrator be interested in engaging our sympathy for either of them? The answer is simply that the story becomes more personally significant for the reader. The petitionary narrative engages us morally; we now have an emotional investment in the outcome, and we are not only intellectually satisfied but also emotionally relieved when Solomon exposes the truth. Stories about court cases are generally not as interested in the neutrality of the judge (which may be impugned or taken for granted) as in the engagement of the reader—not only intellectually but also morally and emotionally—on the side of right. In this story, the petitionary narrative accomplishes that end.

2 Kings 6:24–30

The petition in 2 Kings 6:28b-29 also arises from a dispute between two women but is used to the opposite effect: to demonstrate the helplessness of the monarch.

The city of Samaria is under siege and suffering from a severe famine (vv. 24–25). A woman appeals to (ṣāʿăqâ ʾel) the king as he walks along the city wall: "Help me (hôšîʿâ), your majesty" (v. 26). This is analogous to the written appeal for a hearing at the beginning of the inscription. Originally the king would have understood this as precisely such an appeal and would have responded directly: ma-llāk "What's the matter?" (v. 28; as in 2 Sam 14:4–5).[33] In the present biblical form of the story, however, the king takes it as a general cry for help arising from the present conditions of starvation and replies accordingly—if Yahweh can't help her, how can he? (v. 27). This is part of a prophetic revision of the earlier story, characterizing the king as impious (cf. v. 33b) and now rendering the following introduction of the king's second speech clumsy.[34] The king's invitation to her to proceed leads into her petitionary narrative.

> This woman said to me: "Give up your son, so that we can eat him today, and then we will eat my son tomorrow."
> So we cooked my son and ate him.
> Then the next day I said to her: "Give up your son, so that we can eat him."
> But she hid her son away.

Again, the petition consists exclusively of a narrative. But this, too, is reduced to a minimum. The exposition of the woman's narrative consists of the other woman's proposal for survival—a contract tacitly agreed upon by the speaker—and the execution of the speaker's obligation under the contract. The narrative then concludes with the complication: the other woman's refusal to execute her obligation. The exposition or orientation is an agreement, a verbal contract, which one party has acted upon; the complication is the other party's refusal to keep her side of the bargain. The implied resolution, obvious to king and readers, would be the king's enforcement of the contract.

Since the petition consists entirely of narrative, the persuasiveness of the petitioner's case again depends entirely on her narrative rhetoric. The style of the narrative appears to be direct and factual. On examination, however, its rhetoric is carefully devised. First, the other woman is made solely responsible for the original proposal; the speaker's agreement with it, while implied, is not directly expressed. Second, the reciprocal nature of the agreement and the imbalance between its fulfilment by the one woman and nonfulfilment by the other are emphasized by parallelism: the verbal repetition in the two women's speeches ("Give up your son, so that we can eat him") and the contrast between the clauses expressing the other woman's promise to produce her son on the second day and then her actual hiding of him when the time came. Finally, apart from the repetition, the language is economical. It ostensibly states the facts simply and directly, focusing on the contractual issue and ignoring the human, moral, and emotional issues involved.

The absence of emotion is particularly striking, not so much because petitions probably normally involved some expression of emotion—as noted both in that of the agricultural laborer and of the woman who petitioned Solomon—but because in this case the facts themselves are so shocking. For the petitioner, the form of the petition is calculated to focus the king's attention and get a quick, favorable judgment. But for the narrator it is also calculated to achieve something very different: the horror of the reader at the inhumanity to which this woman—and so presumably the population at large—has been reduced. The narration of such horrific facts with self-interest and lack of feeling and the appeal for enforcement of contract—one mark of civilized society—when the society has so obviously reverted to barbarism, double the horror of the acts described.

The grounds for the reader's horror demand some elucidation. For the petitioner, the agreement to eat the children is the exposition necessary for an appreciation of the complication—the other woman's failure to produce their dinner on the second day. For the reader (and the king), the initial agreement is itself a complication, indeed a crisis, arising from the siege conditions (which, as described in v. 25, are for the reader the exposition behind this complication). That is, the agreement is for king and reader already a crisis eliciting horror. And the horror is sharpened by the speaker's presentation of it not as something which itself needs to be addressed but merely as the necessary background for an appreciation of her present grievance. Further, her present grievance is that the other woman is not complying with her part of the agreement. From the petitioner's point of view, the petition is simply for the enforcement of a contract. The initial horror is thus multiplied by her insistence on compliance with the agreement, and hence the prospect of a second act of murder and cannibalism, and by her complete imperviousness to the ongoing horror.

It has been suggested that such a piling of horror on horror is not cumulative, but comic: the absurdity of the woman's attitude—seeking the enforcement of such a contract under such circumstances—breaks the bounds of high seriousness and becomes comedy (Lasine 1991, 33). Although there is certainly humor in the denouement of the larger narrative (in chapter 7), the immediate context in which the woman's petition appears seems to be devoted to intensifying the seriousness of the initial situation.[35] These verses (24–30) constitute the exposition of the larger narrative (6:24–7:20), introducing the siege and depicting the extremely desperate conditions obtaining within the town. The narrator expresses the extremity of the siege conditions through three voices in these verses: his own in v. 25 (reference to "a great famine" and to the high price of the least desirable comestibles), the woman's (her matter-of-fact account of the two women's pragmatic arrangement to eat their children and insistence on fulfillment of that commitment), and the king's (his reaction to the woman's story—tearing his clothes and the consequent disclosure of his previous response to the famine: the sackcloth next to his skin).[36] The seriousness of the famine, attested to by these three witnesses, is a prerequisite for the reasoning of the outcasts in 7:3–4, who together serve as a fourth witness.

How is the king to respond to the petition? If he grants it and enforces the agreement, he will be normalizing such arrangements. If he denies it, he will be countenancing the breaking of agreements in general. Either judgment undermines the social order, symbolically legitimating murder and cannibalism on the one hand and authorizing disregard of all social contracts on the other. But the petition itself demonstrates that the social order is already more than undermined—"mankind preying on itself." No judgment seems no worse and no better than either judgment. So instead of rendering a judgment, the king rends his clothes.

Whereas the judicial dilemma posed by the petitionary narrative in 1 Kings 3 is used to demonstrate one king's wisdom, that of the petitionary narrative in 2 Kings 6 is used to demonstrate another king's helplessness. In both cases the petitionary narrative is the focal point of the initial exposition of a larger story. (On 2 Kgs 6:24–7:20, see chapter 6.)

2 Samuel 14:1–23

A special problem presents itself when the petitioner wants to appeal against an action or judgment of the king himself. He or she has to devise some alternative to a direct petition.

In 2 Samuel 14, Joab wishes to have Absalom brought back from exile. His only recourse is to petition the king. But the king, as the other interested party, would then be playing the role of judge in his own cause. Joab therefore adopts two measures: he concocts a petitionary narrative in which almost all the particulars are quite different from Absalom's case (so that the king will give an impartial judgment), but which will "change the appearance of the matter" of Absalom (v. 20), that is, place the matter of Absalom in a different light.[37] And he engages a clever woman to present the petition as her own (so that the king's suspicions will not be aroused by Joab's involvement). Only after the king has granted the woman's petition and she has raised the case of Absalom does the king suspect something and guess that Joab is behind her activity. By now, however, he has pronounced an impartial judgment, overruling a local sentence on a fratricide, and so is able to see Absalom's case in a new light. He proceeds to grant what is in reality Joab's petition for the return from exile of the royal fratricide, exercising more promptly and confidently the judicial authority that he somewhat hesitantly assumed in the woman's case (see Bellefontaine 1987).

The success of Joab's ruse depends on the woman's convincingly acting out the role of petitioner. That is why he seeks out a *clever* (*ḥăkāmâ*) woman. Joab's instructions to her spell out what is to be her general role and specific appearance. She is to act as if in mourning, wear mourning dress, abstain from anointing herself, and generally play the part of a woman who has been mourning for some time (v. 2). In this role and garb, she is to go to the king. At this point, the narrator simply says that Joab told her what to say to the king. Like the king, we do not know what she is going to say until she says it. But unlike the king, we know that she is acting and that Joab is her scriptwriter and director. Her performance must convince the king that she is the subject of the petitionary narrative she recounts and that the petition is genuine. It must also be realistic to the reader, who otherwise would question the king's response.

The woman goes to the king and does obeisance to him, saying: "Help, O king" (v. 4; cf. 2 Kgs 6:26). The king responds: "What is the matter?" (v. 5; cf. 2 Kgs 6:28). The following petition consists of two parts: a narrative (vv. 5–7) and a justification of her coming to the king (vv. 15–17). While vv. 15–17 now appear after v. 14, arguments that they are out of place and originally followed v. 7 are compelling. Composed as the continuation of the woman's first speech, they were only later displaced to their present location. It is equally clear that vv. 13–14 trigger the enquiry of vv. 18–19a, as vv. 15–17 do not.[38]

The narrative reads as follows:

(5) I am just a widow woman. My husband has died.

(6) Your maid had two sons. The two of them fought together in the open country, but there was no one around to save them from each other, and one struck the other and killed him.

(7) And now the whole *mišpāḥâ* has risen against your maid and said: "Hand over the one who struck his brother, that we may put him to death for the life of his brother whom he killed."

So they would destroy the heir[39] and extinguish the ember which is left me, leaving my husband neither name nor remnant on the earth.

The exposition, consisting of two nominal sentences, each followed by converted imperfect verbs, first refers to the woman's status as a widow, reinforcing this by mentioning the death of her husband, and then to her status as a mother with two sons, now reduced to one by the outcome of their fighting together: with no one around to intervene, one ended up killing the other. Initially, we might be inclined to interpret this second development as the complication, but it immediately appears that the real complication is in the next development. This is supported by the parallel syntactic structure of the two parts of the exposition and the contrast between the matter-of-fact account of the death of the one son and the extended, more rhetorical account of the threat to the other. If the exposition traces the decline in her fortunes from loss of husband to loss of one of her two sons, the complication (beginning *wĕhinnê*, "and look") brings her face to face with the final loss: her predicament is now threatened by demands from the *mišpāḥâ* that the dead brother be avenged—that the killer be killed. Here is traditional justice with a vengeance. Apparently the local authority has decided to avenge the death of one of its members, even though the killer is also a member—even when, as the woman now spells out, doing so means the end of the line of one of its member families as well as the end of any family support for her.[40] While this situation may seem far-fetched, it is not unique in biblical literature, being also envisaged in the last verses of Genesis 27.[41] There Esau plans to kill his one brother, Jacob, after the death of their father (v. 41b). His mother sends Jacob away for safety, saying to him: "Why should I be bereaved of both of you in one day?" (v. 45b)—anticipating the plight allegedly faced by the woman of Tekoa.

The woman's remark on the absence of anyone else at the fight is not concerned with lack of witnesses: there is no suggestion that anyone doubts or contests what happened. She remarks on the absence of anyone to *intervene*. But, given the life of the family within the *mišpāḥâ*, those most likely to be able to perform that service would be the latter's members. In other words, but for the absence of *mišpāḥâ* members, the death might never have occurred. Without implying any direct responsibility on their part, the woman subtly undermines their judgment. They demand blood vengeance for a killing that, but for chance, they themselves might have prevented. This perhaps pertains to David's supervision of his family.

Beyond stating the facts of the case, the woman quotes the *mišpāḥâ*. In this quotation, we hear her representation of the point of view of the opposing party in the dispute. The quoted speech expresses directly the legal position of that party, a simple legal principle: one who strikes another so that he dies is to be put to death (cf. Exod 21:12). Twice the deceased is referred to as "his brother." For the *mišpāḥâ*, this expresses the heinousness of the crime: fratricide. But for the woman and her audience, it also recalls her dependence on the surviving brother.

She expresses this dependence most directly by setting against the *mišpaḥâ*'s invocation of the principle "a life for a life" the devastating consequences of its application to this situation: the destruction of the "heir," the last male claimant to the family estate, and the extinguishing of "the ember which is left me." Her final reference to the prospective lack of "name" or "remnant" for her husband reinforces the fact that a whole family will be extinguished by this act of vengeance. This would be not just a private loss for her but also a social loss for the group. Her last words, following her quotation of the *mišpaḥâ*'s speech, anticipate one resolution of the plot of her story. She spells out this terrible ending as an incentive to the king to supply an alternative ending. Will he let the tragedy run its course, or will he grant her petition and intervene to provide a happier ending?

While the main thrust of the narrative is to present the woman's dire situation and the prospect of the elimination of her late husband's family, it also implies that the application of a simple, traditional, legal principle to a case involving other serious issues is unreasonable. Both urge the king to overrule the *mišpāḥâ*'s judgment and exempt the surviving son from the death penalty.

The plot of this narrative has the makings of a classical tragedy. Since it is actually a fiction and the speaker is playing the role of the mother, her "cleverness" lies particularly in her ability to play the lead role in such a tragedy. The king's response will show that her performance was convincing.[42] Given the circumstances that she recounts, her petition to the king is realistic.

But as noted before, the end of the narrative is not the end of the petition. Unlike other biblical petitions, but like the field-worker's petition from Mesad Hashavyahu, the narrative is followed by other forms of appeal. In vv. 15–17, the woman explains why she has come to the king. The people, that is, her people— or perhaps, better, the designated kinsman, probably her sons' paternal uncle[43]— are threatening her, so she decided to speak to the king, who, she hopes, will respond to her petition and deliver her from the relative's attempts to destroy her and her son from the ancestral estate.[44] With these last words (v. 16b) she reiterates the theme of the narrative: without the king's intervention, the narrative "plot" will end with the destruction of the family and hence the assumption of the ancestral estate by another—implying the self-interest of the kinsman. But while the narrative states the feared negative outcome, these following words express directly her hope for the king's intervention to prevent that outcome—the petition proper, though indirectly stated. That hope is reiterated at the beginning of v. 17, when she again recalls how she thought that the word of the king would give her relief. Finally, she expresses the reason for her hope: the king is like a divine envoy, hearing right and wrong (cf. the similar flattery in v. 20: the king's wisdom is "like the wisdom of a divine envoy, knowing everything in the land [or on earth]"). The speech concludes with a blessing on the king: "May Yahweh, your god, be with you."

This last part of her speech discloses the specific situation of this petition. The woman is appealing the judgment and sentence of a lower court (the *mišpāḥâ*) to the highest court (the king). But there appear to be no formal procedures, no customary framework within which her petitionary narrative fits. Rather, she has to explain her presumption in coming to speak to the king (v. 15). It is based on two considerations: her fear of the avenger and her hope in the king's readiness to give her relief, the latter in turn based on what she says are his quasi-divine faculties.

Her efforts continue, as the king defers judgment (v. 8) and then assures her that if she brings in the threatening kinsman, he will see that he bothers her no more (v. 10). But this assurance is not satisfactory. She has to get his guarantee of amnesty for her son (the purpose of Joab's ruse). In any case, since the narrative is fictitious, there is no kinsman to produce! But her rejection of this proposal is also realistic under the supposed circumstances: the introduction of the supposed kinsman to the court would allow him to tell the king the story from his point of view and leave the king vulnerable to the rhetoric of his narrative. So she persists until the king swears that he will ensure her son's safety (v. 11b).

Bellefontaine has nicely explained David's reluctance to give a final decision in terms of the transitional nature of early kingship—or chieftainship (Bellefontaine 1987). It is the lack of pertinent custom in the transitional period envisaged by the author that also explains the lengthy justification which the woman appends to her narrative.

While this passage provides another example of an otherwise unknown woman bringing a petition to the king, it also illustrates a more complex technique: the use of a fictitious petitionary narrative to elicit a judgment by the king, through which he can be brought to view in a new light a case in which he is an interested party.[45]

1 Kings 20:38–42

The complexity is further increased in 1 Kings 20. Here a prophet announces Yahweh's condemnation of the king for releasing an enemy whom Yahweh had put at his mercy in the aftermath of a great victory (v. 42). But he prepares the king for this by first having him in effect condemn himself by pronouncing judgment on a man in an analogous situation. The prophet's strategy is to disguise himself and then petition the king for vindication in a situation in which he appears to stand condemned. He must convince the king that he is at the same time *seeking* a favorable judgment and *deserving* of an unfavorable judgment. Here again, though fictitious, the petitionary narrative has to be convincing as such, but for the prophet to succeed in his objective, his petition must be unsuccessful.

Like the Tekoite woman, the prophet both disguises himself and tells a contrived story. Disguised as a wounded soldier with a bandage over his head, he stands near the battlefield waiting for the king to pass by (v. 38). As the king comes, he appeals ($\d{s}\bar{a}^{\varsigma}aq$) to him. His petitionary narrative follows (vv. 39b-40a):

> Your servant had gone out into the battle, and there was someone coming away, and he brought a man over to me and said:
> "Guard this man! If he goes missing, it will be your life for his life, or else you'll pay a talent of silver."
> Then your servant was looking this way and that[46]—and he was gone!

Minimal orientation appears in the first clause: the speaker had been in the battle. The complication follows immediately: someone comes up to the speaker and puts him in charge of a captive. The prophet quotes the man's charge: he is to guard the captive on pain of death or payment of a fantastic, indeed impossible, sum. The speaker does not identify the man as his superior, so presumably his tacit acceptance of the assignment makes it binding. There is no mention of a corresponding reward for fulfillment of the assignment which, the hearers may surmise, was also offered as an incentive to accept the responsibility.[47] His lack of reference to his acceptance is, of course, a device to lessen his responsibility (cf. the similar lack of express agreement to a contract in the narrative of the petitioner in 2 Kings 6, discussed previously), as is his omission of any reference to a reward for fulfillment of the commission.

The petitioner's subsequent activity is described as vaguely and innocently as possible ("looking this way and that"). But while having the appearance of innocence, the vagueness also allows the interpretation that this is an evasion of responsibility. In the climax, the statement of the man's escape is mentioned with maximal indefiniteness (literally: "and he was not"), suggesting not the guard's failure but the inexplicable and mysterious nature of the man's disappearance (in effect: "I can't imagine how he got away"). Again, the vagueness of the narrative, while expressed as a bid for personal innocence, may be interpreted as evasion of responsibility. In any case, the guard's guilt, of whatever degree, in letting the man escape by his negligence will contrast (a fortiori) with the king's in deliberately sending off his enemy after signing a commercial agreement with him.

The aim of the supposed petitioner is to have the king judge in his favor, to exempt him from the penalty imposed by the owner of the captive. The actual aim of the prophet is the opposite: to have the king condemn the petitioner. The prophet is successful. The king is at once convinced by the act and led to condemn the petitioner: "such is your judgment" (i.e., that which was spelled out in your report of the man's speech) "you have decided" (i.e., by your conduct, as you have just reported it).

Having achieved his goal, the prophet quickly removes his disguise, discloses his identity to the king (v. 41), and pronounces his oracle of judgment: "This is what Yahweh has said: 'Because you let go the man I had netted,[48] it will be your life for his life and your army for his army.'" The king, like the petitioner, had let the captive assigned to him get away. As the supposed petitioner's life was forfeit to the man who had handed over the captive to him, so the Israelite king's life (and that of his army) is now forfeit to Yahweh, who had put the Aramaean king in his hands.

The petitionary narrative in this case is used with redoubled subtlety. Though it is not an authentic petition, it is so presented both by the person and words of the prophet; as in the case of the Tekoite woman, the king takes it as genuine. But in addition, it is so conceived and presented that it does not persuade the king to act favorably, but rather leads to his immediate negative judgment, which, unlike the case of the Tekoite woman, was the precedent the prophet sought for his own (Yahweh's) judgment of the king. We have come a long way from the simple narrative of the field-worker from Mesad Hashavyahu.

2 Samuel 12:1–7

A third narrative often grouped with the last two is that of Nathan in 2 Samuel 12:1–4. Like them, it is an imaginary narrative in some respects analogous to the situation of the hearer, the king, and it is used to get a certain judgment from the king that can then be applied to his own situation. But this *use* of the narrative and the fact that the larger stories in which these small narratives are told have a common pattern and may be classified together do not require us to assume that the small narratives quoted in them are of the same genre. The story in 2 Samuel 12:1–4 is more sharply distinguished from the other two than is often recognized.[49] Three features differentiate it significantly from all the other narratives discussed. First, the story is told entirely in the third person. Second, it is set in a vague past: *hāyû*, "there were." Third, it lacks the concrete specificity of a petition.

There were two men in a certain town. One was rich and one was poor. Neither the town nor the men are identified, and the two men are characterized by simple polar opposites. This opening is clearly more characteristic of a parable or fable—or folktale (Gunkel 1921, 36 = 1987, 55)—than a petitionary narrative. But, as we shall see, there are problems in the applicability of those classifications, too. We shall return to the question of the generic classification of the story later.

The narrative continues:

(2) The rich man had very large flocks and herds.

(3) The poor man had nothing but a little ewe lamb that he had acquired. He fostered it, and it grew up together with him and his children: it ate from his piece of bread, drank from his cup, lay down in his bosom, and became like a daughter to him.

(4) Then a traveller came to the rich man, who felt some compunction about taking anything from his flocks or herds to cook for the visitor who had come into his home, so he took the ewe lamb of the poor man and cooked it for the man who had come to him.

The wealth of the rich man is quickly noted, as is the poverty of the poor man who "had nothing" but the one lamb. The narrator draws the hearer into the domestic life of this man, so that he sees the intimate, personal bond the poor man has with his only significant possession. The complication begins with the arrival of a traveler, whom the rich man takes in. Not wishing to sacrifice any of his wealth, the rich man then takes the poor man's only treasure and serves it to the visitor. The rhetoric emphasizes the heinousness of this act, not only by exhibiting the disproportion between the resources of the two men but also by referring to the feelings of the rich man toward his own innumerable animals alongside those of the poor man toward his one animal. There is also an implied contrast between the rich man's feelings toward his own animals and his feelings toward the poor man's ewe lamb. Although the third-person narration exploits an omniscient viewpoint to describe the feelings and motives of both characters, it also pushes the hearer (and reader) to sympathize with the poor man and to condemn the rich man. This is more consistent with the interested point of view of the petitionary narrative than with the parable or fable, which are typically more objective in their presentation.

At this point, David's reaction is described: "David became very angry at the man and said to Nathan: 'As Yahweh lives, the man doing this is a minion of Death! He shall compensate for the lamb sevenfold,[50] because he did this and because had no compunction' " (vv. 5–6).[51] This response is very important for interpretation of the preceding narrative. First, David takes the story quite literally, as he was intended to. Whatever its final use, therefore, the immediate function of the story is not metaphorical: like the two petitionary narratives just discussed, it is neither presented nor received as a parable or fable. Second, David does not draw a lesson from the story but rather pronounces judgment. The "judgment" consists of two quite different elements. The first ("As Yahweh lives, the man doing this is a minion of Death!") is the speaker's personal, moral judgment of the rich man.[52] As such, it is not inconsistent with the formal, legal

sentence which immediately follows ("He shall compensate for the lamb sevenfold"). Thus David responds to the story as to a petition, not a parable.[53]
Third, condemnation of the rich man is what Nathan was looking for: on this,
he is able to build his own (and Yahweh's) condemnation in the next verse ("You
are the man . . .")—the object of the whole episode.

The one reference to this story in the sequel is Nathan's opening declaration:
"You are the man!" This identifies David with the rich man whom David has
just condemned and points David (and the reader) to an analogy between the act
of the rich man and an act of David. Both, enjoying an abundance of the world's
goods, have used their superior power to take what or whom they wanted from
someone to whom it or she is precious. This is the only analogy between the two
stories: beyond this we know nothing of Uriah that would correlate with the
depiction of the poor man; while we know much more about Bathsheba, none
of it corresponds to the fate of the lamb.[54] After these two words (in the Hebrew),
Nathan makes no other reference to the story. The exposure of the analogy between David and the rich man also exposes the deceptive use of the narrative;
hence it is immediately discarded.

A fable or parable that was taken literally by the hearer would have failed.
Fables and parables can achieve their purpose only through the hearer's recognition that they represent something other than what they literally say. They are
didactic, and they survive because they represent some general truth that most
people recognize. The function of the last two petitionary narratives and of this
narrative is the opposite. Their effect depends on their being taken literally. As
soon as another meaning is suggested, they are discarded. Like normal petitionary
narratives, they are ephemera that survive only in consequence of their role in
larger stories of ongoing significance (cf. Gunn 1978, 41).

There is another strong reason for rejecting the category of parable or fable for
this story, and that is its incompleteness (properly noted in Lasine 1984, 111–12).
What were the consequences of the rich man's act? Was he punished for it, or
did he get away with it? And what happened to the poor man? Did he suffer in
silence, or did he appeal to a court—and if so, with what results? If we take
seriously the claim that the story is a fable or parable, we also have to entertain
the claim that it teaches: better rich and powerful than poor and weak; might
makes right, and the sentimental feelings of, or for, the poor are futile. It would
then be comparable with the fable of 2 Kings 14:9 about the crushing of the
presumptuous weakling. But such lessons are clearly at odds with the purpose of
the larger story in 2 Samuel 12.[55] The story does not teach a lesson, because it is
incomplete, and, like a petitionary narrative, cries out for judicial intervention.
David's response is entirely appropriate.

Thus several features of Nathan's story make "parable" a problematic category
in this context: its incompleteness, its one-sided sympathy with one character, its
literal interpretation by the hearer, its eliciting of a legal judgment on the case it
recounts, and its ephemeral nature. It does not teach any general lesson. Being
composed for a unique situation, it is of no significance beyond that situation—
except, as here, in a story recounting that original situation.

But if Nathan's story cannot be classified as a parable, can it be classified as a petitionary narrative? At this point, it is necessary to return to the initial objections raised: the story is told entirely in the third person of two type characters in an undefined location and past time—"There were two men in a certain town. One was rich and one was poor."

To address these objections, we may propose a variation on the standard petitionary narrative that I shall call the hypothetical petitionary narrative. If the king was expected to reach good judgments on the difficult and unusual petitions that made it all the way to the throne, his advisors might give him practice by presenting him with hypothetical cases. There was clearly tension in the court between, on the one hand, the royal ideology of the king as guarantor of justice for the weak, the disadvantaged, and the oppressed, and, on the other hand, the real power and actual practice of the monarch and his court. Those most concerned with the ideology might have been expected to present to the king hypothetical narratives that tested and reinforced the king's commitment to protect the weak and vindicate the exploited. The narrative here presented to David by Nathan would then have been understood by king and readers as such a hypothetical petitionary narrative. It certainly seems to have been so understood in the Lucianic version of the Septuagint, which begins Nathan's speech with: "Tell me this case" (*anaggeilon dē moi tēn krisin tautēn*).[56]

All of the features of Nathan's story—its exclusive use of the third person, its indefinite setting, its representation of the point of view of one character, its incompleteness as a narrative, its literal interpretation, its eliciting of a judgment, its emphemeral nature—fit the proposed hypothetical petitionary narrative, and none militate against it. Everything that the larger story takes for granted now becomes plausible for the reader: that Nathan would come to the king with such a story, that the king would take it seriously and pronounce a formal, legal judgment on the case, and that Nathan could rely on this response.[57]

Further, a hypothetical petitionary narrative would suit Nathan's larger purposes perfectly: it would prompt the king to make the right judgment and be pleased with it—which in turn would enable Nathan, exploiting the analogy between his story and David's recent acts, to move in with Yahweh's judgment of David. The fact that with his words "You are the man!" Nathan points to the analogy, which David then evidently recognizes, does not justify calling the original story a parable. Had David recognized the story as a parable, it would scarcely have achieved its desired effect any more than the stories of the Tekoite woman or the prophet. But if it was not in itself recognized as a parable, then it is impertinent of us to claim it as such. Precisely because it is not recognizable as a parable but is convincing as a (hypothetical) petitionary narrative, it—like the two preceding narratives—can elicit the desired judgment. In all three cases, of course, once the judgment is pronounced, the judicial situation is exposed as a pretense. The king's judgment is then used not as a precedent but to give the king insight into his own situation. Our appreciation of that final turn should not be allowed to ruin our appreciation of the use of the petitionary narrative.

Summary

The narratives surveyed here provide evidence for the reconstruction at the beginning of this chapter of the now otherwise inaccessible oral petitionary narrative as used in ancient Israel. Specific realizations of the genre were found in the written record of an actual petition by a peasant and in a number of artistic adaptations in larger narratives in Samuel and Kings. All except one of the biblical examples discussed were addressed to the king (the exception being addressed to a prophet). Two presented the king with an apparently unresolvable conflict—one used to demonstrate his wisdom, the other to expose his helplessness. Three of the narratives elicited a judgment from the king that was then used to make him see and accept a judgment on his own behavior. Of these three, two were pseudopetitionary narratives presented by people in disguise, one of whom sought to present a case that would be decided *against* him. It was suggested that the third was a hypothetical petitionary narrative—a third-person version used to exercise the king's judgment. The speakers of the last two were prophets—one certainly, the other presumably, a court prophet. The other biblical petitioners were all women: two prostitutes in one case and apparently widows in the other cases, though the substance and purpose of the petition of the woman from Tekoa is to be attributed to the general, Joab.

It is difficult to know how realistic some of these elements were. If the probative, hypothetical petitionary narrative of 2 Samuel 12 is not purely literary invention, it would certainly have been peculiar to the court. The same would be true of the pseudopetitionary narratives. That a general and a prophet appear as their authors supports what we would expect: that the deceptive use of the genre to elicit royal judgments preparing the king to see and accept a judgment on his own behavior was limited to unusually gifted and powerful individuals, especially associated with the court. The pseudopetition would be less necessary at lower social levels, since appeal against interested, biased parties at such levels could always be made to a higher court.

The petitionary narrative is a story normally told by someone in a weak or desperate position to someone in a powerful position, a position to decide the petitioner's fate. Yet in several of the biblical cases, a very different relationship is exposed. The narrator uses the story of the mother during the siege of Samaria to expose the helplessness of the king. The petitionary narrative of Joab and the Tekoite woman succeeds in tricking the king into recognizing Joab's judgment as better than his. The prophet disguised as a soldier tells his story to win the king's recognition of the rightness of his own punishment by the one power higher than he. Finally, Nathan uses a hypothetical petitionary narrative for the same purpose. In these last four cases, the petitionary narrative, which in itself defers to—and sometimes even flatters—the judgment or power of the hearer, exposes the limits of the king's judgment or power. Whether petitionary narratives were actually so used in real life we cannot say. But certainly the Deuteronomistic History delights in the artistic use of the genre, especially to undermine and overthrow the judgment of the king.

The Story of the Siloam Tunnel

Toward the end of the eighth century BCE (if 2 Kgs 20:20 is to be believed), a tunnel was constructed from the Gihon spring, outside the east wall of Jerusalem, through the rock under the eastern hill to a pool on the southwestern side of the hill. Dan Gill, an Israeli geologist, has recently demonstrated that the tunnel followed the course of a fissure that was part of a larger karstic system of fissures, caves, and sinkholes in the limestone and dolomite of the hill (1991; 1994). While this tunnel was only one of several engineering projects undertaken over the centuries to provide water for different pools in the southern part of the ancient city,[1] it was certainly the most ambitious and impressive, involving excavation underground for a distance of about 533 meters (1,748 feet). In comparison, the Siloam channel, running along the western slope of the Kidron Valley, was about 400 meters in length, but was constructed almost entirely above ground. The second longest underground tunnel in Israel (at Gibeon) was only 50 meters in length. Gibeon's entire underground water system, third in length after the tunnel and channel at Jerusalem, was only 127 meters.[2] It is understandable, then, that those involved in the construction of the Siloam tunnel might want to tell the story of this extraordinary achievement and that later generations also might want to give some account of its origins.

The earliest preserved version of such stories appears in an inscription discovered accidentally in 1880. It was written on the wall of the tunnel itself, about six meters from the lower end. A rectangular space on the wall had been carefully smoothed, and the text then written on the smoother, lower half of the polished surface.[3]

The Siloam Tunnel Inscription

(1)   ] the breakthrough.

(1–3) And this was the account of the breakthrough. While [the excavators] were still [working] with their picks, each toward the other, and while there were still three cubits to be broken through, the voice of each [was hea]rd calling to the other, because there was a cavity (?)[4] in the rock to the south and [to the nor]th.

(3–4) And at the moment of the breakthrough, the excavators struck each toward the other, pick against pick.

(4–6) Then the water flowed from the spring to the pool for one thousand two hundred cubits. And the height of the rock above the heads of the excavators was one hundred cubits.[5]

The inscription falls into three parts: two headings, a narrative of human actions, and finally two facts resulting from the preceding actions. The initial situation is described in the first dependent clause: the excavators were working toward each other. The final situation is expressed in the concluding measurements of the completed work. Between these two situations, the narrative consists of essentially three events: the excavators heard each others' voices; they struck each others' picks; the water flowed through the tunnel.

The first heading, perhaps functioning like a title, consists of two words, the first no longer readable. The second word, often translated "tunnel," is probably better understood in the same way as the three later occurrences of this word, that is, as an abstract or verbal noun, referring to the climactic moment of the whole operation, the breakthrough, which is the main subject of the inscription.

The first of three spaces separating different parts of the inscription precedes the second heading, which serves as an abstract of the following narrative, introducing it with the complete sentence: "This was the account[6] of the breakthrough." What is striking in this is the presence of the perfect verb *hyh* "was." Without the verb, the words *zh dbr* . . . are used in biblical literature to introduce laws to be administered in the future (Deut 15:2; 19:4) or the administration of a particular institution in the past (1 Kgs 9:15). In those cases, the sense is: "This *is* an account of the . . ."—a timeless present, which is then followed by verbs referring to actions in the future or the past. In the inscription, however, the expression of the verb in *wzh hyh dbr* renders the account itself in the past— "this *was* the account of . . ."— which suggests that the author is not composing a narrative but referring to something he has heard.[7] In any case, what follows must be based on an eyewitness report by one of the handful of people at the two excavation fronts toward the end of the project. They would have been the first to tell the story.

The remainder of the inscription also falls into three parts: a long complex sentence, a short complex sentence, and finally two simple sentences. The complex sentences begin with temporal clauses: two at the beginning of the first sentence (*bᶜwd . . . wbᶜwd . . .*, "while . . . and while . . .") and one at the beginning of the second (*wbym*, "and at the moment of"). These concentrate our attention on two particular moments. The author could have begun most simply with a general narrative statement, only in a subsequent clause defining the first moment, such as "the excavators worked with their picks, each toward the other, and then, when there were only three cubits to be broken through, . . ." The first clause would then have focused directly on the activities since pick was first put to rock, thus giving a larger temporal scale to this very brief account. But by beginning with a temporal clause, the narrator refers only indirectly to the larger operation. With the first two temporal clauses, the author successively narrows the focus to a particular moment within the operation, thereby suspending the main clause and the disclosure of the event that occurred at that moment.

The first of the two moments was when the excavators were working toward each other with three cubits still to go. At that point, they heard each others' voices. The following causal clause, the narrator's explanation that something in the rock—a cavity or fissure—permitted the voices to be heard, reinforces the realism of the account. Thus the narrative begins in medias res. Our only orientation appears in the clause speaking of the excavators' working toward one another. We can imagine, on the basis of the inscription and the course of the tunnel itself, a fuller, more developed story with an exposition in which the project was commissioned and a complication in which the plan was drawn up to work simultaneously from opposite ends of the projected tunnel and the workers then followed the fault from each end, now this way and now that. A longer account might have made much of the gap between aim and accomplishment. But here we begin almost at the end: when only three cubits separate the two parties. This story would be told not in answer to the request "Tell us about the construction of the tunnel" but, as indicated by the translation of the heading, "Tell us about the final breakthrough in the tunnel."

At this point, the scribe leaves the second major space. This moves us abruptly from the first moment to the second, the climax of the story—the moment of the breakthrough itself, when the laborers' picks clashed against each other. From a long, arduous, and perhaps anxious travail, the narrative picks out only these two critical moments and events at the end of the project. Earlier difficulties and tensions are ignored in favor of these final triumphs. This selectivity suggests the excitement and sense of accomplishment these two moments generated.[8]

Following this concentration on two particular stages at particular locations in the tunnel, the inscription concludes with a move back for a broader perspective. One more narrative event is recorded: the passage of the water along the length of the tunnel. But what impresses the author is not the first passage of the water as *event*, but rather certain enduring facts, namely, the distances involved: the length of the tunnel along which the water flowed and its depth under the ground. The inscription conveys this visually by the last of the three major spaces, which separates the two final sentences from the preceding one and links the sentence about the passage of the water along the length of the tunnel not with the preceding events, but with the following measurements. In narrative terms, these express the concluding state of affairs, following and consequent on the preceding action. What is important for the narrator finally is not the visible result of the excavation or its benefits, but the measurements of the achievement.

As one might expect, this story of the completion of the tunnel ignores the larger context in which a modern historian would be interested: the origins of the project, the plan, the implementation, and the costs and benefits to different groups in Jerusalem. Surprisingly, however, it also ignores the typical interests of ancient building inscriptions. Although it reports the completion of a construction project, it is unlike either of the types of inscription normally serving that purpose in its environment. West Semitic memorial inscriptions are written in the first person by the reigning monarch, who introduces himself and then reports his accomplishments, including buildings. West Semitic dedicatory inscriptions identify the building or other object on which they are inscribed as the gift of the king, to his god. By contrast, the Siloam tunnel inscription expresses nothing of the public piety or political propaganda of the monarch sponsoring the undertaking. It neither gives credit to any monarch nor envisages, either by reference or implication, any relationship between the accomplishment recorded and the deity. It is written entirely in the third person, and the only human subjects are the excavators. They are the sole actors in the narrative, their experience the focus of the two moments captured in the two complex sentences.

The inscription is told from the point of view of someone caught up in the success of the project (the actual meeting of the two parties) and impressed by its scale (the measurements). The structure and content of the inscription betray both an emotional engagement in the outcome and a sense of pride in the success of an exceptional technical achievement. These observations are consistent with two others. First, the inscription is anonymous. Second, it is barely visible in the limited light several meters inside a tunnel through which people did not normally pass. Clearly, therefore, it was not meant for public display.[9]

The most probable explanation of all these facts is that the inscription was produced by or for the "civil engineer" who planned and supervised the project. He would have had the most at stake in the meeting of the two parties excavating from opposite ends of the tunnel, he would have been proudest of the measurements, and he would have been both most interested in recording these things and most anxious that such a record be inconspicuous and that his name not be displayed on it. (Since it was generally only kings who recorded such accomplishments, display might invite royal wrath.) Finally, he would have had the resources to produce such a well-prepared and well-carved inscription.

Stories of the Siloam Tunnel in the Bible

No narrative in the epigraphic record or in biblical literature can be said to be congeneric with the Siloam tunnel inscription. This is, perhaps, not surprising. But the Bible has preserved other accounts apparently of the same project.[10] Although even briefer, they are worth reviewing for the different selections of facts and the different points of view they exhibit.

2 Kings 20:20a

According to 2 Kings 20:20a, Hezekiah "made the pool and the watercourse and brought the water into the city." Here the king is the sole subject of the verbs and sole actor in the narrative. He is responsible for the construction of both tunnel and pool and for the result: the provision of water within the city. Unlike the tunnel inscription, the text is not interested in any aspect of the actual work or experience of the excavators or in the technical achievement that the project represented. On the contrary, construction of the tunnel is granted no more significance than construction of the pool, and both are subordinated to the resulting benefit: the provision of water inside the city. For the author of this statement, the latter is what gives significance to the undertaking.

In contrast with the tunnel inscription, 2 Kings 20:20a is written from an official point of view.[11] It attributes everything to the king and is interested in showing how he benefited the city. The story of the tunnel reflected in Kings was therefore probably first told in the court, initially that of the king responsible, but then, given the significance of the project, probably in that of later Judean kings.

In this case, we are at some remove from the oral origins of the story. Nevertheless, we may be able to say something about its written history. If transposed into the first person—"It was I who made the pool and the watercourse and brought the water into the city"—this account of the construction of the tunnel would fit perfectly into a building inscription. In that form, it is comparable with a similar claim of responsibility for the construction of waterworks by King Mesha of Moab in his memorial inscription (see chapter 4): "It was I who made the retaining walls of the shaf[t to the spr]ing insi[de] the city" (the Moabite Stone, ll. 23–24).[12] The particular wording of the account in Kings corresponds to the style in which such accomplishments are recorded in royal inscriptions. Either it is based on such an inscription, or else it was composed in epigraphic style. We should also note that following this brief account of Hezekiah's provision of water for the city, the author of Kings goes on to claim that "they [this and other unspecified achievements] are written in the chronicles of the kings of Judah." If these chronicles actually existed—other than as part of Kings' historiographic rhetoric—they may have incorporated material from royal inscriptions and thus been a third written stage of this narrative between the other two.[13]

Biblical literature here preserves a narrative statement reflecting what one would expect in a formal building inscription, while the inscription that commemorates the actual construction is unlike any other and of unusual human interest. It is appropriate to contrast the biblical account of the tunnel project as the official story with the epigraphic account as an unofficial version by a—if not the—leading participant in the actual project. The Kings version gives a comprehensive overview of the project—its two parts, its purpose and benefit—but obscures the role of anyone other than the king (as does King Mesha's inscription in referring to the water system constructed in the Moabite city of Qarho). The tunnel inscription, by contrast, ignores the larger context—the king's commission or authorization of the project, the construction of the pool or reservoir at the city end of the tunnel, the final benefit to the city—and describes instead the actual experiences of the workers in the final stages of the excavation and gives the specific measurements of the completed project, thus indirectly expressing the excitement and pride of the supervisor(s) at the completion of their work.

2 Chronicles 32:30a

Much later, 2 Chronicles 32:30a gives the following version of the story: "Hezekiah blocked up the upper outlet of the waters of the Gihon, and directed them down to the west of the city of David." The Chronicler here continues the tradition of attributing such activities to the king (and accepts from Kings that Hezekiah was the king in question). While this account is part of a list of the signs of Hezekiah's greatness and favor with God (vv. 27–30), its language is unusual for the Chronicler, suggesting that it was drawn from some other source (Welten 1973, 39, n. 132).[14] It is certainly not drawn from the Kings account. However, when commentators speak of its adding details to our knowledge of the operation or the tunnel,[15] they exaggerate. Second Chronicles 32:30a concentrates on the *change of direction* of the water. It displays an awareness of a different earlier course, knows that the water now emerges to the west of the city, and provides the physical explanation for the change: the blocking up of the old outlet and redirecting of the water to its present location. But anyone familiar with Kings and the watercourses of Jerusalem would have known or inferred all of this. Thus it is scarcely true that this account gives information otherwise unavailable. There is more additional "information" (though not historical) in the completely separate, more generalized, and almost mythological account provided earlier in 2 Chronicles 32:3–4.

Second Chronicles 32:30a gives a historical account based on observation long after the fact. The activities and objects of interest of the earlier stories have now completely disappeared from view. There is no mention of tunnel or pool, no interest in the means or awareness of the work involved in bringing the water to the pool of Siloam. Any sense that this was an extraordinary accomplishment is completely lost.

Thus the two biblical accounts recall the bringing of water into the city, giving the credit exclusively to the king. Kings notes his construction of tunnel and pool; Chronicles mentions only his blocking up of the old outlet. In both, officialdom has ignored and time has obliterated any sense of the excitement of the human accomplishment or the scale of the technical achievement. For a narrative that gives some hint of those, we have to turn from the biblical literature to the inscription.

Ben Sirach 48:17

Finally, it is worth comparing a poetic account of the construction of the tunnel from the early third century:

Hezekiah fortified his city, directing water into it,
> with bronze he hacked through rocks
>> and dammed up the water into a pool.[16] (Sir 48:17)

In this section of his work, Sirach praises admirable figures of the past through the poetic elaboration of information gleaned from scripture. In 48:17–22 he extols Hezekiah. Verse 17 builds on the basic information provided by 2 Kings 20:20a. It begins with the purpose and consequence of the construction of the tunnel, repeating the motif of bringing water into the city, but seeing this as a part of Hezekiah's fortification of the city (probably in light of 2 Chron 32:2–5). Sirach then builds on the reference in 2 Kings 20:20a to the watercourse and pool. Here his poetic imagination goes behind the official statements of Kings and Chronicles to provide a picture of the work involved: "with bronze he hacked through rocks and dammed up the water into a pool." But Hezekiah remains the subject of this physical labor! There is no trace of the excavators whom the author of the inscription portrayed so graphically in the middle of the tunnel. The poet may sense something of the labor involved, but the tradition has attributed the achievement to Hezekiah, and even this poet's imagination cannot penetrate behind that tradition.

Summary

These four accounts of the Siloam tunnel project not only are different in literary character but also represent different points of view and, ultimately, different interests and social contexts. In the tunnel inscription, the person probably in charge of the project reported with professional pride the final, triumphant stages of the workers' labor and the measurements of the achievement. We can infer from this something of the character of the story as first told by those participating in the project. In 2 Kings, and perhaps earlier in a chronicle or royal inscription, the official record gave Hezekiah the credit for bringing water into the city by making a watercourse and pool. From this, we receive an impression of how the story was told in the court of the kings of Judah.

The two remaining accounts were almost certainly composed in writing, drawing on earlier written accounts, rather than any live oral tradition. In 2 Chronicles, a later Judean historian again credited Hezekiah with the work, which is here described as redirecting the water of the Gihon spring to the west of the city, without even any mention of the tunnel. Finally, in Sirach, a poet in the wisdom tradition imagined the process of cutting through the rock and damming the water into a pool but made Hezekiah the subject of even these verbs, thus faithfully transmitting the tradition of Hezekiah's exclusive responsibility for the project.

Stories of Military Campaigns

Warfare was probably an almost universal experience of the inhabitants of the Iron Age states of Syria-Palestine. Most adult males probably participated in at least one battle during their lifetimes.[1] How much they spoke of their experiences or told the story of this or that battle or campaign we cannot know. But we may be sure that men would have found occasions and audiences for recounting their stories of memorable victories. Certainly kings and generals would have found a ready-made audience at court to hear accounts of their victories. Presumably these would be recounted in the garb of the characteristic royal ideology, presenting the king as the protégé of his god. King, god, or both might be credited with military success, depending on the particular composition of the audience and the particular occasion.

The first topic of royal memorial inscriptions is usually the king's military successes. The fullest preserved collection of such stories in Syria-Palestine appears in an inscription of the eighth-century Moabite king, Mesha. This recounts a series of brief stories of military campaigns, presumably not composed directly from memory of the original events but rather expressing the dominant features of the stories as told in the court.

The following analysis of this inscription explores the narrative techniques of the author and identifies a common structure or pattern to which the stories conform. Similar stories appear in two other inscriptions (from Tel Dan and Sefire). Did the biblical historians also draw on oral stories of campaigns or epigraphic condensations of them? This question is pursued through an analysis of several passages that one might think related to the traditional form found in the inscriptions: two individual narratives in 2 Kings 13 and a series of such in Joshua 10 and 2 Samuel 8 (with an excursus on 2 Sam 10).

Stories of Military Campaigns in Inscriptions

The Inscription of Mesha

The 34–line inscription of King Mesha of Moab was first seen by a Westerner in 1868, when the Bedouin in whose territory it lay showed it to F. A. Klein, a German missionary working in Palestine for an Anglican mission based in England. A complicated series of communications and negotiations—involving interested Prussians, French, and British, and representatives of their respective governments, as well as Ottoman authorities and local Bedouin—ended in the breaking up of the stone monument bearing the inscription. Prior to the breakage, a French scholar, C. Clermont-Ganneau, had commissioned three Arabs to make a squeeze (a facsimile impression on wetted paper) of the inscription. Unfortunately, this also was damaged as a result of the circumstances under which it was taken. Several of the stone fragments were recovered early in 1870. Over the following years Clermont-Ganneau published the inscription on the basis of the squeeze and fragments.[2] However, an authoritative full edition of the surviving material has never been published.[3]

Despite its unfortunate history, the inscription of King Mesha, composed some time in the second half of the ninth century BCE, remains the longest Iron Age inscription ever recovered east or west of the Jordan, the major evidence for the Moabite language, and a unique epigraphic source of stories about military campaigns in this region.

The words of the inscription are separated by dots. There is also a higher level of segmentation of the text by a series of thirty-seven vertical strokes (according to the drawing by Lidzbarski), which displace the dots where they occur. (They are indicated in the following translation by a diagonal line: \.) Most frequently, these mark off pairs of coordinated sentences,[4] thus indicating the writer's awareness of the dominance of a balancing or parallelistic style in the prose composition.

Larger levels of structure may be discerned on the basis of a topical analysis. On the largest scale, there are three major parts: an introduction (A), a series of accounts of how Moab had displaced Israel in various parts of the country (B), and a series of accounts of building activities in various parts of the country (C). The preserved inscription ends with the fragmentary beginning of a fourth part similar to the second (D).[5] These three major parts are easily broken down into smaller sections, often exhibiting some structural parallelism, which we may term paragraphs (separated in the following translation by blank lines).[6] Subsections of these may also be distinguished (here introduced by the line numbers of the original text).

A. INTRODUCTION

(1–3) I am Mesha, son of Kemosh[yatti?], the king of Moab, the Dibonite. \ My father ruled over Moab for thirty years, and I ruled after my father. \

(3–4) And I made this sanctuary for Chemosh in Qarho, \ the Sanctu[ary of the Sa]vior (?), because he saved me from all the kings, and because he let me gloat over my enemies. \

B. EXPULSION OF ISRAEL

(4–6) Omri was king of Israel, and he oppressed Moab for a long time, because Chemosh was angry with his land; \ and his son succeeded him, and he too said: "I will oppress Moab." \ In my time he said so.

(7) But I gloated over him and over his dynasty: \ Israel had finally disappeared for ever.

(7–8) Omri took possession of the land of Medeba[7] and occupied it during his time and half the time of his son—forty years.

(8–9) But Chemosh returned it in my time. \

(9–10) And I built Baal-meon and made the shaft in it, and I built Kiriathaim. \

(10–11) Now the people of Gad had lived in the land of Ataroth for ages, and the king of Israel rebuilt Ataroth for himself (or for them). \

(11–13) But I attacked the town and captured it, \ and killed the entire people: the town became Chemosh's and Moab's.[8] \ And I brought back from there *'r'l dwdh*, and dragged it/him before Chemosh in Kerioth. \

(13–14) And I settled in it people of Sharon and people of Maharith. \

(14) Then Chemosh said to me: "Go and capture Nebo from Israel." \

(14–18) So I went by night and attacked it from crack of dawn till midday, \ and I captured it and killed all, seven thousand men and male aliens, \ and women and female aliens and slavegirls,[9] \ because I had devoted it to Ashtar-Chemosh. \ And I took from there *'[r']ly* of Yahweh and dragged them before Chemosh. \

(18–19) The king of Israel had built Jahaz and stayed in it when attacking me. \

(19–20) But Chemosh drove him out before me. I took from Moab two hundred men, all of its commanders, \ and I took them up against (Lemaire: established them in) Jahaz, and I captured it,

(21) So as to annex it to Dibon. \

C. BUILDING AND OTHER ADMINISTRATIVE ACTIVITIES

(21–24) It was I who built Qarho: the wall of the woods[10] and the wall of the acropolis; \ and it was I who built its gates, and it was I who built its towers; \ and it was I who built a royal palace; and it was I who made the retaining walls of the sha[ft for the spr]ing inside the town. \

(24–25) And there was no cistern inside the city in Qarho, so I said to all the people: "Make for yourselves a cistern each in his own house." \

(25–26) And it was I who cut channels for Qarho with Israelite prisoners. \

(26) It was I who built Aroer; and it was I who made the highway through the Arnon valley.

(27) It was I who built Beth-bamoth, because it was destroyed. \

(27–28) It was I who built Bezer, because [it] was in ruins. \

(28) . . . [And the me]n of Dibon were in battle array, because all of Dibon was a (palace) guard.[11] \

(28–29) And it was I who ruled a hundred [   ] in the towns which I had annexed to the land. \

(29–31) And it was I who built [the temple of Medeb]a and the temple of Dibla-thaim[12] \ and the temple of Baal-meon, and I took up there [   ] flocks of the land. \

D. EXPULSION OF JUDAH? (Cf. B)

(31–32) And as for Horonaim, the House of [Da]vid(?) lived in it[13] [   ]

(32–34) [Then] Chemosh said to me: "Go down and attack Horonaim." \ So I went down [and attacked the town and captured it,(?)[14] and] Chemosh [retu]rned it in my time and . . . from there . . . \ [   ] . . . \ and . .[. . .].

Section A: Introduction   The inscription begins with an introduction (ll. 1–4) in which Mesha identifies himself and refers to the occasion on which the inscription was written.[15] Self-identification is the characteristic opening of memorial inscriptions (M. Miller 1974). Here the king identifies himself by his name (Mesha), his father's name (Chemosh[yatti?]), his office (king of Moab), and his place of origin (Dibon). In a second sentence, he elaborates on his father and office, referring to the length of his father's reign and his own succession: "My father ruled over Moab for thirty years, and I ruled after my father." All of this affirms the legitimacy of Mesha.

In ll. 3–4 the occasion for the inscription is given as the erection of a sanctuary in Qarho in thanksgiving to Chemosh for Mesha's deliverance from and defeat of hostile kings. Until very recently, it was universally assumed that only one enemy is named in the inscription, namely, Israel. However, Lemaire's reading of l. 31 now claims that "the House of David," that is, Judah, is the enemy attacked in the narrative of the last preserved lines of the inscription, and Margalit is proposing that Edom is the enemy referred to there (see n. 13 in this chapter). Could other kings, for example, of Ammon or Damascus, have been mentioned in the remaining lost lines? The phrase "all the kings" in l. 4 does not demand such a conclusion, since it may well envisage potential as well as actual enemies, and, in any case, hyperbole was common in claims of victory (cf. the "seventy kings" in the Tel Dan inscription described later). It was customary in contemporary royal memorial inscriptions to claim resistance to or deliverance from hostile kings (cf. Kilamuwa [chapter 5] ll. 5–7, Zakkur [chapter 6] ll. A2–B3). Mesha's reference to the present occasion serves two literary purposes: it draws attention to the description of his work in Qarho (part C, ll. 21–26), which, because of its length and this early reference, becomes the focal point in the reading of the inscription, and it introduces a pervasive theme of the narrative part of the inscription (parts B and D), namely, the role of Chemosh in Mesha's victories over his enemies.

Sections B and D: The Individual Campaign Narratives   The longest section of the inscription (B, ll. 4–21) consists of five roughly parallel narratives, here marked off as paragraphs. Each concerns Israel's occupation of a certain town or district claimed by Moab, Mesha's recovery of it, and, in most cases, his disposition of the reclaimed territory. The first narrative (ll. 4–7) gives the most general account, of which the following four are particular cases. Where the former concerns Israel's general past oppression of, and recent disappearance from, Moab as a whole, the latter four concern unique historical data and actions in particular towns or districts: Medeba, Ataroth, Nebo, and Jahaz. Within the common pattern of these five stories, the narrative content and techniques vary considerably.

The initial, general narrative begins with the identification of the enemy in terms similar to Mesha's previous self-identification: "Omri was king of Israel . . . and his son succeeded him" (cf. 1 Kgs 16:23b, 28b). Omri was apparently a historical figure of some significance. Although the Deuteronomistic History roundly condemns him (1 Kgs 16:25–26) like most other kings of Israel, it acknowledges that he founded a dynasty (1 Kgs 16:15–28), founded and built what was to remain the capital of Israel for the rest of its existence (1 Kgs 16:24), and was a king whose accomplishments and "valor" (gĕbûrâ) are said to be recorded in the "annals of the Kings of Israel" (1 Kgs 16:27). Even after Omri's dynasty had been replaced on the throne of Israel, the country was still known to the Assyrians as bīt ḫumri, "the household of Omri." Mesha is not embarrassed either to name this prominent antecedent of the present Israelite monarch or to acknowledge his power over Moab: "he oppressed Moab for a long time. . . ." However, credit for Omri's achievement is attributed to Chemosh: "because Chemosh was angry with his land." For the narrator, the only reason why Omri was able to oppress Moab was Chemosh's displeasure with his country, which left it at the mercy of its neighbor. This also establishes that, while Moab may have lost its sovereignty, Chemosh had not lost his.

If the narrator slights Omri's achievement by reference to Chemosh's role, he does not consider his son, the subject of the next two sentences, even worth naming: "He too said: 'I will oppress Moab.' In my days he said so. But I gloated over him and his dynasty: Israel had finally perished for ever." The narrator here uses direct speech to emphasize the contrast between intention and performance, between royal goals and national fate. The Israelite king had proposed to continue his father's policy of controlling Moab but ended up vanishing from the scene, leaving the Moabite king triumphant. The temporal reference following the Israelite king's proposal introduces the narrator: it was in his time that such was intended. Immediately juxtaposed to this is the ultimate outcome, stated in two parallel clauses: it was the narrator who was able to look down on his enemy; Israel was reduced to nothing. The intervening steps—the intervention of Chemosh and Mesha—are here ignored in the interest of contrasting the aims of the anonymous king with the abject disappearance of him and his dynasty.

The structure of this story may be represented as follows: Omri had oppressed Moab, because Chemosh was angry with it (exposition); in Mesha's time his son proposed to do the same (complication), but Mesha saw him off once for all (resolution and conclusion). The three temporal phrases, to which Smelik draws attention (1990, 23–24; 1992a, 69), give appropriate weight to the three distinct stages: Israel's oppression of Moab was "for a long time," the turning point was "in my time," and Israel's departure from the scene is "for ever." The presentation of both Omri and his son exposes their respective weaknesses—not weaknesses of character but weaknesses in relation to the actions of Chemosh. Although only

Chemosh's anger is mentioned here, we know from the previous paragraph that Chemosh is also the one who delivered Mesha; and the mention of Mesha's gloating in l. 7 harks back specifically to l. 4, where it is parallel to Chemosh's deliverance ("because he saved me from all the kings, and because he let me gloat over my enemies"). Thus this overview of the relations between Israel and Moab is linked with the final clauses of the introduction, instantiating their general claim while introducing the theme of the following, more detailed narratives.

The first two thirds of this narrative are expressed by an omniscient narrator, who knows Chemosh's feelings and Omri's son's intentions. But with the reference to "in my time," the interested narrator moves into the frame, and his point of view and interests dominate the conclusion, displacing any reference to actual events. In the midst of this otherwise very summary narrative, the dramatic presentation of Omri's son's speech expresses his point of view, which is immediately exposed by the triumphant narrator as deluded. That speech is also the turning point of the plot. It is the last stage in the Israelite oppression; the following sentence, by introducing the contemporary narrator, discloses the irony of the speech and anticipates the reversal of the two concluding sentences.

The next narrative (ll. 7–10) focuses on the land of Medeba. It consists of three parts, concerned with the Israelite occupation of Medeba, Chemosh's restoration of it, and Mesha's subsequent activity in it.

In the first part, the narrator refers to Omri's initial conquest as "taking possession" of the land and to the duration of the occupation as "his time and half the time of his son—forty years." Historians and chronologists have argued endlessly about the meaning of these words, usually with a view to allowing a new calculation that can be more or less harmonized with one of the biblical chronologies for the Omri dynasty and to correlating some of the events recounted by Mesha with some of those recounted in the Bible.[16] What is generally not recognized is that these two expressions concern only the land of Medeba. The only other chronological data are those of the first, general narrative; and they simply indicate that the resistance to Israel began with the frustration of the intentions of Omri's son and ended with the obliteration of Israel—which could be as late as the reign of Jehu's son, Jehoahaz (see Lemaire 1991).

It is now generally recognized that forty is a conventional number, representing, when used with days or years, a long time (as of Israel's years and Jesus' days in the wilderness, the duration of the flood, and Moses' stay on top of the mountain). The precision of the preceding reference is probably also illusory. It is certainly not literally true that Omri lived in Medeba during his own *and* his successor's reigns! But a king's "time" (literally "days") is imprecise to start with. Further, it is unlikely that the kings of these Iron Age Palestinian states kept careful records of the length of their neighbors' reigns. If they did, the direct way for Mesha to refer to the length of the occupation under Omri's son would be to state the number of years he had been on the throne by the end of the occupation, not by comparing this number with the total number of years of his reign in order to come up with the appropriate fraction! Finally, these phrases cannot be separated from the wording of the previous narrative, which states that Omri oppressed Moab "for a long time" (literally "many days") and speaks of his son as only proposing to oppress it. I conclude that the language of l. 8 exhibits a specious specificity. "His time and half the time of his son" is probably no more than a rhetorical way of saying "from Omri's time until during the reign of his successor," which is then evaluated by the equally rhetorical "forty years" as "a long time"—from the point of view of the narrator. (Cf. the "thirty years" of the reign of Mesha's father, l. 1).

This long, burdensome occupation (again attributed to Omri—the ignominious son who lost Moab remains nameless) was reversed by Chemosh.[17] The narrator says nothing about the form this reversal took. He simply attributes it to Chemosh, associating it with himself by the phrase "in my time." While in the previous narrative that phrase hinted at the delusions suffered by the enemy, in the present context it suggests the divine favor enjoyed by Mesha.

While he ignores the circumstances of the Israelite defeat or withdrawal and claims no credit for it, the narrator goes on to specify the construction he undertook in its wake: "I built Baal-meon and made the shaft in it, and I built Kiriathaim." As is clear from numerous inscriptions, such building activity usually refers to the rebuilding or fortifying of old towns. The shaft would have been a major excavation and construction project providing access to subterranean water within the town (cf. chapter 3). Mesha here records how, in the aftermath of Chemosh's liberation of the land of Medeba, he completed some construction providing for the safety and security of the western border.

In this narrative, the narrator does little more than present Omri as the great oppressor, Chemosh as the sole restorer, and himself as the one who strengthens the now recovered district by his building activities. The roles of Chemosh and Mesha here reflect their roles in the introduction, ll. 3–4, and correspond to the whole of sections B (with D), in which Chemosh delivers, and C, in which Mesha builds. The restoration of Medeba by Chemosh, though the fulcrum of the plot, receives minimal treatment. Recognition of Chemosh's role displaces any attention to details of the campaign. It may have been an arduous, drawn-out war with no single outstanding victory, or Omri may have withdrawn his forces and not resisted Mesha's advance. The only specific information given concerns not the campaign but Omri's previous possession and occupation and, balancing that, the achievements of Mesha's present possession and occupation. The small amount of concrete detail is reserved for the latter subject.

The third narrative (l. 10–14) conforms to the general structure of the second: the Israelite occupation, the recovery for Moab, Mesha's consolidation of his new possession. But its interests are quite different.

The exposition recounts the long occupation of the land of Ataroth by the people of Gad. The expression "for ages" (*m'lm*) distinguishes this occupation from that initiated by Omri. This occupation goes back as long as anyone knows or can remember. The Gadites are thus well established here, which may also imply some rights. But this general exposition is followed by a specific complication: in a recent act of provocation the (again anonymous) Israelite king fortified the town of Ataroth.

Mesha then attacks the town and kills all its population. This confirms that it was not the presence of the Gadites but the fortification of Ataroth that provoked and justified Mesha's action; only the inhabitants of the town are killed, not those of the surrounding district mentioned in the first sentence (l. 10). The town has now become the possession of Chemosh and Moab. The juxtaposition of deity and country indicates the extent to which the interests of Chemosh are now identified with those of the people (in contrast with his past anger with his land, ll. 5–6).

In the following sentence, Mesha speaks of bringing back from Ataroth '*r'l dwdh*—another much discussed but still obscure term—and dragging him or it before Chemosh.[18] After the taking of the town, the slaughter of the inhabitants, and the assertion of its new status as belonging to Chemosh and Moab, this obviously significant dedication to Chemosh is the capstone of the campaign, Mesha's public demonstration before his own people of his complete conquest and dispossession of the enemy, and of his recognition of Chemosh's role and claims.

While the preceding narrative concerning the repossession of a district concluded with the rebuilding of towns in that district, the present narrative concerning the taking of a town and slaughter of its occupants concludes with the repopulation of the town: Mesha settles in it people from two other locations. As the Israelite king's fortification of Ataroth was countered by Mesha's attack on the city and slaughter of its inhabitants, the opening reference to its former occupation by Gadites is balanced by the concluding reference to its new occupation by Sharonites and Maharithites.

In the previous narrative, Israel's expulsion was the briefest element. Here it is the longest and most detailed. While Chemosh was both subject and actor in the second part of the last narrative, the narrator is the subject and protagonist of the corresponding part of this narrative. But the new ownership of the town and Mesha's dedication to Chemosh are the climax of the specific military action. The previous narrative gives Chemosh all the credit for Israel's removal; the present narrative records the specific human actions that put an end to the Israelite presence and that acknowledged Chemosh's sovereignty. The former expresses the present faith of the narrator in the deity as the historical actor; the latter describes the historical acts of the narrator that expressed his acknowledgment of Chemosh at that time. In the first case, the narrative tells us what to believe; in the second, it describes the actions that expressed such beliefs.

The fourth narrative (ll. 14–18) begins with the quotation of a speech by Chemosh: "Then Chemosh said to me: 'Go and take Nebo from Israel.' " The means of communication—dream? prophetic oracle?—is ignored; the speech is presented as the deity's direct word to the king. The divine command implies what in previous narratives was treated independently as exposition: Israel's occupation of the town or district in question. Indeed, the fragmentary beginning of a narrative at the end of the inscription places such an exposition ("And as for Horonaim, the House of [Da]vid(?) lived in it . . .") before a comparable divine command ("Chemosh said to me: 'Go down and fight against Horonaim' "). The present narrative dispenses with such exposition and initiates the action immediately by quotation of the divine command.

The command is directly followed by the obedience of the king: "So I went . . ." (cf. the Horonaim narrative at the end of the inscription: " 'Go down.

. . .' So I went down . . .”). The sequence—divine command and royal obedience—excludes an act that, we learn later, presumably comes between the two: Mesha's promise to devote the entire town to Chemosh, which is disclosed as an analepsis or flashback only after he has carried it out (see l. 17).

We now have the most detailed account yet of Mesha's military activity: “I went by night and fought against it from crack of dawn till midday, and I took it. . . .” The nocturnal expedition, the morning-long battle, the surprise attack, the sustained assault—these suggest the enemy's strength and the measure of Mesha's achievement in taking the town.[19] This is doubtless also conveyed by the following clause: “. . . and killed all, seven thousand men and male aliens, and women and female aliens and slavegirls. . . .” Seven thousand would have been an unusually large population, and it is not clear how many of the listed categories of people are included in the seven thousand.[20] But the number is probably a gross and boastful estimate, no more reliable than other ancient estimates of large numbers of people. The narrator now explains this wholesale slaughter: “. . . because I had devoted it to Ashtar-Chemosh” (the verb is *hhrm,* the same as that used in biblical accounts of slaughter and destruction devoted to Yahweh). In saying that he killed all the inhabitants because he had devoted the town to the god (*ky . . . hhrmth*), the narrator shows that what was involved was a prior commitment (as in Num 21:2; Josh 6:16–17).[21] To this is added a more particular dedication: “And I took from there the '*r'ly* of Yahweh and dragged them before Chemosh.”

The parallels between the previous story and this one are striking. In both, Mesha kills the entire population of a town and removes certain things (or people), which he drags before Chemosh. While the present narrative makes more of the battle, it shares with the previous narrative a special interest in the slaughter of the inhabitants and the dedications to the deity. The question arises whether a distinction exists between wholesale slaughter, as in the previous story, and killing people because one has “devoted” them to Chemosh. The present story is the only one in which there is no conclusion concerning Mesha's administrative activities with respect to the newly acquired territory (rebuilding, resettling, or, as in the following narrative, annexation). Could this be because “devotion” involved complete destruction and abandonment, as in the Bible? Other features of the narrative point in this direction. First, while Mesha kills all the people in the preceding narrative, he kills them in the second, because he has devoted *it* (the city). Second, in the first of these two narratives, the town now belongs to Chemosh and Moab; in the second, he devotes the city to the deity alone (Moab gets nothing because of the wholesale destruction of the city). Third, he spells out that he killed not only the men and women of the city but also male and female aliens and slavegirls (who might otherwise have been ignored, allowed to flee, or taken captive). I am therefore inclined to believe that the “devotion” of this narrative involved the destruction of everyone and everything in the city and that this explains the lack of any concluding adminstrative measures such as appear in the other narratives.

In conclusion, this narrative lacks the expository and concluding parts of the other narratives: it has neither an initial account of Israelite occupation nor a concluding account of administrative measures subsequently taken by the king. It concentrates exclusively on the campaign, which is treated in greater detail than any other, beginning with the initial (quoted) commission by Chemosh, continuing with the reference to the nocturnal expedition and the duration of the battle, spelling out the categories of persons killed and the prior commitment to devote the entire town to Chemosh, and ending with the sacrifice of certain distinguished things (or persons) to Chemosh. By contrast with the account of the Medeba campaign, this story glories in the rapid succession of moves from the divine commission to the dedications to the deity, comprising one swift victory for god and king.

While Chemosh is the subject of the first sentence, the subject of all the remaining sentences is Mesha. But all his actions are a response to the express command and tacit support of Chemosh. Chemosh's speech initiates the action, and Chemosh is finally the beneficiary of Mesha's devotion of the city and of his concluding dedication. Chemosh is more prominent in this narrative than any other.

The fifth and last of this series of brief narratives follows the previous pattern: occupation by Israel, expulsion by Mesha-Chemosh, administrative consolidation. Like the third narrative, it begins with a noun and perfect verb, referring to an antecedent condition or act, in this case: "The king of Israel had built Jahaz." The complication is expressed by reference to the king's ongoing use of it against Mesha: "He stayed in it, when attacking me." In this case, the object of Mesha's concern is the Israelite king's base of operations, presumably implying that this was the most formidable objective that Mesha tackled.

The expulsion of the Israelites is expressed as both a divine act and a human act. At the beginning, we read that "Chemosh drove him out before me," a theological claim not unlike that of the second narrative ("Chemosh restored it in my time") but slightly more explicit. The narrator then reverts to recounting military exploits: "I took from Moab two hundred men, all of its commanders, and I took them up against Jahaz, and I captured it." Contrary to most interpreters, I assume that the two hundred commanders brought their own men with them, not that Mesha's army here consisted of only two hundred men! Mesha is perhaps here claiming a nationwide mobilization appropriate to the target, as compared with more limited forces for lesser objectives. In this case, the scale of his forces is the one detail provided. The juxtaposition of "Chemosh drove him out" and "I captured it" expresses the king's faith in the role of the deity alongside, and enabling, his own role.

The concluding administrative arrangement is minimal, expressed in a purpose clause: "to annex it to Dibon." This reference to Dibon leads into the list of building activities on the acropolis of this city (ll. 21–26.)

The next major part of the inscription (C) records Mesha's administrative achievements, especially the construction of the acropolis of Qarho (ll. 21–26), but then more briefly the rebuilding or fortifying of several other towns and temples (ll. 26–31). Following this part, enough of another narrative is preserved to allow us to recognize in it a story of the same type as those in section B. It clearly represents the first two of the three stages we have found in most of those stories and shares some phraseology with them. While too little remains to permit an appreciation of it on its own terms, it does provide examples of different uses of sentences found in the previous narratives.

Unlike all the preceding narratives, it begins with a place-name[22]: "And (as for) Horonaim, there lived in it. . . ." Perhaps this stylistic shift is reflective of its status as an appendix (see later in this chapter). In other respects, the opening words are reminiscent of the opening of the third narrative ("Now the people of Gad had lived in . . ."). Like the Gad narrative, this, too, tells of an enemy occupation. At this point, the inscription begins to narrate military defeats of an enemy apparently not Israel.[23]

The next preserved piece of text ("[Then] Chemosh said to me: 'Go down and fight against Horonaim' ") recalls the divine initiative with which the fourth narrative began ("Then Chemosh said to me: 'Go and capture Nebo from Israel' "). Where the fourth narrative began abruptly with such a divine command, here the narrator uses it after the more usual expository account of the enemy occupation. Like the fourth narrative, however, this one continues with a notice of Mesha's prompt obedience: "So I went down [and attacked the town and captured it]."

Finally, another sentence is an exact duplicate of one in the second narrative: "Chemosh returned it in my time."[24] There, that one sentence constituted the entire account of Moab's recovery of territory; here, it is juxtaposed to an account of Mesha's military activity. The juxtaposition of divine and human activity recalls the same feature in the fifth narrative's account of Israel's expulsion.

These last fragments suggest that phrases and compositional techniques from earlier in the inscription have been recast to compose a new narrative about a different town and campaign. Perhaps these techniques, formulaic phrases, and constructions were more widely used—at least in Mesha's court and perhaps also, with dialectical variations, in other courts of Iron Age Palestine. Our inscription illustrates how they may be used in similar or slightly different ways to compose individual narratives. Thus "enemy E lived in land L" (or a more detailed account of the enemy occupation) might be used in the exposition of such narratives. "The god G said to me: 'Go and attack/capture L' " (or a more elaborate version of such an oracle ordering and authorizing the military campaign) might initiate the account of such a venture, either following an exposition, as here, or opening a narrative that dispenses with background exposition, as in the fourth narrative. This would be followed by an account of the king's obedient response: "So I went . . . ," as in both these stories. Finally, "G returned it in my time" or something similar (e.g., "G drove him out before me" in the fifth narrative) would express the god's role in the successful outcome of the campaign. The common themes of such stories emerge as the divine oracle authorizing the campaign, royal obedience to the divine orders, and divine action (alongside or displacing royal action).

Two Editions of Mesha's Inscription? The distinction between parts B (together with D) and C has long been recognized and usually characterized as between military activity and building activity. Apart from such obvious differences in subject matter, there are also such stylistic differences as, first, the predominant use of narrative verb forms in B (and D) and the independent pronoun followed by perfect verb forms in C (here translated "and it was I who . . .") and, second, the use of the definite object marker ('*t*) in B (and D) and its absence in C.[25] But the distinction between the two parts can be overdrawn. In part B, three of the four narratives about specific campaigns conclude with administrative (including, in the first case, building) activities by which Mesha established his control over the newly conquered territory. The conquest of Jahaz in the last of these narratives ends with its annexation to Dibon, which leads into the more extended account of the development of Qarho, the acropolis in Dibon, all of which corresponds to the brief administrative measures reported at the end of the earlier campaigns. The material concerning construction in Qarho includes a minimal narrative in ll. 24–25 in which Mesha responds to a lack of private cisterns in Qarho by ordering (narrative verb form!) each household to make its own.

The rest of section C is more complex and difficult to explain. Dibon is left behind in ll. 26–28, which are concerned with other building projects. Then l. 28, though difficult to interpret, seems to concern the function of the personnel of Dibon, describing them as a guard—that is, Mesha's palace guard? Finally, ll. 28–29 apparently summarize (resuming the "it was I who . . ." style) Mesha's rule in the towns he had annexed to the land. Possibly this was the conclusion of an earlier version of the inscription,[26] and the reference to the building of the three temples in ll. 29–31, as well as the account of the Horonaim campaign, were added later. In that case, the so-called building section may be seen as originally an extension of the last of the campaign narratives, consisting of the construction in Qarho, a residual list of three other projects, and a concluding reference to the king's personal support in Dibon and secure rule over all his new territory. The structure of the inscription and the content of ll. 28–29 both commend the proposal that the latter originally concluded the text and that the rest of the present inscription was added after the original composition.[27]

Further observations support this hypothesis. First, two of the three temples mentioned in ll. 29–31 are in localities already dealt with earlier (Medeba and Baal-meon in the second narrative). The fact that these two were not mentioned at the end of the second narrative suggests that they were completed only after the first edition of the inscription. Second, the reference to building activities in ll. 29–31 is stylistically distinguished from the preceding: previously, a separate verb is used for each project, here three projects are the objects of one verb. Third, as noted before, the narrative in section D is both removed from all the earlier campaign narratives and is stylistically distinguished from them by its placement of the name of the site at the beginning of the first sentence (extraposition)—"and (as for) Horonaim. . . ." Again, this passage would not have been included in the original sequence of campaign narratives because the campaign to which it refers took place after the composition of what is now ll. 1–29. Mesha tackled one enemy at a time, turning to expel the occupiers of towns in the south only after ridding Moab of the Israelite presence north of the Arnon. Fourth, it is striking that there is no mention among all the building activities in Qarho (ll. 21–26) of the building of the temple to which the introduction refers (ll. 3–4). Evidently, the original account of Mesha's building activities preceded that undertaking. It is only now, on the occasion of the completion of that temple, that Mesha takes up his former memorial inscription, gives it an introduction fitting to the present occasion, and supplements it with accounts of his more recent construction projects and campaigns.

Summary   In sum, the so-called Moabite stone is a memorial inscription in which Mesha first introduces himself as the legitimate heir of his father and then gives his reasons for making the sanctuary in which the inscription is located: Chemosh gave him victory over all hostile kings. He then illustrates this claim with material from an earlier memorial inscription. He recounts five brief narratives concerning his victories over the king of Israel: initially, a general account of past Israelite oppression and the final disposal of Israel and then four accounts of particular campaigns. Three of the four begin with a reference to Israelite occupation or aggression; the same three end with a reference to some kind of administrative consolidation of Mesha's victory (rebuilding, repopulation, or annexation); all four treat of the recovery of the land from Israel—by Chemosh, Mesha, or both. The third of the five narratives treats of this central process exclusively.

The fifth narrative concludes with a reference to the annexation of Jahaz to Dibon, leading into a list of Mesha's construction projects in Qarho, evidently the citadel of Dibon. Contained in this list is a minimal narrative in which he tells each household to build its own cistern. Three further construction projects are mentioned. The earlier edition of the inscription probably concluded with (now damaged) references to the Dibonites as Mesha's guard and to his rule over all the towns he had annexed. To this is added a notice of the more recent building of three temples and the story of a more recent campaign—the latter, so far as it is preserved, following the pattern of the five distinguished previously. How the inscription finally concluded we cannot say.

Smelik has drawn attention to the different functions of direct discourse in the inscription as representing the roles of the three main actors. Omri's son proposes to continue the oppression of Moab, but the narrator immediately reports that he saw the end of him and his dynasty, indeed, of Israel. The intention of the enemy is quoted to demonstrate its futility: it is not just unfulfilled but reversed. Mesha himself speaks in the building section, in which he is the supreme actor. He orders the people of Dibon to build a cistern in each house. There is no sequel to this order. The narrator takes for granted that his own orders are effective. Finally, Chemosh speaks twice in the military sections of the inscription, directing Mesha to attack particular cities. In each case, the narrator reports his prompt execution of Chemosh's commands and the outcome of the campaign, thus demonstrating at once Mesha's pious obedience and the reliability of Chemosh's directions.

The role of Chemosh in the inscription is particularly significant. The list of building activities in part C (including the minimal narrative in ll. 24–25 and the incomplete ll. 28–29) makes no reference to Chemosh, or any other god, but simply records Mesha's completed projects. Even the deities for whom the temples were built are not mentioned, in contrast with the introductory reference to the making of the present sanctuary for Chemosh. There the reference to the deity is accompanied by an explanation for the construction: Chemosh has given Mesha victory in his military campaigns. Accordingly, Chemosh looms large in all six of the campaign narratives, sometimes as an actor or speaker, sometimes as the object of dedications. This absence and presence of the deity in different parts of the inscription presumably relate to the different role of the deity in the two types of undertaking (cf. the inscription of Zakkur and chapter 6). War is always a life-and-death matter in which the deity's support and direction cannot be taken for granted, and the king's recognition of the deity and the deity's favor are crucial. The representation of the king as obedient agent of the god is a powerful element in legitimizing the king's role as war leader, hence the present accounts of the deity's role in the campaign and the careful spelling out of the king's dedications to the deity after the campaign, and hence also the explanation of Israelite oppression by reference to Chemosh's anger with Moab. Hence, finally, the very existence of the inscription: it is installed in the sanctuary Mesha has erected in recognition of Chemosh's deliverance of him from his enemies.

Once the introduction has stated that Chemosh "saved [him] from all the kings," the narrator represents that divine salvation variously in each individual narrative—directly, by referring to Chemosh's action; indirectly, by referring to Chemosh's instructions[28]; or indeed only by implication, by referring to his own dedications to Chemosh. The narrator seems to be free to use or not use these various narrative ingredients at will.

Finally, we may make some general observations about the campaign narratives. First, they may be contrasted with those of the Assyrian annals and Babylonian chronicles, in both of which there is careful attention to chronology—a listing of the campaigns in chronological order in the former and also a dating by year and often by month and day in the latter. But the courts of Assyria and Babylonia were administratively more complex and more literate than those of Moab and the other small states of Syria-Palestine. The Babylonians clearly kept dated written records of major events, on which the precisely dated events of the chronicles could be based. In the case of the Assyrians, scribes seem to have accompanied the army and kept a kind of journal of the campaigns. These served as the source for the detailed accounts of the official annals, which would then go through several editions as later campaigns were added and earlier ones generally abbreviated. An alternative principle for ordering campaigns is found in Assyrian summary inscriptions (traditionally, but misleadingly, called "display inscriptions"), which ignore chronology in favor of a geographical arrangement.

The inscription of Mesha not only ignores the chronology of the campaigns but also declines any geographical order.[29] The order seems rather to be determined by elements in the stories. Thus the first two are connected by references to Omri and his son. The third is linked to these by reference to "the king of Israel." The third and fourth stories are linked by captured things or persons "dragged . . . before Chemosh." The placing of the fifth story, with its reference to annexation to Dibon, provides a transition to the account of Mesha's building projects in Qarho. Thus literary considerations prevail in the ordering of the campaigns.

Second, the building projects mentioned—which will have taken many years to complete—indicate that the inscription was written long after the campaigns it recounts (though perhaps not so long after the final campaign, if indeed this was written as a supplement to an earlier version of the inscription). Stories of these campaigns presumably circulated in the court over the years, until finally the present synopses or reported stories were committed to writing in this inscription. The concentration on king and deity reflects the common interests of court and temple and the thinking of those who share their ideology. The king freely acknowledges the deity's role while also boasting of his own conquests. He and Chemosh do things for each other: Chemosh drives out the king of Israel before Mesha (l. 19); Mesha captures Nebo at Chemosh's bidding (ll. 14–16) and devotes the conquered to Chemosh (ll. 16–18). Presumably, these stories would have been recounted in the presence of the king's chief military and religious officers, who would appreciate the account of the mutually beneficial relationship of god and king and of the resultant military successes. (Ordinary Moabite fighters would doubtless have told rather different versions of these events.)

Third, though a common pattern runs through the narratives (occupation/aggression, expulsion, administrative sequel), the narrator has treated each account very differently, expanding or contracting each of the three elements. This variety contrasts with the relative monotony of part C. It also reflects not only differences among the original events but also the significance of different aspects of the campaigns in the communal memory of the court over the years, as well as the (aesthetic and political) judgments of the composer of the inscription. But it is not possible to discriminate confidently among these three factors. All we can say is that the original events, as filtered by the memory of the court in their experiences of retelling and rehearing and as shaped by the composer of the inscription, have together produced the variety of narratives now recorded. For whatever reason, the details of the Medeba campaign are completely lost in favor of the simple statement that Chemosh finally returned that territory to Moab (second narrative). By contrast, the battle for Nebo (fourth narrative) is presented as divinely commissioned, as won in one long morning following a nocturnal march and a presumably surprise attack, and as being followed by a sacrificial slaughter of all the inhabitants to Ashtar-Chemosh. Here the divine initiative, the specific military tactic, the quick success, and the dedication of the city to the deity cohere in a great cooperative success. Through all the campaign stories, the consistency of reference to the deity is balanced by the variety of actual events recounted.

Fourth, though the first, general story (ll. 4–6) claims that Mesha has liberated territory oppressed by the Israelites and the second story (ll. 7–8) refers to Omri's and his successor's occupation of land, and Mesha's recovery of such land is stated in that same story and in the final story (section D), it is questionable whether all the territory in question is indeed Moabite land that Israel has taken. In the other three stories, there is no explicit reference to prior Moabite control. The third story admits that "the people of Gad had lived in the land of Ataroth for ages"; in the fourth, Chemosh simply says: "Go and capture Nebo from Israel"; the fifth states that the king of Israel had built Jahaz and was using it as a base of operations against Mesha. The most that can be said is that control of all the territory mentioned was disputed. Nevertheless, a further ideological theme of the inscription is that what Mesha has conquered was Moab's originally.

The Tel Dan and Sefire Inscriptions

There is only one other inscription in Palestine that may have a comparable account of a campaign, namely, that on the stone fragments discovered recently (July 1993 and June 1994) at Tel Dan (Biran and Naveh 1993; 1995).[30] This, too, comes from territory disputed with Israel and also dates from the second half of the ninth century. Unfortunately, it consists of only a portion of the right-hand side and two small pieces from the upper left of a larger monument.[31] However, the remains of lines 3–10 clearly reflect a narrative account of the recovery of Aramaean territory from Israel. After a scarcely preserved account of the wars of his father (only the present l. 2), the royal author refers to his father's death (l. 3) and continues[32]:

> . . . *the king of* [Is]rael earlier entered the land of my father, [but] *Hadad made me king,* yes, me; and Hadad went before me [and] *I went out* . . . , and I killed *[seve]nty kin[gs],*[33] *who harnessed* [thousands of ch]ariots and thousands of horses; [and I killed *Jeho]ram, son of [Ahab],* king of Israel and [I] killed *[Ahaz]iah, son of [Jehoram,* kin]g of the House of David,[34] and I . . .[   ]their land. . . .[35]

As in Mesha's inscription, there is reference to (1) the previous occupation of the land by a hostile neighbor (again Israel), (2) the narrator's coming to the throne (in the newer fragments) and the intervention of the national god (here Hadad) on the new king's behalf, and (3) the narrator's victory over his enemies. It seems safe to claim that behind these broken phrases lies another story of a successful military campaign to recover occupied territory. The narrator is either recounting one campaign against a large array of diverse forces, presumably marshaled by Israel, or summarizing several campaigns. In any case, he is operating on a larger scale than Mesha and so is able to spell out the character of the opposition—the number of the leaders and their chariot forces and the names and patronymics of two particular enemies (according to the two new fragments as filled out by Biran and Naveh). With the exception of the hyperbole of "seventy kings,"[36] this is—so far as we have it!—a straightforward narrative, told consistently from the point of view of the actor-narrator. This ideological viewpoint includes the role of his god as an actor who goes before him in war.

The ideological frame found in the campaign narratives of both the inscription of Mesha and the Tel Dan fragment(s) appears even more prominently in a brief narrative in the stipulations of a treaty preserved in an Aramaic inscription found at Sefire (near Aleppo) and dating from the middle of the eighth century. It is a record of a vassal treaty between Bir-Ga'yah of KTK and Matī'-'Il of Arpad. Since there are no known references to Bir-Ga'yah ("son of majesty")—the overlord!—or his state, KTK, several hypotheses concerning their identity have been mooted (see *RLA* 6, 254–56). An early proposal of Cantineau and Dossin has been recently taken up by Parpola: that these names are cyphers for Ashur-Nerari

V and Assyria, used in the Aramaic version of the treaty to conceal the Assyrian role from anti-Assyrian elements in the local Aramaic-speaking population.[37] This would then be a local edition of the partially preserved Akkadian treaty between Matīʿ-ʾIl and Asshur-Nerari V found in Assyria. The Aramaic version would be designed to protect the prestige of the local king (Matīʿ-ʾIl) before elements of his own population even as he pursued his interest in preventing the Assyrians from invading his territory and displacing him with an Assyrian governor.[38] While not completely satisfactory, this hypothesis seems the most adequate to date.

The paragraph in question reads as follows:

> [Talʾay]m and its villages and its lords and its territory had belonged to my father and to [my father's house for] ages,[39] but when the gods beat down [my father's] house, [it be]came another's. But now the gods have brought about the restoration of [my father's] hou[se and . . .] my father's [house], and Talʾaym has returned to [Bir Gaʾy]ah and to his son and to his grandson and to his descendants for ever. (Sefire III, ll. 23–25)

Certainly this narrative differs in several ways from the narratives previously discussed: "the gods" displace any particular god; they beat down the dynasty, rather than show anger toward the country as a whole, and correspondingly restore the dynasty, as a prelude to restoration of the territory; and the restoration is referred to only by the intransitive verb "returned." The gods are the sole actors, and the theological interpretation of historical events completely displaces any reference to military (or diplomatic) moves that effected the changes in the possession of Talʾaym. Thus there is no explicit reference to a military campaign. But all of these features are explained by the literary context. First, the treaty aims for comprehensiveness in its appeal for divine witnesses and enforcers of its terms.[40] Reference solely to the god of the overlord as the restorer of the territory might disclose the identity of the latter and, in any case, be less effective than a reference that included the gods acknowledged by Arpad. Second, in a context in which the vassal and his dynasty are enjoined to respect the speaker's and his dynasty's control of the territory in question, the narrative emphasizes, not a particular campaign by the overlord, but the divine powers behind the restoration of the dynasty and the reversion of the territory to the dynasty. Despite these particular interests, the same structure is discernible in this little narrative as in the Moabite inscription: the prior claim to territory, divine displeasure leading to the assumption of the territory by another, and return of divine favor, leading to the restoration of the territory. In this case, the story of the recovery of Talʾaym has been adapted to serve as background to a treaty stipulation requiring the vassal to recognize Talʾaym as Bir-Gaʾyah's territory.

Summary

All the narratives reviewed here share not just a common structure—which, after all, may derive from the actual course of events—but a common ideology. Territory conquered by the speaker originally belonged to the speaker's predecessors.

It was conquered by another state, because of divine opposition to the speaker's predecessors (though reference to divine opposition is not preserved in the fragmentary Tel Dan inscription). Now divine intervention has brought about the restoration of the territory. This ideology expresses the legitimacy of the present king's claim on the territory in three ways: it was his originally, it became another's only owing to the temporary displeasure of his god (the gods), and it is now restored to him by his god (the gods). The three inscriptions (and the several stories within the Moabite inscription) inscribe this ideology in various ways, but the underlying message is unmistakable. This is the way the court expresses its conviction of the rightness of the conquest—to itself in the first instance but perhaps also to a larger native population, as well as to other courts into which it enters into treaty relations.

The differences among the inscriptions and their remoteness from one another eliminate any possibility of one inscription having been influenced by another. The similarities among them are best explained on the assumption that these Syro-Palestinian states shared a common ideology of the kind just described and structured their narratives of military campaigns accordingly. Each of the courts of these Syro-Palestinian states would have told such stories of past campaigns. Indeed, the expression and dissemination of oral stories of military campaigns would have begun immediately after the campaigns. Royal memorial inscriptions were usually composed only after lengthy building projects and a long reign. Only then would stories of military campaigns occasionally find written form in a royal stone monument. They would have been preceded by a period of oral narration doing the essential business of which the inscription was only a later, symbolic representation.[41]

So far, we have recovered evidence of campaign stories only from Dibon and Dan. Since these are the only two royal inscriptions of any length to have been discovered in the vicinity of Israel, one may surmise that in the southern Levant only kings strong enough to conquer and hold territory claimed by a strong neighbor would have endured long enough to sponsor such monumental memorial inscriptions.

Stories of Military Campaigns in the Bible

A universal distinction between the epigraphic and biblical sources is between narrators recounting their own acts from their own point of view in their own lifetime and narrators recounting the acts of others from a generally omniscient point of view and at some chronological distance from the time of the characters involved. In the inscriptions, the kings boast of their successes; in the books of Kings, the narrators generally expose the king's failure, or at least lack of success, in battle (Meier 1991). If there is success, it is usually attributed to a prophet or Yahweh at the expense of the king. In its treatment of the united monarchy, the Deuteronomistic History denies Solomon any military activity at all, and in the cases of Saul and David it uses proper military leadership as a measure of royal success or failure (Meier 1991). Further, most biblical war narratives are concerned with defensive campaigns (those of the "judges," Saul, David, and most of those in Kings). Thus the biblical narrators' view of the king at war generally diverges widely from that of Mesha and the Aramaean king of the Tel Dan inscription—and presumably from that of the kings of Judah and Israel.

Mesha's inscription is usually compared, on the basis of its specific historical references, with the narrative in 2 Kings 3, in which Mesha is said to have rebelled against Israel, prompting an ultimately unsuccessful campaign against him by the kings of Israel and Judah (see chapter 6). But here we are interested not in contemporary, related events but in typologically related narratives. Two types of material come into question: first, accounts of campaigns claiming recovery of territory, comparable with the individual narratives reviewed, and, second, sequences of summary accounts of the campaigns of an individual ruler for comparison with the sequence of campaign narratives in the inscription of Mesha. The only narratives in the Deuteronomistic History explicitly devoted to campaigns for the recovery of territory are in 2 Kings 13–14, where we find brief narrative summaries of Israel's reconquest of land previously taken by Damascus. There are also two sequences of narratives summarizing the campaigns of the two early leaders (David and Joshua) that allow comparison with part B of Mesha's inscription, namely, Joshua 10:28–43 and 2 Samuel 8:1–15. We shall consider these narratives in that order.

2 Kings 13–14

According to the Deuteronomistic History, after a period of occupation and oppression by the Aramaeans (2 Kgs 10:32–33; 13:3, 22), Israel was able to drive the Aramaeans off what it considered its own land (as previously, according to the Tel Dan inscription, Damascus had been able to drive Israel off its land). From other sources, we know that this was made possible in part by the weakening of Damascus, evident in its inability to prevail in its assault, with a host of allies from north Syria, on the king of Hamath and Lu'ash in Hadrach (according to the Zakkur inscription; see chapter 6) or to resist an Assyrian attack, surrendering and paying tribute to Adad-Nirari III in 796 (according to Assyrian inscriptions).[42] The biblical texts ignore such factors and recount Israel's repulsion of the Aramaeans from a quite different point of view.

In 2 Kings 13 this recovery is recounted with lapidary brevity.[43] In particular, chapter 13 contains two partially parallel narratives, the first (13:3–5, 7) in the short account of the reign of Jehoahaz of Israel (13:1–9), the second (13:22–25) following two stories about Elisha (13:14–19, 20–21), which are appended to the brief account of the reign of Jehoash (13:10–13).[44]

Second Kings 13:22–25 reads as follows: "Now Hazael, king of Aram, had oppressed Israel throughout the time of Jehoahaz. . . . But then Hazael, king of Aram, died, and Benhadad his son ruled in his stead. And Jehoash, son of Jehoahaz, took back from Benhadad, son of Hazael, the cities which he had taken from Jehoahaz, his father. Three times Joash beat him and so recovered Israel's towns." (Jehoash and Joash are variant spellings of the same name.) Omitting v. 23 for the moment, this follows the pattern of events in Mesha's inscription: previous oppression by neighboring power, succession of a new ruler in both states, recovery of territory by the new ruler of the oppressed state. Since it concerns the recovery of many cities throughout a ruler's reign and makes no mention of administrative consolidation, it is more comparable with the opening, general narrative of Mesha's inscription (ll. 4–7)[45] than with the following specific narratives. It is on a similar scale and has a similar scope to that first narrative overview.

But the correlation is more specific than just a general outline, as can be seen from a comparison of the wording of the two accounts. The first narrative in Mesha's inscription begins: "Omri was king of Israel, and he oppressed Moab for a long time" (ll. 4–5). To this corresponds v. 22: "Hazael, king of Aram, had oppressed Israel throughout all the time of Jehoahaz." Both narratives, having sketched the background of the liberation in terms of oppression by a previous king, mark the end of the oppression by the succession of his heir: "Omri was king of Israel, and he oppressed Moab for a long time . . . and his son succeeded him. . . . But I gloated over him" (ll. 4–7)[46]; and in 2 Kings: "And Hazael, king of Aram, had oppressed Israel during all the time of Jehoahaz. . . . And Hazael, king of Aram, died, and Benhadad, his son, reigned in his place, and Jehoash, son of Jehoahaz, took back the towns . . ." (13:22, 24–25). The turning point of both narratives is the succession of the son of the oppressor.[47]

Nevertheless, there are some contrasts between the two texts. The simple, direct, biblical narrative with the consistent perspective of an external observer contrasts with the hyperbole of the inscription ("Israel had finally disappeared for ever") and its use of the internal perspective of the enemy (quoting the thoughts of Ahab's son) for purposes of irony. The Tel Dan narrative is apparently closer in narrative technique and style, though it also indulges in hyperbole ("seventy kings").

Verse 23 stands out among vv. 22–25 as weighted with specifically Judean traditions: "Yahweh showed them favor and mercy and turned to them for the sake of his covenant with Abraham and Isaac and Jacob and was not willing to destroy them and did not cast them out from his presence until now."[48] The purpose of this verse is to explain Jehoash's success against the enemy by attributing it to the newly favorable attitude of the deity.[49] While it is clearly not in epigraphic style, it functions to distinguish a time of divine favor from a previous time of divine wrath (mentioned earlier in v. 3; cf. 10:32a).[50]

Without v. 23, this narrative reads very much like a third-person version of an account in a royal inscription (with any traditional theology now replaced by v. 23). One has only to put this material into the first person to see the close relationship to the form of the Mesha inscription (and the remains of the Tel Dan inscription):

> Hazael, king of Aram, oppressed Israel throughout all the time of Jehoahaz. . . .
> Then Hazael, king of Aram, died, and Benhadad, his son, reigned in his place.
> Then I took back from Benhadad, son of Hazael, the towns he had taken in war from Jehoahaz, my father.

Conversely, if the narratives of the inscriptions were transposed into the third person and the royal boasting eliminated, they would read very similarly to the biblical narrative. The fact that the only two royal inscriptions recovered from Israel's immediate neighbors commemorate the recovery of territory suggests that such recovery of territory by Israel may have led the Israelite king also to erect a memorial inscription. Could such an inscription lie behind the present account in 2 Kings 13:22, 24–25? The common subject matter, form, and style imply that, if these verses were not drawn directly from an inscription, they were at least modeled on such inscriptions.

We should not leave this narrative without observing how it is used in its present context. Summarizing as it does relations with Aram throughout the reigns of both Jehoahaz and Jehoash, it is placed after the history's treatment of each of those kings (vv. 1–9 and 10–13),[51] giving Jehoash significant credit for actually driving out the Aramaeans. Following the insertion of the prophetic narratives of vv. 14–19, however, Jehoash's success is provided with other explanations beside Yahweh's compassion as expressed in the theology of v. 23. A second explanation appears in the prophetic narrative of vv. 14–17, in which Elisha finally announces: "You will beat Aram at Aphek until you finish them off." Verses 22, 24–25 may now be read as the fulfillment of that prophecy. But then in vv. 18–19 (a supplement to the Elisha narrative of vv. 14–17), we find a more specific link with and explanation of the conclusion of vv. 22, 24–25, based on the wording of v. 25b ("Three times Joash beat him and so recovered Israel's towns"). In v. 25b there is no reservation about the thoroughness of Joash's victory. Indeed, the number "three" suggests completion and finality. But Elisha's concluding announcement in v. 19b ("Three times you will beat Aram") is designed to compromise this account of Jehoash's success, for in v. 19 Elisha makes it clear that Jehoash could have beaten Aram once for all, if he had followed Elisha's instructions with sufficient enthusiasm; as it is, he will beat them *only* three times (see v. 18). Thus the liberator is not now acclaimed for his achievement but exposed as having missed an opportunity to accomplish far more. When the account of the deliverance finally comes at the end of the chapter, what would have been the triumph of an inscription is now lost, indeed, almost reversed: Yahweh showed Israel favor and mercy only because of his covenant with the patriarchs and because he did not want to destroy the Israelites or remove them from his presence (v. 23); and Jehoash beat the Aramaeans only three times (v. 25b) because he did not respond adequately to Elisha's instructions (v. 18).[52]

The reign of Jehoash's predecessor, Jehoahaz, is treated in 2 Kings 13:1–9, where it is framed by the usual Deuteronomistic formulae for the beginnings and ends of the reigns of Israelite kings (vv. 1–2, 8–9). The intervening vv. 3–7 may be summarized as follows:

(3) Yahweh was angry with Israel, and so handed them over to Hazael and Benhadad.

(4) Jehoahaz pleaded with Yahweh, and Yahweh responded, because he saw the oppression of Israel by the king of Aram.

(5) Yahweh granted Israel a savior, so that they came out from under the control of Aram and lived at peace.

(6) They did not turn from the sins of Jeroboam and the Asherah was still in Samaria.

(7) For he had left Jehoahaz only a small army, and because the king of Aram had finished them off.

Verse 6 has clearly been inserted to counter the favorable view of Jehoahaz and Israel appearing in vv. 4–5 by reiterating and extending the opening condemnation of v. 2. Verse 7 is problematic. The versions all read "no forces were left Jehoahaz except . . . ," which sits tolerably well after v. 6, both grammatically and substantively. But the MT reads: "he did not leave any forces . . ." with no suitable antecedent in v. 6 for the third-person reference. While the versions can all be explained as smoothing the transition between the two verses, there is no discernible reason why a smoother text should have been changed to what is now the MT. Thus the MT of v. 7 is probably the more original. But what verse does it presuppose? Verse 7 could follow v. 3: Yahweh handed them over to the Aramaean kings without intermission, (v. 7) "for he had not left Jehoahaz any forces except. . . ." Thus both verses describing Israel's extremity would precede Jehoahaz's appeal to Yahweh (v. 4) and Yahweh's response (v. 5). According to Montgomery, vv. 4–5, as well as v. 6, are "an awkward intrusion" that would have been inserted into a historical narrative consisting of vv. 3 and 7 (1951, 433). Verses 3 and 7, recording only the oppression under Jehoahaz, would then be consistent with vv. 22–25, which, while referring to the same oppression, attribute the recovery of Israelite territory to Jehoash. Verses 4–5 were added to explain why Yahweh did not obliterate Israel in his anger: the king played the role of intercessor for the people, Yahweh responded and gave them a savior so that they again dwelt in peace (McCarthy 1973).[53] According to this explanation, vv. 3 and 7 were a historical notice into which were inserted first vv. 4–5 and then v. 6.

The other possibility is that v. 7 depends on v. 4: "(4b) Yahweh heard him [Jehoahaz], because he had seen the oppression of Israel, that [or for] the king of Aram had oppressed them, (7) for he had not left Jehoahaz any forces except . . . ." The subject of v. 7a would then be the king of Aram, and v. 7 would add two causal clauses explaining how the king of Aram had oppressed Israel. By contrast, v. 4a—Jehoahaz's appeal—would follow immediately on the divine anger and resulting oppression in v. 3. Verse 5 would then have been inserted to adumbrate the consequences of Yahweh's "hearing" Jehoahaz in v. 4a, anticipating the eventual deliverance recorded in v. 25.

Whatever the final resolution of this problem, vv. 3–5 (+ 7) have some common ground with Mesha's inscription. The inscription explains Moab's oppression by Israel theologically: "he oppressed Moab for a long time, because Chemosh was angry with his land" (ll. 5–6; cf. the Tal'aym narrative); the same explanation is given in v. 3: "Then Yahweh became angry with Israel and handed them over to Hazael and to Benhadad the son of Hazael without intermission" (v. 3).[54] This may appear to support the claim that the supposed historical notice, vv. 3 and 7, is from an independent source. However, this claim founders on the fact that v. 3 is thoroughly Deuteronomistic in its wording. *Wayyiḥar-ʾap Yahweh beYiśrāʾēl wayyittĕnēm bĕyad* . . . (then Yahweh became angry with Israel and handed them over to . . .) corresponds to Jdg 2:14a to the letter and is almost identical to Jdg 3:8a and 10:7 (which have *yimkōr* instead of *yittēn*). Again, though the wording is quite different, the explanation for the present king's success against the enemy is attributed in Mesha's inscription (and the Tal'aym narrative) and the present biblical narrative to a newly favorable attitude by the deity (ll. 4, 8–9; vv. 4b-5a). Finally, both Mesha and this narrative speak of a country being "finished off" by military defeats: Mesha thus dismisses Israel (l. 7), and v. 7b speaks of Israel's fate at the hands of the Aramaean king in the same terms[55]—though one narrator is describing the fate of the enemy and the other that of his own people.

But these few common features are insufficient to relate the narrative of vv. 3–5 (+ 7) in any specific way with the form of the royal inscription. Apart from the last detail, they are theological elements common throughout the ancient Near East, while their particular expression in this narrative is peculiarly biblical. Although vv. 3–5 (+ 7) are built on the background of divine anger and military oppression (vv. 3, 4bβ, 7), they focus now on Jehoahaz's intervention with Yahweh (v. 4a) and especially Yahweh's compassion and provision of a savior (vv. 4b-5). For the Deuteronomistic historians, the successful liberation of Israel from Aram in the early eighth century was bothersome. Why would Yahweh give such success to one whom they regarded as a bad king? The traditional royal appeal for deliverance (cf. the Zakkur inscription and see chapter 6) was certainly one possible explanation. But though this explanation is used (v. 4), Yahweh's response is based on his view of Aram's oppression of Israel, not on his approval of Jehoahaz (v. 4b; contrast Zakkur's inscription in chapter 6). Further, the people, not the king, are the object of the anticipated deliverance (v. 5).

Finally, in the present form of the text, there is a significant delay between, on the one hand, Jehoahaz's successful appeal to Yahweh and Yahweh's provision of a savior (v. 4–5a) and, on the other, the historian's later account of the actual deliverance in Jehoash's recovery of the occupied towns (v. 25). Both appeal and divine response appear in the reign of a king one generation before the deliverance. As readers now read vv. 3–7 and proceed to vv. 22–25, they must construe v. 5 as proleptic, rather than in chronological order, and v. 7 as describing, not conditions prior to v. 5 or even v. 4, but the ongoing extremity of Israel through the reign of Jehoahaz. They realize that whatever the transaction between Jehoahaz and Yahweh and the final outcome of Yahweh's response, the *experience* of liberation was delayed by one generation. Finally, we should note that the full restoration of Aramaean land to Israel is registered only later with the reign of Jeroboam (14:25–28) and that it is again due to Yahweh's concern, not for the king, but for the people (14:25b–27). Verses 26–27 resume the theme of 13:4b and 23: Yahweh's compassionate observation of the oppression of Israel and his refusal to order its obliteration.

In conclusion, there are echoes of the traditional royal terminology and ideology in 13:3–5a and 7b, but they have been thoroughly transmuted into biblical phraseology and theology. Verses 13:22 and 24–25, however, exhibit striking similarities to elements of ll. 4–9 in Mesha's inscription (although the present v. 23 displaces any previous theological similarity) and, if they do not draw on such an inscription, may at least have been modeled on such epigraphic narratives. But they are now incorporated in a larger presentation of Israel's recovery of its freedom from Aram in 2 Kings 13–14. This extends over the reigns of three kings and involves a number of narratives and theological perspectives, the dominant thrust of which is to depreciate the achievements of the kings and to thematize Yahweh's compassion on the people.

Joshua 10

We turn from individual narratives concerned with recovery of territory, to sequences of campaign narratives, summarizing the campaigns of one ruler. While these campaigns are presented not as acts of "liberation" or recovery of territory but as conquests, they are legitimated by being carried out under divine direction, and the larger present context presents the land as a divine gift to leader and people (Josh 1:2–4, 6). Thus the theological, if not the historical, claim on the land is similar to that in the inscriptions.

Joshua 10:28–39 is a summary list of Joshua's conquests in the south of the country, including Makkedah, Libnah, Lachish, Eglon, Hebron, and Debir. The six campaigns in this list almost all conform to the following pattern: "Then Joshua and all Israel with him (verb of motion) from (place A) to (place B) and attacked it and took it and beat it with the sword and every person in it, letting no one escape, just as he had done to (place A or C)."[56] There are two significant divergences from this. First, v. 28, referring to the conquest of Makkedah, omits the first part of the pattern, since it presupposes the preceding lengthy narrative about the same city. It is, in fact, a redactional link between that narrative and the following list of conquests (David 1990, 219). Second, v. 33 introduces a unique development after the conquest of Lachish: the king of Gezer goes to help Lachish (v. 33). This episode is concluded with a very abbreviated selection of the formula: "Then Joshua beat him and his army, letting no one escape." This is the one substantial divergence from the pattern that appears to be arbitrary, introduced purely for the sake of variation. David is probably correct in seeing this as a later addition (1990, 211). Omitting these two episodes, we are left with a sequence of five battle accounts. Among these there are two additions that occur more than once. In the first two accounts, the clause "attacked it" is followed by the sentence: "Then Yahweh handed it (and its king) over to Israel" (vv. 30, 32); in the last three cases, the city is devoted to destruction (ḥerem; vv. 35, 37, 39). The former is the one expression of the divine role and the one departure in the list from the external observer's point of view.[57]

The references to Yahweh's gift of some cities and to Joshua's devotion of others are reminiscent of Mesha's attribution of his recovery of territory to Chemosh ("Chemosh returned it in my time" [twice], "Chemosh drove him out before me") and his devotion of Nebo to Ashtar-Chemosh. But the consistency of form and content running through these narratives stands in stark contrast to the variety among the narratives of Mesha's campaigns. The historical particularity suggested by the narrative diversity of Mesha's campaign narratives is completely absent from this summary of Joshua's southern conquests. Van Seters has compared the Deuteronomistic account of Joshua's campaigns in Joshua 1–12 with the Assyrian annals (1983, 330–31; 1990). Yet even the most formulaic sections of the Assyrian annals[58] scarcely reach this level of monotony. There is virtually no interest here in narrative (or historical) diversity or complexity. The one significant narrative variation in v. 33—the intervention of the king of Gezer to help Lachish—illustrates how even an unexpected initiative from an enemy still issues in Joshua's standard, thorough victory. The campaigns are basically a cycle of formulaic actions.

But the formulaic repetition serves two distinct purposes in this context, known to readers of the larger work and reiterated in the concluding summary of vv. 40–42. First, according to v. 40, throughout the territory covered, Joshua simply executed Yahweh's instructions. The monotony of Joshua's actions in vv. 28–39 illustrates and emphasizes the consistency of his obedience. The unity of his actions is further expressed in the words of v. 42a: he took all the cities *pa'am 'eḥāt,* "at one time," which here almost has the sense of "in one move." Further, Yahweh's instructions, as we are reminded in v. 40, included administering the *ḥerem,* so that the mention of this act in some of the individual accounts is simply an occasional reminder of what was standard practice. This also explains why there is no mention of spoils or new administrative arrangements in any of the individual campaigns. Second, Joshua took all these kings and territories "because Yahweh, the God of Israel, fought for Israel" (v. 42b). Hence there are no setbacks, no surprises, no needs for special strategies or tactics. The two previous references to Yahweh's handing over the town in question to Israel (vv. 30, 32) were simply reminders of what Yahweh did for Israel throughout Joshua's campaigns.

Like the concluding summary, the list of formulaic narratives is an unimaginative illustration of Deuteronomic law. Yahweh is really fighting for Israel (Deut 20:4, 16), and Joshua is simply acting on divine orders to destroy completely all the towns Yahweh is giving them (Deut 20:16–17). Thus antecedent conditions or acts of provocation, particular strategies or tactics, and unique spoils or administrative arrangements after the victory are all irrelevant, as are the points of view of the participants. We are here far removed from court stories of campaigns and their condensation in royal inscriptions.

However, the present Deuteronomistic setting of this campaign list raises some questions. Other references to the conquest of Hebron and Debir attribute it not to Joshua coming from Gilgal in the north but to individuals or tribes (Caleb, Othniel, Judah) situated in the south (Josh 14:6–15; 15:13–20; Jdg 1:9–20). David has nicely shown how several peculiar details in Josh 10:28–39 are explicable if the battles were originally recounted in the reverse order. A few examples will illustrate his evidence and argument. First, the last campaign (in the present order) against Debir is the only one that does not include a reference to the previously conquered city (v. 38). This would be quite appropriate if Debir was originally the first city in the account. Second, the first of the two references to Yahweh's handing over the city to Israel includes the word *gam* "also" (v. 30). This, too, would be perfectly appropriate if it originally followed what is now the second reference (v. 32). Third, v. 35 refers to Joshua's devotion of Eglon, as of Lachish (the now preceding city). The *ḥerem,* however, is not mentioned in the treatment of Lachish (v. 33)—but is in what is now the following city (Hebron, v. 37). Similarly, in v. 37 Joshua "left no survivor" in Hebron, just as in Eglon.

Again, the quoted phrase is not used of Eglon—but is of the following city.[59] David concludes that an earlier version recounted the campaign by moving in the reverse order, from south to north (Debir, Hebron, Eglon, Lachish, Libnah), which would be consistent with the traditions about a conquest from the south in the other sources.[60] But since the historian now has Joshua conquer the entire country from his base at Gilgal, this original order was reversed so as to make military sense of the campaign in the present historiographic context. This reversal, involving the necessary substantive changes in the names of the cities, overlooked the several details that support David's explanation (David 1990).

Thus there was an earlier form of this campaign list in which the cities appeared in the reverse order. The three references to the consecration of the city to destruction then came in the first three campaigns, and Yahweh's gift of the city in the last two. Whereas in the present order Joshua's consecrations may be read as his grateful response to Yahweh's gifts, in this earlier version Yahweh's gifts may be read as a reward for Joshua's consecrations.

Yet even in this earlier form, Joshua 10:29–39 would still be a mechanical account using formulaic Deuteronomistic phraseology and consistently expressing the Deuteronomistic theology of war in land claimed by Israel (Deut 20:16–17). It would thus bring us no closer to the sequence of campaign narratives in the royal inscription, which, by comparison with these verses, is marked by variety in form and substance, narrative complexity, and interesting details.

2 Samuel 8

A more promising candidate for a series of campaign narratives related to those in the Moabite inscription is in 2 Samuel 8:1–15. This is loosely connected with the preceding chapter by the vague "after this" (8:1aα) and followed by the quite distinct list of royal officers (vv. 16–18; cf. 20:23–26; 2 Kgs 4:2b–6).

Second Samuel 8 contains four campaign narratives, of which the first, second, and fourth are brief (against the Philistines in v. 1 the Moabites in v. 2, and the Edomites in vv. 13aβ–14a), and the third is lengthy (against the Aramaeans in vv. 3–13aα). As the commentators recognize, the Aramaean narrative is composed of different kinds of material that have accumulated around a briefer campaign narrative (see most recently Stoebe 1994). The core of the latter involves two battles, one with a named Aramaean king, Hadadezer of Zobah, the other with a second army that comes to his assistance from Damascus.

David's first victory is over the Philistines: "and he subjugated them, and David took the *meteg hā'ammâ* from the possession of the Philistines" (v. 1). The untranslated Hebrew expression has not been satisfactorily explained.[61] In light of the Moabite inscription ll. 12–13 and 17–18, vv. 7 and 8 discussed later, and the retrospective summary in v. 11, we may reasonably suppose that it refers to something (or possibly someone) of economic or religious value that was dedicated to the deity.[62] Beyond the bare fact of victory, the narrator is interested in the subsequent subjugation of the population and acquisition of this trophy.

David's second victory is over the Moabites (v. 2). Here the disposal of the defeated on the battlefield is the focus of attention: "he measured them off by

line, making them lie down on the ground; and he measured off two lines to be put to death and one full line to be allowed to live"—that is, executing a random two thirds. This has the heartless character of a soldier's boast that might also be taken up in popular tales.[63] The narrative concludes with a reference to more permanent arrangements: "and Moab became David's servants, tributary to him." The details of David's unusual treatment of Moab's army on the battlefield overshadows this concluding administrative arrangement.

The third campaign concerns the Aramaeans (vv. 3–8). "David beat Hadadezer of Rehob, king of Zobah, as he was going to set up[64] his monument at the river." There are two debatable referents here: who was on his way to the river, and which river? If it was David whose goal was the establishment of his monument at the river, the narrator would be suggesting that this battle was a diversion from his main purpose. Since in all the other narratives in this sequence, David's purposes are military, it seems more likely that they are so here and that he attacked the Aramaeans while *they* were on their way to the river. Tradition identifies the river as the Euphrates, the usual referent of "the river" when used as a geographical reference in the Bible, Akkadian sources from Neo-Assyrian times, and contemporary Aramaic inscriptions (see Eph'al and Naveh 1989, esp. p. 195). But it is unlikely that the narrator would have either David or Hadadezer setting up his stela there. The geographical horizon of David's conquests in 1 Samuel 8 is Palestine and southern Syria, the territories of the usually hostile neighbors of Israel. The northernmost area mentioned is that of Hamath (vv. 9–11) in central Syria. But that is not within David's territorial ambitions: the king of Hamath takes the initiative in sending a friendly embassy to David—evidently in Jerusalem—in recognition of his disposal of their common enemy, Hadadezer, not in recognition of a triumphal march by David to the Euphrates, which, indeed, the king of Hamath might have been expected to protest. It is even less likely that Hadadezer would have been on his way to the Euphrates—in the opposite direction to the kingdom of Israel!—when David attacked him. Then again, if Hadadezer was proceeding toward the Jordan or Jabbok rivers to establish his monument, this would be seen by the narrator as encroaching on Israel's borders and inviting David's intervention (cf. 2 Sam 10:16–17). This last scenario is altogether more fitting in the immediate literary context (as well as in historical fact) than the farflung imperialistic aspirations suggested by the alternative. In this case, then, David's attack was provoked by an expedition by Hadadezer to establish his border at the Jordan or Jabbok River.[65]

The narrative goes on to a summary of the mopping-up operations, listing the military forces that David captured and adding that he hamstrung the chariot horses, leaving only one hundred. An Aramaean force of Damascus now appears, coming to assist Hadadezer. The narrator reports that David beat them also and gives the number he killed. Administrative arrangements follow: David establishes garrisons in Aram of Damascus and it becomes "David's servants, tributary to him" (cf. the end of the second narrative).

At this point, there is a general summary statement: "Yahweh gave David victory wherever he went" (v. 6b). This first mention of Yahweh casts a new light on the preceding accounts. The external perspective thus far is suddenly replaced by an omniscient viewpoint: these are not simply David's conquests, but Yahweh's gifts to David. The first three narratives thus have a general conclusion that puts David's military successes in the context of divine favor.

In the present form of the texts, however, this theological interpretation interrupts David's activities following his victory over the Aramaeans, which now continue with an account of the booty.[66] David takes from Hadadezer's servants gold bow and quiver cases which he brought to Jerusalem (v. 7). Verse 8 reports that he had also taken a large amount of bronze from two of Hadadezer's cities. This is followed by a discrete episode: the embassy of the king of Hamath, who sent his son to David with silver, gold, and bronze objects, to felicitate him on his victory over their common enemy (vv. 9–10). Next comes a report that David had consecrated these gifts to Yahweh, along with the gold from all the other nations he had subdued (v. 11). The nations are then listed (v. 12). As noted before, it is doubtful that all these verses were part of the original campaign narrative. Not only do they follow the concluding statement in v. 6 but also their connections with one another are rough.[67] Verses 8, 11, and 12, for example, not only use a different word order and perfect verbs (here with the force of the English pluperfect) but also refer to David as "the king, David." The latter expression is probably introduced by association with its use in the account of the diplomatic visit of vv. 9–10, where it is quite fitting. Elsewhere in this section the king of Israel is always called simply "David."

Verse 13 then returns to the narrative of David's conquest of Aram: "Then David made a memorial when he returned from beating Aram."[68] Finally, there is one more narrative about a victory over the Edomites (vv. 13–14). The beginning of this has been confused in the various textual witnesses with the end of the sentence about the memorial; that is, one or another of the originally juxtaposed references to beating Aram and beating Edom has been lost due to the graphic near-identity of the two names.[69] Again, the number of dead is noted, David appoints garrisons in Edom (as in Aram of Damascus, v. 6a), "and all Edom became David's servants" (the clause is used of Moab and Aram in vv. 2b and 6a, but here lacks the additional phrase that appears there: "tributary to him"). The passage ends with a repetition of the general summary statement of v. 6b: "Yahweh gave David victory wherever he went."

The four discrete campaigns—against the Philistines (v. 1), Moabites (v. 2), Aramaeans (vv. 3–13a, perhaps earlier 3–6, 13a), and Edomites (13–14)—range in scope from the brevity and simplicity of the first to the length and complexity of the third, which includes not only the campaign against Hadadezer but also the intervention of the auxiliary force from Damascus and the setting up of a memorial inscription. Omitting the material added to the Aramaean campaign (vv. 7–12), we find that the narrative material is remarkably homogeneous. All four campaigns begin, "David (or he) beat . . ." with the name of the specific enemy (vv. 1, 2, 3—and probably something similar originally in v. 13 [see McCarter 1984, 243, 246]). In v. 5, the same phrase follows a clause announcing the arrival of the second Aramaean army. All four campaigns include notice of the new administrative relationship with the conquered territory: the minimal "he subjugated them" in the case of the Philistines, the installation of garrisons in the cases of the

Aramaeans and Edomites, and the definition of the defeated as "David's servants, tributary to him" in the cases of the Moabites, Aramaeans, and, without the last phrase, Edomites. The number of enemy dead is given for both the Aramaean auxiliary force and the Edomites. More distinctive are the taking of the mysterious *meteg hā'ammâ* from the Philistines, the manner of execution in the case of the Moabites, and the details of the captured forces and the treatment of the chariot horses in the case of the Aramaeans.

Unlike the campaign narratives in Mesha's inscription, these have virtually no references to an antecedent situation or act of provocation. (The exception would be the Aramaean expedition to set up a monument at the river.) These are wars, not of liberation, but of conquest. There is no detail about the strategy employed or the battle itself. In each account, it is the aftermath of victory that is of interest, especially the fate of the enemy forces and the new administrative relationship between victor and vanquished.

The Hebrew campaign narratives are thus more homogeneous than those in the Moabite inscription: more consistent in subject matter and wording, structurally less complex, and consistent in their external point of view. They contain no direct speech. There are distinctive developments only in the extended form of the Aramaean section, especially in the embassy of Toi. Here, in vv. 9–10, there is a shift to an internal perspective, the narrator taking us into the court and the motivations of Toi through the subordinate clauses that disclose what he had heard (that David had beaten Hadadezer), the purpose of his son's embassy (to congratulate David on his victory), and the reason for the congratulations (Hadadezer had been at war with Toi). Here we see the narrator's knowledge of information received by and the motivation of another court, as distinct from large public actions and the arrangements accomplished by the Judean court. The nearest thing to this in the inscription is the expression of Omri's son's intentions in line 6.

Yahweh appears in none of the individual campaign stories, only in the summary statements of vv. 6b and 14b.[70] This refrain—"Yahweh delivered David wherever he went"—compares with Mesha's opening statement: "he (Chemosh) delivered me from all the kings" (l. 4). Both make similar theological claims (using the same verb *yš'*), attributing the victories, respectively, to Yahweh and Chemosh. In his introduction, Mesha cites Chemosh's intervention as a reason for building the sanctuary for him, but also as an announcement of the theme represented in various ways in the following narratives. The Deuteronomistic historian uses his statement as a retrospective summary of the preceding narratives. This limited reference to Yahweh contrasts with the initial generalization and the subsequent interweaving of divine and royal responsibility in the narratives of Mesha's inscription.

Following the sequence of campaign narratives in vv. 1–14, we read the general statement: "Then David ruled over all Israel, administering justice and fairness to all his people" (v. 15). This is commonly grouped with, and understood to introduce, the following list of David's officers (vv. 16–18).[71] But it is worth asking whether it is not preferable to understand it as the conclusion of the preceding. Two other passages are pertinent. First Kings 4:1 ("King Solomon was king over all Israel"), which is very similar to the first part of 2 Samuel 8:15, has been generally recognized as redactional. It has both retrospective and prospective functions. On the one hand, 4:1 complements the immediately preceding recognition by "all Israel" of the new king's divine skill in administering justice (3:28, referring back to the story of vv. 16–27, which in turn illustrates the divine gift to Solomon in vv. 4–15). On the other hand, it introduces the organization of the kingdom under Solomon (the rest of chapter 4). This organization consists of two lists (vv. 2b–6 and 8b–19). However, unlike the list at the end of 2 Samuel 8, each list here has its own introduction (vv. 2a and 7–8a). Thus the first list, the list of chief officers (vv. 2b–6), has the fitting heading: "Now these are the officers he had:" (v. 2a). Second Kings 4:1 is not, therefore, required as an introduction to what follows. The case is even clearer in 2 Samuel 20:23–26, where the list of David's officers reappears without any introduction at all. Thus, in neither passage is the list of chief officers dependent on a general statement about the king's rule over his entire realm.

While 2 Samuel 8:15 may have provided an appropriate context for inserting the list of officers, the inclusion in that verse of the additional statement concerning David's administration of justice confirms the looseness of the connection with the following list: none of the officers has any specific relationship to the king's administration of justice to all his people. However, v. 15 builds on the preceding account of David's campaigns. Having conquered his surrounding enemies, David could now rule over all Israel and attend to its internal regulation. It is not without relevance that what has been proposed as the original conclusion of Mesha's inscription (ll. 28–29) gives a summary statement concerning Mesha's general rule over his expanded realm: "And it was I who ruled over a hundred [   ] in the towns which I had annexed to the land." Other memorial inscriptions give extensive attention to the king's governance of his realm, with particular emphasis on his just and beneficent administration.[72] Thus, while it has no essential relationship to what follows, v. 15 forms a fitting conclusion to the sequence of campaign narratives, particularly in light of royal memorial inscriptions.

One other feature of this pericope invites further comment. The conclusion of the Aramaean campaign, "David made a memorial when he returned from beating Aram" (v. 13a), while without a precise counterpart in the Moabite inscription, corresponds to what Mesha actually did after his campaigning and building. The Hebrew text, while part of a literary work, refers to the occasion and the act. The Moabite text, while referring to the occasion (ll. 3–4), constitutes the product of such an act. (Other inscriptions, e.g., those of Zakkur and Azatiwada, refer explicitly to the inscribed memorial itself.) As Mesha erected his memorial inscription sometime after the last victory he records, the Hebrew text envisages David's doing the same after the last of his victories over the Philistines, Moabites, and Aramaeans: his last act after his last victory was the erection of a memorial—on which an account of his victories, broadly comparable to Mesha's, might have been inscribed. By referring to this occasion and act, the Hebrew of v. 13 may wish to suggest that this memorial was the source of the preceding narratives. Moreover, as Mesha's inscription is probably an extension of an earlier edition— the present form including the supplement taking account of the recovery of

Horonaim—so the Hebrew passage may be read as an extension of an earlier account inscribed after the Aramaic campaign and ending in v. 6 with the recognition of Yahweh's role, now including a supplement taking account of David's subsequent victory over Edom and reiterating that general theological recognition. This would support the suggestion that the form of the memorial inscription might have influenced the shaping of 2 Samuel 8:1–15.

Stoebe is surely correct in his conclusion that 2 Samuel 8:1–14 as a whole is composed of materials of various origins and so cannot have been extracted from a chronicle (1994, 246).[73] I would add that the differences in content and style— even without the material appended to the Aramaean campaign—are too great to claim that 2 Samuel 8:1–15 was drawn from an actual inscription like that of Mesha. But what other model would a narrator have in mind for such a list of successful royal campaigns? I conclude that the passage is not taken from an inscription but was probably modeled on this genre of the monarchic period, the reference to the memorial being included to imply an ancient testimony to the events the narrator is recounting. Second Samuel 8:1–15 shows Israelite historians, wanting to give a summary account of the victories of a famous king of the past, using as their model royal inscriptions like that of Mesha.

Excursus: 2 Samuel 10

With the exception of the extended Aramaean narrative, the campaign narratives of 2 Samuel 8:1–14 are both simpler and more repetitive than the stories written on Mesha's stela. We have argued that the Aramaean narrative goes back to a core of vv. 3–6. Another much longer and more complex account of a victory over Hadadezer by David appears in 2 Samuel 10. The question arises how this material is related to 8:3–6.

The differences between the two stories about the same Aramaean king are too great to permit the hypothesis of an antecedent literary relationship. In chapter 8, Hadadezer is defeated by David, and the Aramaeans of Damascus then come to his assistance. In chapter 10, the Ammonites, fearing an attack by David, hire Hadadezer's forces to come to their assistance; then, after David's initial defeat of both Ammonites and Aramaeans, Hadadezer brings auxiliary Aramaean forces from "beyond the river" for a second confrontation with David. David reduces to tributary status the Aramaeans of Damascus in chapter 8 (v. 6a) and the Aramaeans of Beth Rehob and Zobah and "beyond the river" in chapter 10 (v. 19).

There are, however, several striking commonalities in the material of the two stories. Second Samuel 10 speaks of "the Aramaeans of Beth Rehob and the Aramaeans of Zobah" (v. 6) and later of Hadadezer (vv. 16–19); 2 Samuel 8 introduces Hadadezer as "of Rehob" and "king of Zobah" (v. 3). The Aramaean force in 10:6 consists of twenty thousand foot soldiers; David captures twenty thousand foot soldiers from Hadadezer in 8:4a. David crossed the Jordan to attack Hadadezer in 10:17a; he attacked Hadadezer "on his way" to the river in 8:3b. Chapter 10 includes two stories involving the use of Aramaean troops brought in from another area; in chapter 8 also, additional Aramaean forces move in from another area (v. 5). While there is no reference to the numbers of Ammonites defeated in chapter 10, the Aramaean numbers are given (v. 18), as they are in 8:4. Both chapters record the subjection of the auxiliary Aramaean forces to tributary status (10:19a and 8:6a).

This common material is sufficient to suggest that the different accounts in these two chapters derive from variant oral stories of a campaign or campaigns by David against Aramaeans, involving auxiliary troops and the leadership of Hadadezer. Whether there were originally two different campaigns and so two separate stories between which there has been some mutual or unidirectional influence, or whether stories about a single campaign have been developed in different directions in combination with other materials, it is impossible to say.[74] In either case, the narrative in 2 Samuel 10 supports the claim that there is an original core of material in 8:3–6 (as distinct from 8:7–12) with which it shares several motifs and details. While chapter 10 has now been built onto a story concerned with Israel's relations with the Ammonites, 8:3–6 has been reduced to the scale of the other campaign narratives in chapter 8 and later expanded with other kinds of material (vv. 7–12).

Summary

We have a uniquely long and well-preserved series of campaign narratives in the inscription of Mesha, disclosing narrative variety and complexity and also a high degree of consistency of basic structure and ideology. Something of that structure and ideology appears also in the fragmentary Tel Dan inscription and—though excluding human agency—in the story of Tal'aym (Sefire inscription). The stories in the memorial inscriptions, in which the first-person narrator recounts his and his god's successful expulsion of foreign forces occupying land he claims as his own, will be distillations of stories told in the courts of the kings in whose names the inscriptions were composed later in their reigns.

The few comparable stories in the Deuteronomistic History have varying relations with the royal memorial inscriptions, reflecting clearly or faintly some of the structure and ideology of the epigraphic stories, if not their narrative complexity and royal rhetoric. Second Kings 13:22–25 is similar to the first, general story in the inscription of Mesha (ll. 4–7). If the language of v. 23 had replaced a more traditional expression of divine favor on the new king of Israel, the whole of 13:22–25 could have been derived from such a royal inscription—or at least been directly modeled on such inscriptions. Since the two inscriptions from Israel's immediate vicinity—indeed, from contested territory—were produced to commemorate the expulsion of occupying Israelite forces, it is certainly thinkable that Israel's successful expulsion of Aramaeans from the contested territory in the northeast might also have occasioned the production of a royal memorial inscription.

Of the two sequences of campaign narratives in the Deuteronomistic history, Joshua 10:28–39, on the one hand, even in the earlier form with the conquered cities in reverse order, is a formulaic, Deuteronomistic recital of the fulfillment of the Deuteronomic law concerning war against territories given by Yahweh to

Israel. It clearly has no connection with epigraphic accounts of such campaigns. Second Samuel 8:1–15, on the other hand, while distinguishable from the sequence of campaign stories in Mesha's inscription in many respects, has some features which suggest that the composer(s) of at least 8:1–6 and 13–15 was or were at least aware of such inscriptions—and may have implied such a source by the reference in v. 13a to David's setting up of a memorial after his campaign against Aram.

The rarity of material in the Deuteronomistic History that is at all close in form or style or narrative technique to the stories preserved in the one virtually intact royal inscription from southern Syria-Palestine or the fragments from Tel Dan argues against the supposition that the Judean historians in general quoted extensively from—or indeed were significantly influenced by—campaign narratives preserved in Israelite or Judean royal inscriptions. The most we may safely conclude is that they may have been generally aware of such royal inscriptions and occasionally disclosed that familiarity when the subject of their narrative evoked it—that is, in the restoration narrative of 2 Kings 13:22–25, for which the strongest case can be made for an actual epigraphic source, and in the summary of campaigns in 2 Samuel 8. The significant similarities in these two cases are the more striking for their rarity.[75]

It is clear from all the inscriptions and biblical passages reviewed that stories of military campaigns and claims to land were expressed in theological language. Loss of land was the result of the deity's anger. Recovery of land and military success were the result of the deity's favorable intervention on behalf of the new ruler and of the latter's acting on divine instructions and duly acknowledging the deity as the giver of victory. Such divine favor and human acknowledgment appear in the two biblical sequences of campaign narratives. Thus, even in a text as far removed from royal inscriptions as Joshua 10:28–39, essentially the same ideology is used to legitimate Israel's occupation of its land.

Stories of Appeals for Military Intervention

The stories of which we have just been speaking all concern military victories and conquests. In this chapter, we turn to stories in which the protagonist is on the defensive and initiates diplomatic moves to dispose of the force that threatens him. While the deity was always involved in the campaigns of the preceding stories, he is notably absent from all the stories that follow.

The small states of Syria-Palestine responded in various ways to threats from more powerful neighbors. The threat of a siege following the invasion of the country and the taking of towns outside the capital might prompt the king and his court to submit rather than undergo a lengthy ordeal. They might judge some economic deprivation better than the prolonged suffering of a full-scale siege, with possible eventual breach of the walls and ensuing slaughter. As a first strategy, then, they might buy off the invader: accept whatever terms he might impose and pay tribute out of the royal (and divine) coffers, the palace and temple treasuries. For the invader, the receipt of satisfactory tribute would be preferable to the expense of time and resources demanded by a long siege.[1] Not surprisingly, while the Assyrian kings often mention the receipt of such payments in their inscriptions, the Northwest Semitic royal inscriptions are all silent on that subject. The Deuteronomistic History, however, recounts four occasions on which the courts of Judah and Israel responded to a military threat by disbursements to the invader from their treasuries, in order of increasing narrative scope: 2 Kings 17:3; 18:13–16; 12:18–19; 15:19–20.

A second possible strategy entailed a similar economic sacrifice, but to a different end: an appeal to an even more powerful king to attack the threatening neighbor. The appeal would be accompanied by a substantial present. The king to whom the appeal was made would happily accept the present and then normally undertake the requested intervention against the invaders, expecting to benefit from the usual fruits of conquest as well as the initial gift. To the initially threatened party, the benefits might appear more attractive than those of the first strategy: not only could they expect immediate relief but also they stood to gain economically in the short term from the defeat of the invaders (as noted later in this chapter) and might reasonably expect that the latter would be unwilling or unable to invade them again after their treatment at the hands of the third party. This strategy obviously depended on the existence of a stronger power than the invader and was not an option when the invader was the strongest power in the world—Assyria during most of the period with which we are concerned. Assyria was the invader in three of the four accounts listed here as examples of the first strategy[2] and in none of the situations reviewed in the rest of this chapter.

The story of the successful appeal for outside intervention would be told rather differently in the courts of the three kings involved. We are best informed on the story as structured and expressed by those who successfully brought in a third party to dispose of a threatening power. Two Northwest Semitic royal inscriptions from Zinjirli tell of such events, one very briefly, by the king himself, the other at some length in a third-person version by the son of the protagonist. The books of Kings include two stories of the same general sequence of events from a point of view sympathetic with that of the threatened court.

We would expect to see the point of view of the force posing the initial threat only in a story critical of the strategy. The first part of such a story appears in the mouths of a besieging army in a longer imaginative narrative in 2 Kings 6:24–7:20. Otherwise, it is only when the anticipated assistance is not forthcoming or is unsuccessful that the initial aggressor recounts the tale. Assyrian royal inscriptions provide several examples of the former outcome. In a standard introduction to several of the building inscriptions of the early thirteenth-century Assyrian king, Adad-Narari I, appears what A. K. Grayson identifies as "the first real narrative of military conquest in the Assyrian royal inscriptions." This narrative includes an account of a "rebellion" against—that is, a bid for independence from—Assyria by a new king of Khanigalbat (the immediate western neighbor of Assyria at that time). Of this king, the account says at one point: "He went to the land of Hatti for aid. The Hittites took his presents, but did not render him assistance." The sequel narrates Adad-Narari's conquest and destruction of the rebel's cities, imposition of forced labor on the population, and deportation of the king's family and staff in bonds to Asshur, the Assyrian capital (Grayson 1987, 135–36). Thus, according to the Assyrian king, the rebellious king of Khanigalbat, in anticipation of an Assyrian attack, sought to buy the assistance of the Hittites, who took his gifts but then left him to the mercy of the merciless Assyrians. Such an outcome is also reported in several Neo-Assyrian royal inscriptions. Obviously the Assyrian army and court delighted to tell such stories. In two very different literary contexts (2 Sam 10 and Deut 23:5b–6), the Bible preserves tales of such assistance procured by a king who felt threatened by early Israel. In both cases, the assistance is unsuccessful.

Finally, the point of view of the party to whom the appeal is made is represented in the historical narrative in the vassal treaty drawn up by Suppiluliuma, king of Hatti, and imposed on Niqmaddu II of Ugarit. This recalls the invasion and devastation of the land of Ugarit by three neighboring kings, quotes Niqmaddu's appeal to Suppiluliuma, and recounts the repulsion of the invaders by Suppiluliuma's troops, Niqmaddu's presentation of gifts to the Hittite commanding officers, and his formal submission to Suppiluliuma in Alalakh.[3] In this case, the verbal message of submission is sufficient to elicit the Hittite response, the presents following later. In the context of the treaty, due weight is given to each stage in these developments. In other contexts, the structure of events may not have been remembered in the same way, or at least the court in question would not construct a comparable plot. While the payment and the invasion might both be counted among the superior king's achievements, they may be recorded without mention of any connection between the two. The king of a mighty imperial power such as the Neo-Assyrian might not wish in his own inscriptions to record his policy decisions as prompted by appeals and gifts from a small, weak state on the periphery of his empire. (Appeals for assistance by Kuwait and Saudi Arabia did not figure largely in the pronouncements by the United States or the United Nations concerning their military moves against Iraq.) We have no such story from a Syro-Palestinian king to whom such an appeal was made.

This chapter reviews stories of the use of this strategy in two inscriptions referring to events in the narrator's lifetime or that of his predecessor, in two passages in the books of Kings referring to events in the more distant past, and in three other narratives in Deuteronomistic literature concerned more with literary, religious, and moral interests than with historiography.

Stories of Appeals for Military Intervention in Inscriptions

The Inscription of Kilamuwa

In the ninth–eighth centuries there was in what is now south-central Turkey a small Neo-Hittite and Aramaean state called Sam'al, whose kings resided in a small town where the present village of Zinjirli is found: near the modern Turkish-Syrian border east-northeast of the Gulf of Iskenderun (Alexandretta). The German excavators of Zinjirli discovered the pieces of the inscription of King Kilamuwa on the left side of the gateway of the northwest palace (Palace J) in 1902 (von Luschan 1911, 374).[4] It was carved on a stone orthostat, the upper left corner of which is occupied by an Assyrian-style relief of the king, who faces the upper half of the inscription and points with his right hand to four symbols carved in front of his head: a horned helmet, a yoke, a winged sun disk, and a moon. These represent, respectively, the high god, Hadad; the god of the dynasty, Rākib-El; the sun god, Shamash; and the moon god, known as Baal-Harrān, "the

Lord of Harran," according to one of the inscriptions of the last known king of Zinjirli, Bir-Rākib (Tropper 1993, 24–26). The inscription was clearly carved after these reliefs, as the text of ll. 1–7 and 9 moves to a new line when it meets the reliefs. It is written in the Phoenician script and language and is the oldest of the Semitic inscriptions found at Zinjirli, dating from around 825 (Tropper 1993, 12, 27). It falls into two parts, divided by a double horizontal bar. In the first part, Kilamuwa boasts of achieving things his predecessors had not and then refers to his disposal of inimical neighbors. In the second part, he reports his parental care of a previously disadvantaged segment of the population, which now owns livestock and personal adornments it had never seen before. The inscription ends with curses on anyone damaging it.

On the basis of this inscription, Fales has characterized King Kilamuwa of Zinjirli as "a shrewd storyteller" (1979, 16). The inscription is certainly a very literary work, and, as Fales especially has shown, a carefully constructed piece of royal propaganda. Most of it consists of what may be described as a series of parallel minimal narratives, contrasting the way things were before Kilamuwa's reign with the way they are now. The three clauses in lines 7–8, however, constitute a minimal story (a state of affairs, an action, and the resulting [different] state of affairs) on the subject of an appeal for military intervention.

(1) I am Kilamuwa, son of Ḥayyā.

(2–5) Gabbār was king over Sam'al[5] and he accomplished nothing. There was BNH[6] and he accomplished nothing. And then there was my father, Ḥayyā, and he accomplished nothing. And then there was my brother, Sha'il, and he accomplished nothing. And I, Kilamuwa, son of TML,[7] whatever I accomplished, those coming before did not accomplish.[8]

(5–7) The house of my father was among powerful kings, and each began to do battle.[9] But I was in the hands of the kings like fire burning up the beard and like fire burning up the hand.

(7–8) And the king of the Danunians was more powerful than I (or too powerful for me), so I hired against him the king of Assyria[10]: they gave a girl for a sheep and a boy for a garment.[11]

—— [12]

(9) I, Kilamuwa, son of Hayya, sat on the throne of my father.

(9–13) Under the former kings the Muškabīm[13] lived[14] like dogs. But I, to one I was a father, to another I was a mother, and to another I was a brother. And whoever had not seen the face of a sheep, I made him the owner of a flock; and whoever had not seen the face of an ox, I made him the owner of a herd; and ⟨whoever had not seen . . . I made him⟩[15] the owner of silver and the owner of gold; and whoever had not seen a tunic[16] from his youth, in my time they covered him with fine linen.[17] And I took the Muškabīm by the hand and they looked to me like a fatherless child to its mother.[18]
(The inscription ends characteristically with curses on anyone who damages it.)

After his opening self-identification, Kilamuwa goes on in the first lines of the inscription to list his predecessors, each of whom, he says, "accomplished nothing" (bl p'l). But, he proclaims, he accomplished what was unprecedented (ll. 2–5).

His father's house, he continues (ll. 5–7), was situated among powerful, hostile kings, but any of them who laid hands on him got "burned"—he was "in the hands of the kings like fire burning up the beard and like fire burning up the hand." [19] He then turns from this general account of his situation and reaction to a specific, particularly difficult, situation and his specific response (ll. 7–8). He begins by identifying one king whom he could not repel: "The king of the Danunians was more powerful than I (or too powerful for me)"; continues by describing his own response to the danger: "so I hired against him the king of Assyria"; and concludes by describing the consequences: "they gave a girl for a sheep and a boy for a garment."

This last expression requires comment, since it has garnered several different translations (see Fales 1979, 16–21; O'Connor 1977, 19, 22, and 24–26; and more recently Sperling 1988, 332–33). O'Connor takes it to describe an inflated economy—citing the high cost of sheep and clothing—but then has to admit that the line "is out of chronological sequence." A second proposal is that the king of Assyria is the subject of the verb (thus "he gave") and that Kilamuwa is boasting by metaphor of what a good bargain he got from him (so Rosenthal in *ANET*, 654, n. 2). This implies an agreement in which Kilamuwa paid a small price (= a sheep, a garment) for a large good (= a girl, a boy), that is, the Assyrian king's attack on the Danunians and destruction of Kilamuwa's oppressors. Fales extends this to include the economic benefits to Kilamuwa subsequent to the Assyrian victory, quoting approvingly the interpretation of Collins (1971, 186). But in Collins's interpretation, the image refers not to the bargain, which would be limited to a payment by Kilamuwa and the removal of the Danunian threat by the Assyrians, but to the economic conditions following the Assyrian conquest of the Danunians. This interpretation is supported by an Assyrian text from which Fales also quotes and a biblical text cited by Collins, as well as others. A review of these texts will show that they all refer to similar conditions from three different points of view.

The first point of view is that of the conqueror. Fales quotes lines from the inscription of Assurbanipal (on the Rassam Cylinder, VIII, 12–22), in which the Assyrian king boasts of how, after his Arabian campaigns, his land was filled to the borders with "cattle, sheep, asses, camels, slaves without number," which his army had captured. "Throughout my land camels were bought for a shekel, indeed a half-shekel"; camels and slaves could be acquired by a brewer for a jug of beer or by a gardener for a basket of vegetables. [20] This is an account of the economic consequences of a conquest—the abundance and cheapness of slaves and domestic and exotic animals—from the point of view of the conqueror.

Other texts speak of similar conditions from the point of view of the conquered. The text to which Collins refers is Joel 4:3. Here Yahweh speaks of the conquest of his people, in which the conquerors scattered them among the nations, divided up his land, threw lots for his people, and "gave a boy in exchange for a prostitute, and a girl they sold for wine and drank." This is a vivid depiction of the aftermath of conquest: on the large scale, exile of the people and new administration of the land; on the small scale, the conquerors throwing lots for captives and selling children in exchange for (the price of) "sex and booze." But the conquerors' sale of captured children is only an immediate consequence of defeat. In the famine that follows, people may resort to selling their own children to keep alive.[21] Thus we find in a city lament: "All her people are groaning, seeking food. They gave their darlings for food, to keep alive" (Lam 1:11; for translation and justification see Hillers 1992, 62, 87–88).[22] In Lamentations 4 a vivid description of famine conditions—especially for children (v. 4)—is preceded by a comparison of the people of Zion with gold that is now worthless (vv. 1–2). While these two verses do not expressly mention sale, the economic parallel is telling. The common theme of these passages is the sale of young people as slaves—and at low prices.[23] Unlike the Assurbanipal inscription, all these cases reflect the point of view of the defeated.

The third point of view is that of the neighbors of the conquered, who are able to take advantage of depressed conditions. Thus Judah's neighbors, such as the Edomites (whom the Judeans never forgave for their perfidy), were able to benefit from the conditions following the taking of Jerusalem. From these neighbors' point of view, as for the conquerors', there were significant economic benefits resulting from the conquest of Judah. They were the ones who, according to Joel 4:3, could acquire a young male or female slave for a prostitute's hire or a jug of wine. There is an explicit connection between an appeal for military aid against an invading neighbor and the economic prosperity that follows for the king making the appeal in a Hittite text (written in Akkadian) known as "The Siege of Urshu" (Liverani 1991, 181).[24] In this, a refugee from Urshu quotes the besieged king of the city as saying that he has gathered together silver, garments, cattle, and herds that he is going to give to the Hurrians (to engage their intervention against his attackers) and that, if they go along, he expects to recover sevenfold. Here, as in Kilamuwa's inscription, is the point of view of the initially threatened king. But where this king's view is prospective, Kilamuwa's is retrospective. Kilamuwa claims that, following the Assyrian conquest of the Danunians, their neighbors, the Samalians (Kilamuwa's people), could acquire a male or female slave for a sheep or garment. Either the Assyrian army that conquered the Danunians flooded the labor market with captives, or conditions following the conquest were so bad that the Danunians themselves sold their children into slavery. In either case, the Samalians benefited from the cheap price of slave labor as a consequence of the Assyrian conquest of their neighbor.

Kilamuwa—canny politician that he seems to have been—would have been quick to exploit this, first, economically, and later, as material for his propaganda. So he boasts here of his ability to benefit from the economic conditions prevailing after the Assyrian defeat of the Danunians. In the series of contrasts in the second half of the inscription between former conditions and the conditions that he has introduced, Kilamuwa goes on to claim: "Whoever had not seen the face of a sheep, I made him the owner of a flock; and whoever had not seen the face of an ox, I made him the owner of a herd; and ⟨whoever had not seen . . . I made him⟩ the owner of silver and the owner of gold; and whoever had not seen a tunic from his youth, in my time they covered him with fine linen" (ll. 12–13). The prosperity established by Kilamuwa, and here elaborated by repetition and parallelism, is anticipated in the last line of the preceding section, where he is concerned with external affairs and with what a sheep or a garment could buy after the Assyrian king had done the work he was hired for. In the second half of the inscription, the subject shifts to internal affairs, and Kilamuwa boasts that people who had never even seen certain basic commodities were now enjoying abundance and luxury goods. The coinage by which Kilamuwa measures both prosperity and poverty includes especially sheep and garments.

The story of ll. 7–8 is now clear. The three clauses refer, respectively, to the military danger faced by Kilamuwa (the king of the Danunians was too strong for him), to his political countermeasure (he "hired" the king of Assyria against his enemy), and the economic consequences for his people (there was a cheap supply of slave labor). The first clause does not admit that the hostile king accomplished any particular defeat on Kilamuwa, invaded his territory, or confined him to his capital city. He may have demonstrated his superior force in any of those ways, but Kilamuwa admits only his relative superiority. That is the motivation and justification for Kilamuwa's initiative. According to the second clause, Kilamuwa did not appeal to the Assyrians for help. Rather, he paid for the services of ("hired") the Assyrian king. The word certainly expresses the presumptuousness of Kilamuwa's point of view.[25] The king of Assyria would scarcely see himself as Kilamuwa's hireling. What one party records as the successful use of gifts to win the intervention of the Assyrians against an oppressor, the Assyrians may simply record as the receipt of tribute (see later in this chapter). And the acceptance of gifts by no means compelled the recipient to respond as requested. As noted previously, several Assyrian inscriptions record the failure of kings to respond to the pleas and presents of other kings whom the Assyrians were threatening.

The structuring of the plot further contributes to the rhetorical effect of Kilamuwa's inscription, presenting the events from a carefully defined and limited viewpoint. Much of its expository material has appeared already in the first few lines of the inscription. The first clause of ll. 7–8 then introduces the antagonist and the crisis now faced by Kilamuwa. The second clause serves as complication and climax and even suggests the resolution of the story, for the word "hired" expresses concisely a whole sequence of events: at least Kilamuwa's gifts and proposal to the Assyrian king, the king's acceptance of both, and his subsequent action—the attack on the Danunians.[26] Kilamuwa says nothing about these individual actions, even though in this section of his inscription he is concerned with external relations. The third clause moves directly to the conclusion of the story. By passing over the details of the Assyrian actions and speaking immediately of the economic aftermath of the Assyrian attack, he confirms the success of that attack—the defeat of the Danunians—but, more important, leads directly into what he most wants to demonstrate in this inscription, namely, the benefits of *his* actions for his people. As already observed, the economic benefits of his engagement of the Assyrians here anticipate the subject of the immediately following second half of the inscription: the peace and prosperity of his people under his paternal, fraternal, and especially maternal care (ll. 9–11, 13).

This inscription is a masterfully composed representation of Kilamuwa's reign as one set apart from those of his predecessors by his establishment of secure borders and his provision of peace and prosperity for his people (see already Fales

1979). The story in ll. 7–8 is quite consistent with this and indeed represents the larger themes in miniature. We can imagine that others in Sam'al may have told the tale in rather different terms: Kilamuwa's personal rule was threatened by a more powerful neighbor, so he sacrificed precious resources to pay the Assyrians to keep him in power. But Kilamuwa's story shows his cleverness by the vagueness of its initial admission of the superiority of the Danunian king, by its use of the word "hired" with reference to the great king of Assyria, and by its immediate shift to the economic benefits of this move; vulnerable to a more powerful neighbor, Kilamuwa nevertheless managed on his own to procure the assistance of the greatest power on the horizon and to enrich his country. This surely reflects the story as it would have been told in Kilamuwa's court, bolstering the stature of the king and his supporters. The location of the inscription at the main entrance to the palace also suggests that the inscription was designed to impress at least symbolically all who entered the palace.[27] Doubtless prior oral communication of the content of the inscription was adapted for even larger consumption. The economic benefits of Kilawuma's reign, as here spelled out, reflect a message to the larger population: in the words of a modern political campaign, "You've never had it so good."

But the end of the inscription more directly implies another audience. The concluding curses are invoked on "whoever among my sons sits (i.e. rules) in my place and damages my inscription" and "whoever destroys this inscription." The curse on the first is to face civil discord and that on the second to have his head smashed by the gods of the state (ll. 13–16). Although these curses are worded in the third person, they are warnings directed to any heir who tries to change or otherwise deface this record of Kilamuwa's achievements and any other person (rebel, invader) who would do away with it altogether. Kilamuwa here attempts to constrain such successors from in any way depriving posterity of access to this record. This conclusion to the inscription tells us that the ideal reader is someone who respects and preserves this account of Kilamuwa's accomplishments.

The story in Kilamuwa's inscription is closer to the events referred to than any of the other stories we are about to review. Its brevity and rhetoric disclose relatively little of the historical events behind it, only that, when threatened by the king of the Danunians, Kilamuwa made a major donation to the king of Assyria, who subsequently attacked the Danunians and disposed of the threat against Sam'al.[28] As a story, the account elevates the protagonist-speaker (Kilamuwa) and focuses on the economic benefits of his move, rather than on the military facts (which would tend to extol the king of the Danunians and then the king of Assyria). It conceals the military activities, disguises the diplomatic developments, and highlights the economic benefits by a synecdoche: the availability of a male or female slave for a sheep or garment, respectively.

The Inscription of Bir-Rākib for His Father Panamuwa

During the first archaeological campaign at Zinjirli in 1888, the lower half of a dolerite statue was found. Two feet protrude from under a long robe, on the front of which was written an inscription in the local dialect (Samalian).[29] Dating to about a century later than that of Kilamuwa, c. 730 BCE, the inscription records that it was dedicated to Panamuwa II after his death by his son, Bir-Rākib. Since the honored king was already deceased, the monument was probably originally located in the royal necropolis in nearby Gerçin, but it was found about three kilometers from there in an abandoned Islamic cemetery, where it had been re-used (upside down) as a gravestone (von Luschan 1893, 48). The statue would have been a representation of the dead king.

While the inscription is certainly an act of piety, a tribute by the son to his deceased father, it is also an extraordinary piece of historiography. Its range, both temporal (from the events preceding Panamuwa's assumption of the throne to those following his death) and social and economic (covering not only the deeds and fate of the king but also conditions and events in the country as a whole and, indeed, further afield), marks it as unique among the recovered inscriptions of the kings of Syria-Palestine. Although it is badly damaged, so that no line is easily read and most have gaps, its narrative and historical significance demand attention, and its size and the number of complete sentences preserved permit at least a partial narrative analysis. The larger part of the inscription is devoted to the story of Panamuwa's engaging the Assyrian king to dispose of his enemies and secure his rule.[30]

(1) Bir-Rākib set up this monument for his father Panamuwa, son of Bir-Ṣūr, king of Sam'al in . . . the year [of his death?].

(1–2) Because of his father's right conduct, the gods of Sam'al delivered my father Panamuwa from the destruction that occurred in his father's house,[31] and Hadad stood by him.

(2–6) . . . .[32] destroyed/the terrible thing . . . from/in his father's house, and he killed his father Bir-Ṣūr, and he killed his father's seventy 70[33] brothers. But my father mounted a chariot and . . .[34] and he filled the prisons with the rest of them,[35] and he made ruined towns more common than inhabited towns, . . .[36] "and if(?) you bring the sword into my house, and kill one of my sons, then I will release the sword in the land of Sam'al." Then he/they slew(?) . . . the curse(?) of Panamuwa son of QRL . . . my father Pana-mu⟨wa⟩, son of Bir-Ṣūr, (they) fled from the land.[37] And sheep and cattle and wheat and barley [were rare]; and a half-mina stood at (only) a shekel, and a ŠṬRB(-weight?) of onions(?) at a shekel, and two-thirds of a mina of oil (?) at a shekel.

(6–8) Then my father Pana[muwa, so]n of Bi[r-Ṣūr], brought [a present][38] to the king of Assyria, who made him king over his father's house and killed the stone of destruction from his father's house and . . .[39] from the treasure of the houses of the land of Sam'al from. . . . Then he broke open the prisons and released the prisoners of Sam'al.

(8–11) Then my father arose and released the women from the [neckstocks?] . . . the house of the women who had been killed, and he buried them in (?). . . . [Then he took] his father's house and made it better than before. And wheat and barley and sheep and cattle were abundant in his days. And all [   ] ate from . . . the price was cheap. And in the days of my father Panamuwa he appointed masters of villages and masters of chariots. And my father Panamuwa was counted among mighty kings. . . . And my father was rich in silver, yes, and rich in gold.

The inscription continues with an account of Panamuwa's faithful service of the Assyrian king and the rewards he received, and then of his sickness and death and the general mourning for him, including Tiglath-Pileser's honoring of him. It ends with Bir-Rākib's own accession, setting up of this monument, performance of a ritual, and prayer for blessing.

This is not the first-person account of a king's doings typically found in memorial inscriptions. The narrator stands outside the story (apart from the first and the last four lines, when Bir-Rākib introduces himself as Panamuwa's successor and donor of the present monument). The story that concerns us here occupies the first half of the twenty-three-line inscription and falls into three sections corresponding to the three clauses of Kilamuwa's story: the threat to Panamuwa, his appeal to and the intervention of the Assyrian king, and the subsequent conditions of peace and prosperity. Beside the minimal story of Kilamuwa, this is rich in details.

The opening sentence of the inscription is neither that of a memorial inscription ("I am so-and-so, king of such-and-such") nor that of a dedicatory inscription ("The X that so-and-so set up/built/made, etc., for such-and-such a god"). It begins with the name of the author in the third person and states that he set up this monument for his father. The distinctive introduction serves the distinctive purpose. This is neither a typical memorial inscription nor a typical dedicatory inscription, but a memorial dedicated by the son to the father.

Panamuwa's story begins with an abstract (ll. 1–2) that speaks of a terrible thing that occurred in his father's house and of his deliverance from it by the country's gods. This tells us less and more than the rest of the narrative. It reveals almost nothing of the plot: something terrible happened from which Panamuwa was delivered. But it gives a theological dimension to the story that is not present in what follows: it was the gods, and especially Hadad, who delivered him.[40] This abstract alone provides the theological perspective from which Bir-Rākib would have the audience see the following mundane events.

As in Kilamuwa's story, the author must have introduced the antagonist immediately. After a further reference to the terrible thing that occurred in Panamuwa's father's house, we learn that the antagonist kills Panamuwa's father and "seventy brothers." The author is certainly drawing on traditional motifs here, like the Israelite author of Judges 9, who has Abimelech kill his seventy (half-) brothers, or the author of 2 Kings 10:1–11, who has Jehu accomplish the killing of the seventy sons of Ahab. The number is not stated in 2 Kings 11:1–3, in which Athaliah destroys "all the royal seed"; but there, as in Judges 9 and the story of Panamuwa, one escapes. Bir-Rākib is fitting his story into a well-known pattern. "Seventy" comprises the entire family; if one escapes the slaughter, he is the only legitimate heir. This also suggests that there is something miraculous or providential about the survivor's escape.

The narrator goes on to recount the depredations of the antagonist: filling the prisons and laying waste the towns, the extent of latter expressed by the comparison that the number of desolate towns surpassed the number of inhabited ones. Where Kilamuwa referred vaguely to the greater strength of the king of the Danunians, Bir-Rākib spells out the antagonist's slaughter of Panamuwa's family and ravaging of his people.

Panamuwa I, the protagonist's antecedent, must have been introduced in the following damaged part of l. 4 (and the name is hesitantly read there by Tropper) because, when continuous text reappears, he is evidently being quoted in a conditional threat: to bring about bloodshed in the land if one of his sons is killed. This is worded as a matching retribution: "If you bring the sword . . . then I will release the sword . . ." (l. 5). The certain reference to Panamuwa I later in line 5 may refer to these words as his "curse" (*'lt*). It is not clear when Panamuwa I uttered this threat—earlier, prior to his death, or through an oracle after his death. It may echo lines in the inscription dedicated to the god Hadad by Panamuwa I, in which he says: "Whoever of my sons/house takes the sceptre in Sam'al and sits on my throne and rul[es   let him not ta]ke up the sword . . . let him not kill . . ." [ll. 24–26]. In any case, the threat is quoted here to anticipate—and contribute to the justification of—the later military intervention of the Assyrian king at Panamuwa II's urging.

The fate of Panamuwa II is now taken up again: we learn that he fled the country. This section ends with examples of the economic hardship in the land from which the protagonist has been driven—the shortage of livestock and cereals and the debased value of standard weights.[41]

Now the story reaches its turning point: Panamuwa, whom we saw mounting a chariot and fleeing, reappears bringing a present to the Assyrian king. This is immediately effective: the king puts Panamuwa on the throne and kills his antagonist, freeing up the treasures(?), breaking open the prisons, and releasing the prisoners. In these clauses, the antagonist is objectified and vilified as "the stone of destruction/the destructive stone," and the legitimacy of Panamuwa, the Assyrian's puppet king, is emphasized by the repetition of the phrase relating him to "his father's house." The legitimacy and right conduct (*ṣdq*, l. 1) of Panamuwa contrasts with the destructiveness (*šḥt(h)*, ll. 2 [twice], 7) of the antagonist. Several elements of the complication are reversed here: the father's house that was deprived of heirs now has an heir on the throne; the antagonist who killed is now himself (itself!) killed; the prisons he filled are now emptied.

These reversals apparently continue in the last section. Panamuwa undertakes his own measures of restoration, releasing certain women, and burying others who had been killed (the surviving complication has not preserved the actions that now required these steps). His restoration of "his father's house"—now referring to the palace—produces something better than what was there before.[42] In place of the economic deprivation suffered before his critical intervention with the Assyrian king, there is now an abundance of cereals and livestock (the two pairs in reverse order) and prices are cheap.[43] Thus Panamuwa brings peace and prosperity to his land. The story concludes with reference to Panamuwa's administrative measures (appointing officers in charge of villages and chariotry), his international standing (being ranked among mighty kings), and his personal wealth (rich in silver and gold).

With this, Panamuwa's engaging of Assyrian intervention is vindicated. The wrongs of the antagonist are as far as possible righted, the dynasty is reestablished, those who have not been killed are restored to their former condition, wretched economic conditions are reversed, a new order is imposed, and Panamuwa's royal status is established. From here, the inscription goes on to detail Panamuwa's subsequent service to Tiglath-Pileser and the Assyrian king's favors to Panamuwa.

While the antagonist seems to have been internal rather than external—a usurper rather than an invader—in other respects, the general situation and developments recounted are broadly comparable to those reflected in Kilamuwa's inscription: A threatens B, B procures the military intervention of C by appealing to him with presents, A and his country prosper as a result. But here the story is recounted in much more detail: in ll. 2–6, the various misdeeds of the antagonist, Panamuwa's flight, and the miserable economic conditions ensuing; in ll. 6–8, Panamuwa's present to the Assyrian king and the latter's actions in response; and in ll. 8–11, the various beneficent deeds of Panamuwa and the flourishing economic conditions prevailing after his assumption of the throne. The narrator uses the cost of animals and grains both to express the hardship experienced during an interregnum of military oppression and the prosperity enjoyed during the subsequent restoration.

Despite the elaboration of the actions involved, the three actors arc characterized by type: the nameless antagonist is an objectified malefactor; Panamuwa and the Assyrian king are pure benefactors of the country. From the preserved text, it appears that the narrator holds back the protagonist in the first part of the story, impressing readers with the details of the devastation wrought by the antagonist (and its economic consequences) and with the quotation of the curse of Panamuwa I. We are afforded only two glimpses of the protagonist (in two sentences of the surviving text): mounting a chariot in the middle of l. 3 and fleeing the country toward the end of l. 5. His fate through this section is left largely to the reader's imagination, although traditional associations, as well as the curse of Panamuwa I, raise expectations that, despite the bleak picture, he will be avenged and restored.

For all its poor state of preservation, the inscription establishes clearly that this story is presented as an act of filial piety: it is the faithful son's account of the near destruction of his dynasty and land, and of his father's restoration of both. It thus represents the story of these events as told in the second generation, in the son's court. Bir-Rākib, like his father, owes his place on the throne to Tiglath-Pileser, a fact he graciously acknowledges (l. 19; in his other inscriptions, he reiterates this debt and emphasizes his own faithful service to the Assyrian king). The stories behind these eighth-century inscriptions might have been told with representatives of the Assyrian court in the audience, and the inscription itself might have been readable by local Assyrian officials. Hence, in contrast to Kilamuwa's boast of using the Assyrian as a hireling, Bir-Rākib gives full recognition to the role of the Assyrian king in establishing his father and himself on the throne and in liberating political prisoners.

Then again, the initial abstract suggests a somewhat different interpretation. There it is not the Assyrian king who is credited with Panamuwa's deliverance but the gods of Sam'al, especially Hadad, motivated by the good conduct (*ṣdq*) of Panamuwa's father. Bir-Rākib is quite deliberate in his references to the gods in this inscription. At the end, he calls upon all the gods of Sam'al, including "Hadad and El and Rākib-El, the lord of the dynasty, and Shamash" (l. 22). Here, appropriately in a blessing, appears the most extended, specific list of deities. A little earlier, when he introduces himself in the manner of a memorial inscription, he says that it is because of his father's and his own good conduct that "[his] lord Rākib-El and [his] lord Tiglath-Pileser" set him on his father's throne (ll. 19–20).[44] Here the dynastic deity and the Assyrian king are set side by side and given joint responsibility for Bir-Rākib's reign. But that synergistic view of the forces at work on his own reign is not imposed on the older story. His recognition of the divine role in his father's career is stated only outside the story, as an introductory thematic statement; the narrative itself remains on a strictly human plane, like Kilamuwa's. It is as if the story has its own established form and authority: the historical facts and political exigencies and moral judgments, the structure of the plot and the structure of the rhetoric—all cohere in a whole that ignores the gods. Thus the role of the gods, which Bir-Rākib now recognizes, must be stated in the introductory abstract. The singling out of Hadad for recognition, which occurs only here in the inscription, perhaps reflects Panamuwa's special allegiance to this deity. In any case, the story is now viewed as an illustration of the gods' deliverance and Hadad's support. Thus the abstract confers on the story in its present setting a different view of causation and responsibility from that which it expresses in itself—and presumably expressed in oral versions prior to its incorporation in this inscription. This secondary interpretation of the story anticipates the work of the Deuteronomistic historian (see later in this chapter).

The historical background of this story was apparently an internal revolt against the reigning dynasty and an oppressive rule by a rival of the protagonist. (We should remember, however, that the protagonist of such stories may himself be a usurper, legitimating his rule by claiming that he is the heir of a prior ruler and that his immediate predecessor was a usurper; see Liverani 1974). Panamuwa fled and appealed for assistance to the Assyrian king, who destroyed the rival and put Panamuwa on the throne as his vassal. Again, these events may have been told very differently by the Assyrians, by those who were defeated, and by any who were opposed to Bir-Rākib's reign.

Tadmor has argued that royal autobiographical apologies in Assyrian literature were written around the appointment of the author's successor (1983). In this case, we have a biographical apology—or, better, apologetic biography—written by the son. Could the son's accession have prompted renewed questioning of the father's legitimacy (and therefore the son's) by the old opposition or by a new anti-Assyrian movement? Certainly, the inscription addresses the questions both of the legitimacy of father and son and of the benefits of Assyrian overlordship. Bir-Rākib leads off by claiming that Panamuwa enjoyed the support of the gods and goes on to recount the benefits of his father's service of the Assyrian king. He was a benefactor of the country, a clever and good man whose virtues were appropriately rewarded with wealth and status, and a favored and honored servant of the king of Assyria. The latter, along with Rākib-El, has now installed Bir-

Rākib as Panamuwa's heir. He portrays the antagonist, by contrast, as destroyer not only of Bir-Ṣūr's family, but also of the people and the land. Moreover, the quotation of the threat of Panamuwa I suggests that the killing of the antagonist was the fulfillment of that threat and that Panamuwa II and his Assyrian sponsor were the faithful executors of Panamuwa I. The inscription thus counters any opposition by claiming that Panamuwa II and Bir-Rākib, even under Assyrian overlordship, are true heirs of the dynasty and benefactors of the country. Panamuwa's piety toward his father is not unrelated to his vindication of his own position.

Stories of Appeals for Military Intervention in the Bible

Historiographic Accounts

In 2 Kings, there are two stories that recount the same strategy, though somewhat further removed from actual historical events. In both 1 Kings 15:17–22 and 2 Kings 16:5–9 the narrator stands outside the story, but focuses on the initially threatened king, his interests, and achievements. Unlike the inscriptions of Kilamuwa and Panamuwa, neither of these stories has an interest in the economic conditions before or after these events. Instead, they concentrate on military and diplomatic events: military threat, appeal to a third force, and that force's military response.

1 Kings 15:17–22 "Baasha, king of Israel, went up against Judah and built Ramah, so as not to allow anyone to leave or go in to Asa, king of Judah" (1 Kgs 15:17). The building of Ramah, a border fortress only eight kilometers (c. five miles) from Jerusalem, clearly implies control of Jerusalem's northern environs, the main north-south route, and the main approach from the west, but it would not be clear from this alone that more is involved—that is, that Asa is completely hemmed in by a full-scale siege of Jerusalem. Certainly, the fortification of Ramah might be perceived as a bridgehead for an attack on Jerusalem. The narrator, however, in his explication of Baasha's purpose in the second half of the verse, insists that Jerusalem and its king were isolated.[45]

Asa, however, was able to send envoys to Benhadad of Damascus. "Then Asa took all the silver and gold left[46] in the treasuries of the temple of Yahweh and the treasuries of the palace of the king and handed them over to his servants. And King Asa sent them to Benhadad, son of Tabrimmon, son of Hezion, the king of Aram, who ruled from Damascus" (v. 18). The present is accompanied by the message: "There has been a treaty between me and you and between my father and your father.[47] Look, I am sending you a present (*šoḥad*) of silver and gold. Go and break your treaty with Baasha, king of Israel, so that he withdraws from me" (v. 19). The speech discloses to us the already existing relations among the kings and Asa's thinking and strategy in the present situation. The treaties between Judah and Damascus, on the one hand, and Israel and Damascus on the other would presumably require that Damascus remain neutral in conflicts between Israel and Judah. But Asa's introduction of the treaty between Judah and Damascus as one that has endured for two generations is the first argument for Benhadad's favorable response. The implication is that Benhadad's treaty with Baasha is of more recent origin and therefore less deserving of respect. Asa reinforces this statement of long-standing common interests by drawing attention to the accompanying present, designed to shift Benhadad's goodwill away from Israel and toward Judah. After this preparation, Asa makes his specific request that Benhadad violate his treaty with Baasha—which therefore must have bound him to nonaggression against Israel[48]—and expresses his final objective: Baasha's withdrawal. Unlike the stories from Zinjirli, this story is more interested in the argument that accompanies the present than in the present itself.

The correct understanding of the connotations of "present" or "gift" (*šoḥad*) is as important in this story (and the next one to be discussed) as of the word "hire" in the inscription of Kilamuwa. It is in many contexts used to refer to what we would call a "bribe," and many commentators read the connotations of "bribe" into such passages as this. But in English a "bribe" is always viewed negatively (except in jocular contexts). This is not so of the Hebrew word.[49] Certainly, when it is used in legal contexts, it may have negative connotations. (The same is true in English of such words as "present" and "gift": if a party to a lawsuit gives "presents" to the judge or jury, the implication is negative.) But we are not justified in claiming that the Hebrew word's roots are in legal parlance and that its connotations in other contexts are therefore necessarily negative. A reading of the various contexts in which the word *šoḥad* appears reveals several in which it has positive significance.

Before considering contexts in which the noun occurs, we may briefly take note of the two biblical contexts in which the cognate verb is found.[50] It is used of the giving of presents by a promiscuous woman (representing Jerusalem) to get her lovers to come to her (Ezek 16:33) and of the paying of a ransom to deliver a friend from an enemy (Job 6:22–23). In Ezekiel 16:33, the parallel clause reads: "you have given your gifts (*nātatt nědānayik*) to all your lovers." This practice is contrasted with the otherwise universal one of giving gifts (*nedeh*) *to* such women. However negatively such behavior is viewed, the gifts would not appear to have the associations of bribes. The ransoming of someone from an enemy, as in Job 6:22–23, is also in the background of Isaiah 45:13. There Yahweh says he is responsible for arousing Cyrus and easing his way and announces: "He will rebuild my city and dismiss my exiles—not for a price, and not for a present (*šoḥad*)." While Job has not asked his friends to come up with the money to ransom him, and Cyrus has not demanded ransom money, neither text suggests that such gifts would be wrong or even inappropriate. Certainly, Yahweh would not be depicted as considering a bribe. In any case, there is no question of injury to third parties. In both cases, from the point of view of the speaker, the present would release worthy people from their oppressors.

Proverbs 21:14 reads: "A secret gift (*mattān*) appeases anger; and a present (*šo-ḥad*) kept close, a wild rage." Here such presents are commended as a way of dealing with someone in a bad temper. The same strategy is envisaged in Proverbs 6:35, although there it is said that it will not work on a jealous husband if one has committed adultery with his wife. As much as the adultery is condemned, there is nothing to suggest that once a man had committed that offense, it would be wrong of him to try offering such presents to appease the enraged husband. As the previously quoted text makes clear, to give presents to someone who is angry with you is proverbial common sense. In Proverbs 6:35 the word *šoḥad* is parallel to *koper* "ransom," which, while it, too, may be used in a blameworthy context (e.g., Num 35:31), also has a perfectly respectable meaning, even in legal contexts like Exodus 21:30, where, as an alternative to the death penalty, the *koper* placed on the guilty party is the equivalent of the expression "redemption for his life," which the law approves.

Proverbs 17:8 is more ambiguous: "A present seems like a lucky stone to the presenter—wherever he turns he succeeds." This could be commending generous giving of presents by members of the class to which the writer belongs, in recognition of the effectiveness of the practice in oiling the social machinery one needs to use in everyday life and business. (We need to remember that this is much more important in traditional than in modern societies.) Then again, the expression "seems . . . to the presenter" could be intended to suggest that the present is not what he thinks it is—that for others it is more like the evil eye. In the latter case, presumably the text would imply the narrower meaning, "bribe." But then it is surprising that some more direct form of disapproval is not expressed. Unfortunately, as so often in Proverbs, the context is of little help—unless we choose to link this verse with the following one, which concerns getting on well with people. This would support the first interpretation.

Finally, we may consider Proverbs 17:23: "A wicked person takes a present surreptitiously to pervert the course of justice." Here, clearly, wrong behavior is the subject. But that is unambiguously conveyed by the expressions: "a wicked person," "surreptitiously," and "to pervert the course of justice." If the word *šoḥad* denoted precisely a "bribe," the proverb would be defining the obvious. Such pleonasm seems out of place (except in the case of synonymous parallelism) among these usually pithy proverbs. Either half of the verse—"A wicked person takes a bribe" or "a bribe perverts the course of justice"—would alone be a truism. But it seems that *šoḥad* has to be modified by the adverbial "surreptitiously" (Hebrew *mēḥēq*) to emphasize the illegitimacy of the present in this case. The longer sentence merits its place in this collection of proverbs only if *šoḥad* alone means "gift, present."

In conclusion, it seems clear that the Hebrew word in question is a common word for "present," the good uses of which include ransoming the oppressed, appeasing the enraged, and, probably, generally smoothing one's way in society and business. In legal contexts, presents are, of course, a threat to impartial justice and, hence, judged and condemned.[51] But the propriety or impropriety of the present is made clear by the individual context. I conclude then, that the word *šoḥad,* like the English word "present" and unlike "bribe," does not in itself express a condemnation. While "bribe" may be an appropriate translation where the context determines that meaning and connotation, "present" may serve everywhere as an adequate translation, since the context clearly determines the particular attitude toward, or moral valuation of, the present.

In 1 Kings 15:19 the word *šoḥad* is used not in a legal context, but in the context of international relations. Further, it is used by the person sending the present in an address to the person receiving it, not by someone—whether outside observer or threatened third party—who might view the act negatively. There are, therefore, no grounds for claiming that the use of *šoḥad* by Asa is an expression of the narrator's condemnation of the act. Certainly this *šoḥad* was understood by both parties to require something in return, as in modern political life. But in Asa's message, it remains distinguished, as a present, from the opprobrium of a "bribe," as also from an enforced gift or "tribute." Asa's speech and gift together *aim* to accomplish what Kilamuwa claims he *actually* accomplished when he says more laconically and presumptuously that he "hired" the king of Assyria. Asa's *šoḥad*, like his speech, is an instrument of persuasion.[52] By his double appeal, Asa aims to tip the balance between the two alliances Benhadad has with Israel and Judah.

Benhadad "responded" to Asa by sending his officers against several northern Israelite towns and through most of Israel's northeastern territory (v. 20). The actual deliverance of Asa is also spelled out directly: when Baasha gets news of Benhadad's invasion, he stops his aggressive construction and settles back in Tirzah (v. 21). Aggressive action elsewhere in the besieging king's territory draws him off. But the narrator has no further interest in the outcome of the Aramaic invasion or the fate of Israel. Only the subsequent actions of Asa are considered relevant.

According to v. 22, Asa calls up all Judeans, with no exemptions, to remove the stones and wood of Ramah, and "with them King Asa built up Geba of Benjamin and Mizpah" (respectively, nine kilometers northeast and thirteen kilometers north of Jerusalem). Instead of beginning the sentence with the verb form typically used to express the next action in a sequence (the converted imperfect), the author begins with the subject, followed by a perfect verb form.[53] This disconnects the construction work of v. 22 from the preceding. Such construction work was certainly a long-term activity distinct from the military moves of the preceding narrative and in royal inscriptions is often treated separately from military affairs. But here the clause modifying Ramah ("which Baasha had built") links the verse with the preceding narrative. In this respect, it corresponds to the references to administrative consolidation that appear at the end of several of Mesha's campaign accounts (see chapter 4). Thus it is presented as a further step to ensure a long-term solution to Baasha's threat by pushing the fortified boundary back north.

This account of a weak king's appeal to a strong king for intervention against a threatening neighbor spells out the nature of the initial threat, the precise argument used to persuade the strong king to intervene (including the history of the relations between the three parties), the effects of the intervention, and, ultimately, the delivered king's consolidation of his new position over the long term. The narrator of this story insists that the threat to Asa is much more serious than simply a shift of the border to only eight kilometers north of Jerusalem: all movement to and from Jerusalem is cut off. The story depicts Asa draining the already depleted treasury to reinforce a relationship with Damascus to the detriment of Israel. Finally, it shows the efficacy of this move by listing all the Israelite towns and districts ravaged by Benhadad's forces and noting the withdrawal of the offending king. While Baasha's withdrawal in v. 21 reverses his advance in v. 17, the addition of v. 22 extends this reversal of his initial aggressive action: Baasha's construction project had moved the fortified frontier southward; Asa's now moves it northward. The larger structure of the story may be outlined as follows:

1   A Baasha's attack on Judah (17aα)
     B Baasha's construction (17aβ)
2   Asa's voluntary gift of treasures to Benhadad (18)
3   Asa's speech to Benhadad (including references backward to 2 and forward to 2'
     and 1A') (19)
2'   Baasha's involuntary loss of land to Benhadad (20)
1'   B' Baasha's abandonment of construction (21a)
     A' Baasha's withdrawal from Judah (21b)
     B'' Asa's construction (22)

We already noted the discontinuity between v. 22 and the preceding. As it now appears, v. 22 also stands outside the strict chiastic structure of the story. These two observations suggest that it may not have originally been part of the preceding narrative. While the references to construction maintain the traditional epigraphic role of the king as directly responsible for the achievement—Baasha builds Ramah, and Asa builds Geba and Mizpah—elsewhere the narrator extends the dramatis personae. Having taken the silver and gold from the treasuries, Asa "handed them over to his servants and sent them" to Benhadad. Rather than leading the invasion himself, Benhadad orders his military officers to attack parts of northern Israel. Asa conscripts every Judean to participate in the dismantling of Ramah. Thus royal servants, military officers, and the Judean populace all have roles in the story. While they are all mere functionaries, they make explicit the activities of the larger social world in a way that most inscriptions do not (but cf. Panamuwa).

This narrative presents Asa as effectively shifting the balance of power in his favor and as accomplishing something more permanent than the cessation of a siege. The historian's approval of Asa in vv. 11–14 is not inconsistent with this account of his success. However, some inconsistency appears between this story and the summary statement immediately preceding it: "There was war between Asa and Baasha, king of Israel, all their days" (v. 16). This is reiterated in v. 32 and, indeed, is a refrain in these accounts of the early reigns of the two monarchies (cf. previously 14:30; 15:6, 7). By this refrain, the historian renders the resolution of the story in 15:17–22 a mere interlude in an ongoing conflict, diminishing the impact of Asa's accomplishment as portrayed in the story. But if the story is not then the creation of the historian, neither does it have the stamp of Asa's court or that of his immediate successors. There is no trace of the personal involvement or colorful rhetoric that we find in the inscriptions of Kilamuwa and Panamuwa. Instead, we have a straightforward account in simple language (including the quotation of Asa's message) by a more objective, external observer, with prosaic elaboration of details not essential to the plot ("so as not to allow anyone to go out or come in to Asa, king of Judah," "all the silver and gold remaining in the treasuries of the house of Yahweh and the treasuries of the house of the king," "he sent the officers of the troops that he had against the towns of Israel," "king Asa summoned all Judah with no exemptions and they took the stones and wood of Ramah, which Baasha had built"). It is more neutral than the stories of the Samalian kings and more aware of the various groups of people on whom the kings rely. It seems unlikely that the historian is drawing on an old royal inscription or on any other written source directly reflecting an oral court story of the ninth century. This is confirmed by consideration of the skillfully constructed speech at the center of the present account, which reads like something written according to Thucydides' famous claim: the writer has made the speaker say what, in his view, was called for by the situation (*The Peloponnesian War* I, 22). While probably too blunt in its language to be an actual diplomatic appeal, it provides an appropriately argued message for a king attempting to engage the military intervention of a possibly unwilling ally.

2 Kings 16:5–9   The similar story in 2 Kings 16:5–9 treats events roughly contemporary with Panamuwa. Whereas in 1 Kings 15 Judah appealed against Israel to Damascus, here Judah appeals against Israel and Damascus to Assyria. "Then ('*āz*) Rezin, King of Aram, and Pekah, son of Ramaliah, king of Israel, went up to Jerusalem for battle, and besieged Ahaz, but could not do battle" (2 Kgs 16:5). Here and in Isaiah 7:1, the last word (*lĕhillāḥēm*) probably refers to bringing the siege to an actual battle by making a breach in the gate or wall of the city, which would normally lead to the immediate defeat of the defenders.[54] If there were no sequel, this verse could stand on its own as a summary account of an unsuccessful siege of Jerusalem. There is then in v. 6 a parenthesis (beginning "at that time," *bāʿēt hahî*) concerning the recovery of Elath by the Edomites.[55] The temporal connectives opening each of these two verses are the writer's means of weaving into the history materials without a precise historical connection to the preceding.[56]

Following these two minimal historical narratives, the subject of the Syro-Ephraimite siege of Jerusalem is taken up again to provide an explanation for its ultimate failure. "Then Ahaz sent messengers to Tiglath-Pileser, king of Assyria, with the message: 'I am your servant and your son. Come up and deliver me from the power of the king of Aram and the power of the king of Israel, who are attacking me.' And Ahaz took the silver and gold which was in the house of Yahweh and in the treasuries of the king's house, and sent a present (*šoḥad*) to the king of Assyria. The king of Assyria responded to him, and the king of Assyria went up to Damascus and took it. He exiled its inhabitants to Kir, and killed Rezin" (vv. 7–9). Whether or not v. 5 ever existed independently,[57] vv. 7–9 certainly depend on the account of antecedent events in v. 5, where the joint attack on Jerusalem signals the military danger, and the failure to conquer the city suggests a long siege (a suggestion now indirectly reinforced by the interlude in v. 6).

In his appeal to Tiglath-Pileser, Ahaz presents himself as his vassal ("servant," "son"), calls on him to save him from his enemies, and sends a handsome "present" (*šoḥad*). The message and present are recounted as separate, successive actions. Tadmor and Cogan claim that Assyrian vassals—and, indeed, members of the Assyrian court—always refer to themselves as the "servant," never the "son" of the Assyrian king. In assigning to Ahaz the expression "your servant and your son," the writer has him put his relationship to Tiglath-Pileser in terms normally reserved for the relationship between king and Yahweh. Thus this wording is the work of the Deuteronomistic historian interested in exposing Ahaz's faithlessness and contrasting him with the faithful Hezekiah (Tadmor and Cogan 1979, 504–7; Cogan and Tadmor 1988, 192; followed by Irvine 1990, 87–90; cf. Na'aman 1995).[58] But both words are traditional expressions of subservience and respect in Syria-Palestine, going back to the El Amarna correspondence: 'Abdi-Kheba of Jerusalem and 'Aziru of Amurru both refer to themselves as "your servant [and] your son" (EA 288:66) and "your son, your servant" (EA 158:2) when writing to the king of Egypt and one of his officers, respectively (Kalluveettil 1982, 129). Biblical literature recognizes this. David, for example, speaks of himself as Nabal's son in seeking a favor from that unworthy—without any trace of Deuteronomistic disapproval (1 Sam 25:8). This suggests that "your son" may simply be a rhetorical device used alongside, or instead of, "your servant" to express at once submission to and a claim on the addressee. Thus, while the language of Ahaz's speech may not have been used in real addresses to the Assyrian king, it apparently conformed to traditional expressions of subservience in Syria-Palestine and in that context was in no way inappropriate.

As noted, the word for "present" need not carry any negative connotations. Most pertinently, in 1 Kings 15, it was put in the mouth of the king who was sending it (Asa, judged favorably even by the Deuteronomistic historian). In all the Assyrian passages cited by Tadmor and Cogan in support of the negative evaluation of presents (1979, 499–503), the presents were sent by one king to engage the support of another *against* the Assyrian king. The latter certainly viewed such acts negatively,[59] as did, in the present instance, Rezin and Pekah or, in 1 Kings 15, Baasha. But in the two biblical passages there is nothing to suggest that the *sender* of the present or the *narrator* viewed the moves negatively. The Deuteronomistic History reports that several kings of Judah used the treasures of both palace and temple for diplomatic purposes, whether to buy off an invader, as in 2 Kings 12:18–19 (Jehoash) and 18:13–16 (Hezekiah), or to engage the intervention of a third party against an invader, as in the two passages in Kings discussed in this chapter. These actions are never condemned. The Deuteronomist accepted the common understanding that temple treasures (generally donated by the king), as well as palace treasures, were at the disposal of the monarch precisely for such occasions. Thus, pace Tadmor and Cogan—and Na'aman 1995, 44–45[60]—there is no evidence in 2 Kings 16:5, 7–9 of any negative judgment of Ahaz by the narrator. Rather he, like Asa in 1 Kings 15:17–22, was here recognized as having successfully negotiated Jerusalem's deliverance. The courts of Syria-Palestine did not see resort to a superior power for assistance as a sign of weakness, as is clear in different ways from the wording of the inscriptions of Kilamuwa and Bir-Rākib.

The major difference between Kilamuwa's and the Judean narrator's views of the western kings' relations with the king of Assyria is reflected in their choice of words. Kilamuwa's *škr* and the Judean narrator's *šōḥad* both refer to the use of royal resources to procure Assyrian intervention. But Kilamuwa, who is not addressing the Assyrian king, may speak of "hiring"—that is, making temporary use of him—while the Judean narrator has Ahaz, who is addressing Tiglath-Pileser directly, express his submission to him: "I am your servant and your son."[61] Kilamuwa presents himself as in charge, making use of the Assyrians. Ahaz is presented as submitting to the Assyrian king in his appeal for assistance. According to Bir-Rākib, Panamuwa did the same.[62] Ahaz and Panamuwa would have had comparable respect for Assyrian power.

Tiglath-Pileser's response to Ahaz's appeal is to attack Damascus. The narrative ends with the fate of that city, its inhabitants, and its king. As in Kilamuwa's account, and unlike the story about Asa, there is no direct reference to the threatened king's deliverance. Once the response of the Assyrian king is registered (implicitly in Kilamuwa's inscription by the word "hired"; explicitly in the Hebrew narratives by "he responded"), the defeat or withdrawal of the attackers in the Kilamuwa inscription and the Ahaz narrative is taken for granted.

We know from the Assyrian Eponym Chronicle that Tiglath-Pileser campaigned for two years in the territory of Damascus before the city finally fell. The story in 2 Kings 16 telescopes these events, balancing the attack of the Aramaean king on Jerusalem at the beginning of the story with the Assyrian destruction of Damascus at the end to suggest that the latter is the fitting punishment for the former. Further, by its focus on Ahaz's message and gift—quoting the former and spelling out the nature and sources of the latter—it shows that through his message and gift Ahaz was the one who brought about that fate. Ahaz not only saved his city but also accomplished the final destruction of a powerful and hostile neighbor.

There is no reference to any Assyrian attack on Israel, the other party besieging Jerusalem. One might expect, from the reference to both parties in the account of the attack on Jerusalem and in the appeal of Ahaz, that the narrator would have recounted Assyria's invasion of Israelite as well as Damascene territory. The reference to Tiglath-Pileser's conquest of significant areas traditionally belonging to the northern kingdom and his deportation of their population to Asshur in 2 Kings 15:29 has been understood to refer to the other part of Tiglath-Pileser's response to Ahaz. It has been suggested that 2 Kings 15:29 was originally part of the conclusion of our story, paralleling the account of Tiglath-Pileser's destruction of Damascus, and was later moved to the account of the reign of Pekah (Tadmor and Cogan 1979, 507–8) in order to explain the coup of Hoshea, who presumably represented a pro-Assyrian party willing to pay tribute to the Assyrians before they could invade the Israelite heartland. But Irvine has argued that the territories listed in 2 Kings 15:29 were in Aramaean control at this time (Irvine 1994), in which case this verse would not supply the missing attack on Israel sought at the end of our story. Comparable territorial references listed as incorporated into the empire in Tiglath-Pileser's summary inscriptions are there clearly identified as Aramaean territory (nos. 4:5'-7'—Tadmor 1994, 138–39 and 9: rev. 3–4—Tadmor 1994, 186–7).[63] Thus the present narrative capitalizes on the Assyrian devastation of a long-standing, powerful enemy and ignores the conquest of large areas of Israelite territory.[64] By placing the conquest of Damascus immediately after Ahaz's appeal to Tiglath-Pileser, it portrays Ahaz as an effective power broker who at once saved Jerusalem and secured the destruction of Damascus.

This contrasts with the Assyrian view of the matter. The one reference to Ahaz's "present" appears in summary inscription 7: rev. 7'-13'. This is a list of the rulers and states of Syria and Palestine, followed by the materials that Tiglath-Pileser received from them as tribute. Among the other rulers, and in no way distinguished from them, is Jehoahaz (a longer form of the name Ahaz) of Judah (l. 11'). From the retrospective Assyrian point of view, Ahaz sent tribute like all the other submissive kings. (Similarly, Panamuwa appears only in lists of rulers paying tribute to Tiglath-Pileser.[65]) Further, it is inherently unlikely that the Assyrians' resolve to incorporate Damascus fully into the empire and so control the trade that flowed through the city would be seriously influenced by gifts from a minor state in southern Palestine (Irvine 1990, 107–8). But there is no reason why the Judean court would not have boasted of such influence later, when the king to whom they had sent treasure had destroyed Damascus. In this case, then, we have evidence of two of the three different attitudes toward Ahaz's act: that of the narrator (and presumably the Judean court), who saw it as a present that produced the desired result, and that of the Assyrian court, which saw it as just another payment of tribute.

Unlike Kilamuwa's story, this one is not interested in inflating the besieged king's role in relation to the Assyrian. On the contrary, it emphasizes his submission and appeal to Tiglath-Pileser. In these respects, it bears comparison with Bir-Rākib's account of the relations between Panamuwa and Tiglath-Pileser and, indeed, with Bir-Rākib's own memorial inscriptions, in which he boasts of his service to Tiglath-Pileser.[66] By the latter part of the eighth century, when both Bir-Rākib and Ahaz ruled, independence from the great Assyrian king was no longer a serious proposition for most of the lesser kings of Syria-Palestine, who were content to boast of the favor they enjoyed with the Assyrian king and of their relative superiority to their fellow kings. In the later eighth and the seventh centuries, Jerusalem court circles continued to waver between a policy of independence and one of submission. This story appears to reflect the views of those who favored the latter policy.

Summary   This account of Ahaz's successful diplomacy[67] contrasts with the hostile introductory Deuteronomistic judgment of his reign in 2 Kings 16:2b–4. Thus, neither the story of Asa nor that of Ahaz fits well with its present context. The disjunction between both stories and their present contexts suggests that neither was invented by the historian. Then again, the two stories have many features in common, not only of plot but also of language and interests. These may be suggested initially by the following schematic summary:

1 KINGS 15

(17) Then RN_1, king of GN_1 went up against GN_2 . . . so as not to allow anyone to leave or go in to RN_2 king of GN_2

(18) and RN_2 took the silver and gold that were left
in the treasuries of Yahweh's temple and . . . the king's palace
and handed them over to his servants
and sent them to RN_3 . . . king of GN_3 . . . :
(19) "(nominal sentence describing present and past relations)
Look, I'm sending you a present . . .
(request for assistance—imperatives and jussive)"
(20) Then RN_3 responded to king RN_2
and sent officers against . . . and struck. . . .

2 KINGS 16

(5) At that time RN_1 king of GN_1 went up to Jerusalem . . .
to do battle and laid siege against RN_2 . . .
(8a) and RN_2 took the silver and the gold that were
in Yahweh's temple and in the treasuries of the king's palace
(7a) RN_2 sent messengers to RN_3 king of GN_3:
"(nominal sentence describing proposed relations)"
(8b) and he sent to the king of GN_3 a present
(7b) "(request for assistance—imperative)"
Then the king of GN_3 responded to him
and the king of GN_3 went up . . . and took. . . .

The common features of the two biblical stories may most fruitfully be reviewed by way of contrast with the two epigraphic stories. First, there are significant differences in content. Unlike the inscriptions, the biblical stories make no mention of the economic benefits enjoyed by the country as a result of the kings' actions. These are not works of public propaganda. Nevertheless, they share certain distinctive narrative elements missing from the inscriptions: quotation of the diplomatic message, statement of the nature and source of the presents, and account of the military actions undertaken by the third party. These interests in diplomatic argument, in disbursements from the coffers of Jerusalem temple and palace, and in the Judean king's success in defending Jerusalem and getting invaders invaded, as well as the lack of interest in the general economy, suggest Jerusalem court circles as the general matrix for the production of these stories—specifically those in the court committed to international involvements, not to isolationist policies or apolitical quietism.

Second, there are differences in rhetoric between the two pairs of texts. There is no trace in either of the Judean stories of the rhetoric of the central actor or his successor, no direct expression of the interests of the particular monarch's court, as in the Zinjirli inscriptions. Both stories stand at an objective distance from the passions of lived history—without, however, being excited by literary passion or theological conviction. They are examples of that extraordinary dispassionate prose that we find here and there in the Deuteronomistic History and in contemporary Babylonian chronicles. Further, their extensive common phraseology suggests their origin in a common social and cultural circle.[68]

To conclude thus far: the Zinjirli inscriptions present us with two stages in the transmission of court stories: one a report from the court of the king in question, the other an account from the successor of the king in question. The historical Kilamuwa has the story of his own achievements written in his own lifetime. Bir-Rākib relates the story of his father. The two biblical narratives present us with accounts composed by court officials of later generations, historiographic rather than propagandistic in character and interest. Further, as Bir-Rākib provided in his opening statement a distinct, theological perspective on the story of his father, so the Deuteronomistic historians give a distinct, religious evaluation of the two Judean kings in the opening assessment of their reigns (1 Kgs 15:11–14; 2 Kgs 16:2b-4).

Didactic Literary Accounts

2 Kings 7:6   The passages discussed so far give accounts by the king making the appeal (the inscription of Kilamuwa), his son (the Panamuwa inscription), or later narrators sympathetic to him (in 1 and 2 Kings). The remaining biblical references to such stories of appeals for military intervention appear in the mouths of those who pose the initial threat (in a larger narrative) or in the words of narrators sympathetic with those in that role. While the last three stories spoke of sending a present, the next three references, like the inscription of Kilamuwa, speak of "hiring" assistance. As in the case of sending presents, hiring may be viewed positively or negatively, depending on the position of the speaker. As the hirer, Kilamuwa could boast of his accomplishment. Those against whom the intervener has been hired may be expected to regard the hiring with less favor.

In a richly developed story of divine deliverance from a siege in 2 Kings 6:24–7:20 (see chapter 6), Yahweh caused the Aramaeans besieging Samaria to hear the sound of chariots and horses and a great army. Under this delusion, the Aramaeans say to each other: "The king of Israel has hired against us the kings of the Hittites and the kings of Egypt[69] to come against us" (7:6). These kings are presumed to be not currently hostile toward the Aramaeans, who may therefore conclude that the besieged king of Samaria must have "hired" them to intervene. In other words, the author has the Aramaeans reconstruct for themselves the same sequence of events that Kilamuwa claimed to have set in motion when he used the verb: a threatened king sent an appeal with presents to a third party who agreed to respond and marched against the threatening force. The narrator shows the effectiveness of the supposed "hiring" in the immediate flight of the Aramaeans (v. 7). The writer's use of their assumption (that the Israelites have hired reinforcements against them) and their reaction (flight) clearly presupposes that both would be realistic, given the initial perception.[70] What makes Yahweh's ploy so effective in this story is the reasonableness of their reaction, which, like the subsequent reasonableness of the Israelite king—who suspects a trick when he discovers that the Aramaeans have gone—provides a nice foil for the divine deliverance of the Israelites actually effected in this story (see chapter 6). In the context of the larger story, the delusion caused by Yahweh and the explanation assumed by the Aramaeans constitute the narrator's disclosure to the reader (and to none of the characters) of how Yahweh had disposed of the besieging Aramaeans.

Here the point of view of the initial aggressors is expressed. But for them, too (according to the author), the word "hired" is appropriate. The besieging forces attribute to the besieged king of Israel the same degree of responsibility for the intervention that the besieged king of Sam'al (Kilamuwa) claimed for himself. But the sudden reversal of the Aramaeans' fortunes—their panic-stricken flight, in which they abandon everything, just when they were about to conquer the city—suggests that their reconstructed story expressed not only their fear but also their resentment at this (supposed) move. The same word describes an action of which one speaker boasts and another decries. In the same way, we saw that the words for "present" (*šoḥad*; Akkadian *ṭātu*) are neutral descriptions of an action of which one speaker may approve and another disapprove. Point of view is here expressed not by these words but by the relations among the characters and their actions.

Stories of such defeats are not likely to be told at court or in subsequent historiography. This "story" is told as part of the fictitious world of the surrounding literary-theological narrative. But when the bid to hire a third party does not result in the defeat of the party perceived as a threat, then the latter may well enjoy telling the tale. In the inscription of the Assyrian king, Adad-Narari, mentioned previously, he recounts the attempt of the king of Khanigalbat to hire the Hittites against him, the Hittites' acceptance of the gifts—and their subsequent abandonment of Khanigalbat to its fate. This all redounds to Adad-Narari's glory: the Hittites were afraid to intervene; Khanigalbat's desperate attempt to keep the Assyrians at bay was futile. The viewpoint of the initial invader is similarly reflected in the remaining biblical passages, in which the third party accepts the gift and responds to the appeal but is unable to inflict harm on those against whom it has been "hired."

2 Samuel 10:6   In 2 Samuel 10:6, the Ammonites, believing (wrongly, v. 2) that David of Israel is planning to conquer their city and knowing that they have insulted and offended him (vv. 4–6a), "sent off and hired" the forces of a number of Aramaean states (v. 6b). After an initial defeat, further reinforcements are summoned in v. 16 in vaguer language: "Hadadezer sent and brought out *(wayyōṣe')* Aram which was beyond the River." Both hirers and hired are defeated by Israel (vv. 7–18). The story ends, however, not with the destruction of the Ammonites— Joab abandons the fight after the Ammonites have fled into their city—but with the defeat of the hired Aramaeans and their conclusion of a vassal treaty with Israel so that "Aram was afraid to help the Ammonites any more" (v. 19b).[71]

The story provides an early example of diplomatic misunderstanding leading to war. The reader might suspect that David had sent his servants to spy on the Ammonites, as the latter suspect, but the omniscient narrator dismisses this charge by revealing David's motives (through a quotation of David's thoughts [v. 2aα] and the narrator's own statement of the purpose of the embassy [v. 2aβb]). The Ammonite misinterpretation of David's intentions (v. 3) is thus exposed as such and their subsequent shaming of the envoys (v. 4) as undeserved. The narrator further reinforces the reader's belief in David's decency by depicting his considerate treatment of his embarrassed envoys (v. 5). It is again the Ammonites' perceptions, which the narrator discloses in v. 6a, that lead to the further escalation of hostilities. As their suspicion of David's motives led them to mistreat his envoys, their beliefs about his subsequent attitude toward them prompts them to "hire" the Aramaeans. Given the narrator's emphatic demonstration of David's innocence and of the Ammonites' misinterpretation of David's actions, the "hiring" of the Aramaeans against David is clearly regarded by the narrator as a perverse act. It introduces the battles between Aram and Israel that are the focus of attention in the rest of the story. With the final subjection of the Aramaeans (not the Ammonites, who started it all!), the narrator emphasizes the fate of those who let themselves be hired to fight against Israel.[72]

Deuteronomy 23:5b–6   Finally, the same word occurs in the little narrative cited to justify and motivate obedience to the prohibition against admitting Moabites into the convocation of Yahweh in Deuteronomy 23:5b–6. This narrative refers to the strategy of Balak of Moab when he felt threatened by Israel. His response to the perceived military threat was to hire not, in this case, a military, but a religious force—the seer, Balaam.

According to Deuteronomy 23:4, no Ammonite or Moabite is to enter the congregation of Yahweh. Verse 5 gives two reasons for this: "They did not receive you with bread and water on your journey out of Egypt, but hired against you Balaam, son of Beor, from Pethor (Pitru) of Aram Naharaim, to curse you."[73] The verse refers to two different traditions,[74] the first referring to the Ammonites and the second to the Moabites. Both traditions must have been stories familiar to the audience; references to unknown events of the past would scarcely be compelling justifications or motives for the law. A complex version of the second story, concerning the hiring of Balaam, is recounted at considerable length in Numbers 22–24.[75]

In Numbers 22:2–21, the Moabites are alarmed by the Israelite presence, having seen what Israel has just done to the Amorites (22:2–4a). It is in reaction to this perceived threat that the king of Moab appeals—with a fee for divination in 22:7, the promise of a rich reward in 22:17—not in this case to a stronger military power, but to a religious power: the seer, Balaam. In relation to Balak, Balaam is free to decline or accept this proposal. Once he has accepted, he is committed to speaking a divine word on Israel. (As a seer, however, Balaam must, according to this tradition, accept or reject the proposal only in accordance with divine direction.) There the analogy between the preceding situations and this ends, since Balak wants Balaam to attack and weaken the Israelites with the power of his word, not to provide military assistance. In the event, Balak did not get from Balaam the word against Israel that he had bargained for, and Balaam used the classic prophetic defense, that he could not determine what the deity would say.

How much of this was known, or at least used, by the authors of Deuteronomy 23:5b? The "hiring" refers to the Moabites' payment and Balaam's agreement to perform a service. The other contexts in which we find the verb, as well as Numbers 22:2–3, suggest that the hiring here would have been occasioned by a (perceived) threat from Israel. Further, the condemnation of the Moabites in this context is certainly grounded in the belief that the hiring of Balaam was a powerful threat against Israel. This is confirmed by the conclusion of this story in v. 6: "But Yahweh your God was not willing to listen to Balaam, and Yahweh your God turned the curse into a blessing for you, because Yahweh your God loves you." Whereas Yahweh intervenes at various points in the complex story of Numbers 22–24, in the summary telling of the compiler of this law, Yahweh intervenes at the final critical moment. The Deuteronomistic writer uses the story not only to motivate Israel to obey the law concerning the Moabites but also to illustrate Yahweh's love for Israel. It is that love that intervenes to counter the intervention of the hireling. A higher power reverses the role of the hired power.

Four comments may be made about this case. First, the relationship between the two versions of the Balaam story in Numbers and Deuteronomy illustrates how the bare story invoked by the word "hires" may correspond to a long and complex narrative in another context. Second, the narrators of Deuteronomy 23:5b (and Neh 13:2), like the authors of 2 Kings 7:6 and 2 Samuel 10:6a, use the word "hire" to express the point of view of those against whom the outside force is brought in, and to fix the responsibility of (and condemn) the "hirers" for bringing in the supposedly greater power (contrast Kilamuwa). Third, the use of the same word to describe these actions taken in response to a perceived military threat points to the authors' perception of a narrative analogy between the hiring of a military power to attack one's enemies and the hiring of a powerful seer to curse them. Fourth, because of that religious threat, this is the one story that moves the plot into the theological sphere. When Balaam agrees to intervene, the God of Israel supervenes.

While the story of Balaam in Numbers is a typical third-person narrative with an external omniscient narrator, the story in Deuteronomy is a second-person narrative with the expressed audience in the role of the threatened Israelites and the omniscient narrator identified in the larger context as their leader, Moses. The Israelites in the story of Numbers 22–24 are completely oblivious of Balaam's and Yahweh's activities. Only Israelite hearers of the story in Numbers learn what threatened and saved their ancestors. In the Deuteronomic version, by contrast, the Israelites are the addressees, told directly by the narrator what had threatened them and what had saved them. The narrative thus puts the expressed audience in the position of having been directly threatened by Balaam's curse and having benefited directly from Yahweh's love, which turned curse into blessing. While readers of Numbers know more than any of the characters in the story, readers of Deuteronomy find themselves addressed as characters in the story. Thus, the difference between the ignorance of the characters and the knowledge of the readers is eliminated. The implied readers' recalled experience of danger from the Moabites and salvation by Yahweh is the motivation for them to obey Yahweh's directive that no Moabite be permitted to enter the convocation of Yahweh.

Summary

All these stories presuppose a similar sequence of events: A threatens B; B sends gifts to C appealing for intervention against A. If the appeal is successful, C attacks A. In the complex narrative of 2 Kings 6–7, A presumes this sequence of events (as far as C attacking A) and withdraws. In the two Zinjirli inscriptions and the stories of Asa and Ahaz, A is defeated or withdraws, and B's rule and security are assured. In the remaining two biblical texts, C is unsuccessful and A prevails.

Stories of successful intervention were told in the courts of those who made such appeals (e.g., Kilamuwa's) and of those who enjoyed the ongoing benefits of the outside intervention (e.g., Bir-Rākib's). Written distillates of such stories appear in the two inscriptions. Kilamuwa, in a minimal story of three clauses, boasts of hiring (škr) the great king of Assyria to reduce his overbearing neighbor and of thus securing economic benefits for his people. He expresses his pride in his own cleverness in getting the great Assyrian king to do a job for him. The consequent economic well-being is expressed in a pithy saying referring to the availability of slaves for the price of a sheep or a garment. The story accords with the larger interest of this ninth-century inscription in contrasting the ineffectiveness of Kilamuwa's predecessors and the previous poverty of the native people with his own accomplishments and the people's present prosperity.

A century later, Bir-Rākib recounts his father's experience. The appeal for assistance here takes the form of a present, which generates a prompt response on the part of the Assyrian king. This is the pivotal move between longer accounts of the prior malefactions of the enemy and his father's subsequent benefactions. Like Kilamuwa, Bir-Rākib refers to specific economic values to express the general prosperity following his diplomatic move (and the wretched conditions preceding). The son emphasizes his father's virtue and the pure destructiveness of the enemy. But, like his father, Bir-Rākib is a vassal of the Assyrian king and so portrays also the goodness of his lord, who intervened in response to his father's appeal (Tiglath-Pileser III). But while the story itself is a straightforward secular account, Bir-Rākib introduces it with an abstract that attributes the deliverance and prosperity of Panamuwa to the gods, especially Hadad. The inscription as a whole is at once a pious tribute to Bir-Rākib's father and an apologia for his own rule, a defense of his legitimacy as king and vassal of Tiglath-Pileser.

The rhetoric and sense of personal investment in the stories of Kilamuwa and Bir-Rākib contrast with the more dispassionate, colorless accounts now incorporated in the books of Kings. These are as close as we come to the stories that would have been told in Jerusalem's (or Samaria's) court, and they are clearly at a much further—but indeterminate—remove from actual events. Ahaz was roughly contemporary with Bir-Rākib. It is altogether plausible that he, too, would have sought Assyrian intervention against his immediate oppressors and that the Judean court would later have interpreted the destruction of Damascus as a successful outcome of his appeal, even though there was doubtless little connection between the two. The Deuteronomistic historian, however, casts a pall over the story in its present context by his express disapproval of Ahaz.

The story of Asa's appeal to Benhadad to attack Baasha is a more polished piece of literature, chiastically structured. At the center is a carefully worded message from Asa to Benhadad, designed (with the gifts) to move him away from loyalty to Baasha. The mismatch between the success and finality of Asa's actions in the story and the belittling comments of the historian in the larger context suggests that this story, too, existed in some form before the historian incorporated it in his work. Both stories might have been used in later reigns not least by those favoring appeals for outside intervention on other occasions.

Whereas the Samalian inscriptions claimed that the kings had economically and socially benefited their people, these two biblical narratives ignore general social and economic conditions to focus instead on the king's verbal diplomacy and stewardship of central economic reserves. The former are primarily political documents, the latter historiographic accounts.

The remaining three references (all using the verb *škr*, "hired") express the point of view of the party representing the initial threat (the Aramaeans in the story of 2 Kgs 7:6) or the community identifying with that party (the Israelites in 2 Sam 10:6 and Deut 23:5b–6). Accordingly, they are all hostile to the appealer and therefore to the appeal. But they have the literary characteristics neither of the propagandistic royal inscriptions from Zinjirli nor of the historiographic texts in Kings. They are essential parts of larger literary units (2 Kgs 6:24–7:20; 2 Sam 10; Deut 23:4–7) in which each serves a moral or theological purpose: as a mistaken story assumed by the Aramaeans besieging Samaria when they hear noises produced by Yahweh (in 2 Kgs 6:24–7:20), in an illustration of the fate of such hirelings when they agree to attack Israel (in 2 Sam 10), and in a recollection of Yahweh's direct intervention against such a hireling out of his love for Israel (in Deut 23:4–7).

The stories of this particular diplomatic move characteristically make no reference to the gods. Only in a story in which the threat is transferred to the religious sphere, as in the story of Balaam, does the deity appear. However, the contexts in which such stories are later used may speak of the gods' blessing of the king in question, as in the Panamuwa inscription (ll. 1–2), or the king's displeasing of the deity, as in the Deuteronomistic historian's account of Ahaz (2 Kgs 16:2b).

Stories of Miraculous
Deliverance from a Siege

The last refuge of a king losing a war or fleeing in battle and the first refuge of a king wishing to avoid a confrontation with a far superior army was the fortified city. Here a king determined not to submit to the power of another might hope to hold out until the besieging forces gave up or a relief force arrived. In general, the besieging forces had the advantage. They could move freely, plunder the neighboring countryside for provisions, and bring in reinforcements and might, by technique or ruse, break into the city or tempt the occupants out. By contrast, those inside the city had limited power to harass the attackers and could hold out only as long as they had food and water.[1]

Sometimes, despite the odds, the besieged might be able to drive off the besiegers, or the besieging forces might pack up and go, perhaps finding their resources exhausted, or drawn away by more urgent business elsewhere or at home. From the point of view of those fearing, and perhaps expecting, the worst, such a withdrawal might be nothing short of a miracle. Indeed, in some cases, they regarded it as a miracle too good to be true and suspected a ruse, a strategic withdrawal to tempt the city to open up its defenses and pour out into the countryside, rendering city and army vulnerable (see 2 Kgs 7:12). Israel's literature more than once recounts Israelite armies' use of such a ruse (Josh 8:3–29; Jdg 20:29–48). When in such cases the departure was real and final and the deliverance undeniable, the experience had to be told. Survivors would have recounted first-person narratives that might have been spread by others in third-person form to other towns and subsequent generations.

Consistent with such experiences and stories was the belief that the deity, given an appropriate appeal or promises of devotion by the city or its king, might drive off the invader. Hence a cultic text from the Late Bronze Age city of Ugarit near the north Syrian coast promised:

> When a strong force attacks your gates,
>> A warrior your walls,
> You shall raise your eyes to the Lord[2]:
>> "O Lord,
>> [I]f you will drive the strong force from our gates,
>>> the warrior [from] our walls,
>> A bull, Lord, we shall consecrate,
>>> A vow, Lord, we shall pay,
>> A [ma]le/[fir]stborn (animal), Lord, we shall con[se]crate,
>>> A *ḥtp*-offering, Lord, we shall pay,
>> A banquet, Lord, [we shall gi]ve,
>> We shall go up to the sanctuary of the Lor[d],
>>> We shall walk the paths of the house of [the Lord]."
> Then [the L]ord will list[en] to [your] prayer.
> He will drive the strong force from your gates
> [The warrior] from your walls.[3]

The besieged community is told to pray to the deity to remove the threat, promising appropriate religious gifts and service. It is assured that the deity will respond to such prayers. The cultures of Israel and Judah and their neighbors in the first half of the first millennium subscribed to the same belief in the appropriateness and effectiveness of prayer to their deity when threatened with a siege. Stories of such divine relief from a siege are recorded in an Aramaic inscription from northern Syria and in several places in the books of Kings.

The Inscription of Zakkur

Four pieces of the inscribed stela of King Zakkur were found by H. Pognon in 1903 in Afis, about forty-five kilometers southwest of Aleppo.[4] They fit in a vertical sequence. It is not clear that the stela did not continue below the bottom piece, but it is clear that it continued above the top piece. The top two blocks bear the lower part of a relief: the bottom of the robe and the feet of a figure standing on a plinth. The preserved part of the figure is about 20 centimeters. high. Pognon estimated that the height of the whole figure must have been about 1.25 to 1.3 meters. Taking into account the ca. 85 centimeters. from the bottom of the feet to the bottom of the lowest block, he estimated that the whole stela must have stood at least 2.1 meters high.

The bottom two blocks contain the beginning of an inscription (A). It is continued on the left side (B), where twenty-eight lines are preserved, covering all four blocks. Since there is no relief on the side, the inscription here probably began near the top of the stela, so that another thirty or so lines would have preceded what is preserved.[5] Three words are preserved at the top of the right side (C). Pognon thought that this was a different inscription on C, perhaps very short, but it is now generally regarded as the conclusion of the inscription on the other two sides. Consequently, another thirty lines must be missing from the top of this side.[6]

Many of the preserved lines are incomplete, but enough is preserved to permit the restoration of most of them. However, there remain two large lacunae: at least thirty short lines between A and B and the same between B and C. From the structure and genre of the rest of the inscription, however, the general content of those missing portions is clear. The inscription is probably to be dated around 800 BCE.

(A1) [S]tela that Zakkur, king of [Ha]math and Lu'ash, set up for Ilu-wer, [his lord].

(2) I am Zakkur, king of Hamath and Lu'ash.

(2–4) I am a pious man. And the Lord of the Heavens [delivered?] me and stood by me and the Lord of the heavens made me king in Hadrach.

(4–9) And Bir-Hadad son of Hazael, king of Aram, formed a confederation against me of s[ix]teen kings: Bir-Hadad and his army, and Bir-Gush and his army, and [the king] of Quwe and his army, and the king of 'Umq and his army, and the king of Gurg[um and] his [ar]my, and the king of Sam'al and his a[rmy], and the king of Milid and [his a]r[my, and the king of   and his army, and the king of   and his] a[r]my, and seven [other kings—th]ey and their armies.

(9–10) And all these kings laid siege to Hadra[ch] and raised a wall higher than the wall of Hadrach and dug a ditch deeper than [its] dit[ch].

(11) Then I lifted my hands to the Lord of the Heavens.

(11–B3) And the Lord of the Heaven[s] answered me, [and] the Lord of the Heavens [spok]e to me [th]rough seers and through prophets, [and] the Lord of the Heavens [said to me]: "Fear not, for I have made [you] kin[g and I will st]and by you and I will deliver you from all [these kings who] have laid siege to you." Then [the Lord of the Heavens] spoke to [me: "I will   ] all these kings who laid [siege to you, and I will   this ditch] and this wall whi[ch

(gap of at least thirty lines)

    ]Hadrach[   ]for chariot(s) and horse(s) [   ]its king in its midst.

(B3–15) I [built up] Hadrach and [I] added [to it] the whole district of [   ] and I established it [   ] these [str]ongholds throughout [my] territ[ory and] I [bu]ilt temples for the gods through[out] my [land] and I built up [   ] Apish and [   ]s temple [and] I established this stela before [Ilu-Wer] and [I] wr[ote on] it what I have accomplished.

(16–) (CURSES)

(gap of at least thirty lines)

(–C2) (BLESSINGS)

At first sight, this appears to be a dedicatory inscription: a gift to the deity requesting a blessing in return. Thus it begins: "Stela that Zakkur, king of Hamath and Luash, set up for Ilu-Wer, his lord" (A1) and ends by invoking blessings on the king. Only part of the final one is preserved: "May the name of Zakkur and the name of [his dynasty last for ever]" (C1–2). However, apart from this introduction and conclusion, the inscription has the form characteristic of memorial inscriptions.[7] It now begins: "I am so-and-so, king of Hamath and Lu'ash" (A2); the body concerns a military confrontation and the king's building activities (A2–B15); the final section consists of curses on anyone damaging the stela (B16–28 and beyond). This suggests that in this or a similar form the text had been used previously as a memorial inscription and then adapted for this particular occasion—the dedication to Ilu-Wer—by the addition of the clause in A1 and the blessings at the end. It was probably on this occasion that the account of the king's building activities—his establishment of control over Hadrach, his construction of fortresses and temples throughout the land—was extended to include reference to his rebuilding of Apish, to his installation of this stela before Ilu-Wer in that god's temple in Apish (B10–15), and to his inscription on it of his achievements ("And [I] wr[ote on] it what I have accomplished"—B14–15).[8]

This suggestion is supported by the fact that the military narrative and the first part of the building section are concerned with Hadrach, and the building section continues with generalizations about building in Zakkur's territory in general. Only the conclusion of the building section turns to another specific city: Apish. Thus, it seems likely that a memorial inscription commemorating the deliverance of Hadrach and Zakkur's building of it (and perhaps other fortresses and temples) has been adapted for a new site and occasion: the completion of the building activities in Apish and the restoration of its temple. This is not surprising in view of the well-attested Assyrian practice of adapting the content of earlier inscriptions to new occasions and new contexts.[9]

Further support for this hypothesis comes from the fact that in the account of the military crisis it is the Lord of the Heavens who saves the king from disaster, while in the building narrative there is no mention of any god until Ilu-Wer is introduced toward the end as the object of this dedication.[10] Thus, the present inscription honors two different deities: the god Ba'alshamayn, "the Lord of the Heavens," who made Zakkur king and delivered him from a military threat, and the god Iluwer, whose temple and city Zakkur has recently restored and to whom he is now dedicating this stela.

The two parts of the body of the inscription are both first-person narrative accounts, but very different in other respects. The building section (B3–15) is a list of activities in the form of short sentences, each beginning with a first-person verbal form. There are eleven first-person-perfect verbal forms (including restorations)—of which five are *wbnyt* "then I built" and three are *wšmt* "then I established"—followed by objects and in several cases prepositional phrases. Thus, the building section consists entirely of a catalogue of things "I" have done, concluding with the writing of this record of "my" accomplishments.[11] As already mentioned, the only deity who is referred to is Ilu-Wer: "[then] I placed this stela before [Ilu-Wer]." (This restoration is certain, not just because of the dedication of the stela to Ilu-Wer in A1 but also because the following curses speak of someone who might remove "this stela from before Ilu-Wer.")

The siege narrative (A4–B3) differs in several significant respects from the building narrative. It consists of at least seventeen lines, each twice as long as those in the building section, and just over thirty lines the same length as those in the building section. Thus, the account of the siege narrative is several times longer than that of the building activities, which consists of only thirteen of these shorter lines. Further, the syntax of the preserved part of the siege narrative is much more complex than that of the building section: it has both first- and third-person verb forms, both with varying subjects; sentences of varying structure and word order; and two speeches.[12]

It seems safe to conclude that the siege narrative would first have been composed and told independently as an account of a unique deliverance of Zakkur by the Lord of the Heavens.[13] When the memorial inscription was first erected, this story was given pride of place, distinguishing the inscription from the more common accounts of military victories and building activities. In this context, it would have served as a paradigmatic exhibition of the Lord of the Heavens's favor toward the king. The final testimony to its persistent importance for Zakkur and his court is its replication, along with its framework from the memorial inscription, in the present complex inscription dedicated to another deity.

We turn now to the narrative itself. It is introduced by a reference to Zakkur's piety[14] and a thematic statement or abstract acknowledging the Lord of the Heavens's support and specifically his responsibility for Zakkur's becoming king of Hadrach: "The Lord of the Heavens [delivered] me and stood by me and the Lord of the Heavens made me king of Hadrach" (A 2–4).[15] Since the protagonist is the narrator, and information about his status as king of Hamath and Luʻash was supplied in A1–2, it is unnecessary to introduce him further.

The long first sentence of the narrative introduces the pluriform antagonist, Bir-Hadad and his sixteen allies, and begins the complication, the forming of a confederacy against Zakkur. The individual mention of nine of these confederates, each with his army, emphasizes the range of forces opposing Zakkur. Neither Bir-Hadad nor his confederates are characterized; nothing is said of their motives or goals. The narrator similarly ignores any military encounters or diplomatic moves that may have preceded or followed the formation of the confederacy and moves directly to the crisis: "All these kings laid siege to Hadrach, and they raised a wall higher than the wall of Hadrach and dug a ditch deeper than its ditch." No sooner is the siege introduced than we are brought to the critical moment: two graphic details inform us that the attackers have rendered Zakkur's defenses ineffective. Again, there is no reference to any countermeasures or to any consultation with advisors. In this crisis, Zakkur turns immediately to the deity. His appeal is expressed not by a speech, but a gesture: "I lifted my hands to the Lord of the Heavens."

This moves us directly to the beginning of the resolution: "The Lord of the Heavens answered me. . . ." The narrator reports that the god spoke to him through two classes of prophets. The divine response is treated at greater length than any other part of the preserved narrative in two separate divine speeches: A13–A15 and A15–A17 (and following?). The first speech is an oracle of salvation:

"Fear not, for I made you king and I am standing by you and I will save you from all these kings who have laid seige against you."[16] Three reasons are given to justify the initial reassurance, one referring to the god's past achievement on behalf of the king, one to the god's present support of him, and the third to the god's imminent deliverance of him. At least the first two of these resume the second and third of the characteristics of the relationship between god and king as stated by the narrator in the introduction.[17] The reiterated phraseology underlines the identity of the ideology expressed by deity and narrator. The narrator's claims in the introduction are supported by their foundation in the earlier divine promises; the deity's promises and their fulfillment are confirmed by the previously stated present testimony of the narrator. In the introduction, the title of the deity—there the subject of the verbs—was supplied for two of the three verbs. Here the first-person independent pronoun is expressed all three times, giving maximal emphasis to the role of the deity. The personal role of the king is also emphasized, not only as the object of the deity's interest in each of the three clauses but also in the final adjectival clause. Whereas in the original reference to the kings' attack the narrator spoke of their laying siege to the city, Hadrach, the god now refers to them as laying siege "against you," the king. Thus, the god sees the siege as a personal attack on his protégé. Having made him king in the first place, he will now stand by him and save him.

Only the fragmentary beginning of the god's second speech to Zakkur is preserved: "[I will   ] all these kings who have laid [siege against you and I will   this ditch] and this wall whi[ch ...]." As the restoration suggests, it appears that the god now announces what he is going to do to the invading kings and their siegeworks. The god takes up in this speech precisely those elements of the invasion signaled in the narrator's original account of it as representing the imminent conquest of the city (A9–10). He thus responds directly to the specific threat of the city's collapse. Although the verb is missing, it is certain that he reverses that threat.

At this point, at least thirty shorter lines are missing. Traces of the conclusion of the narrative appear in what are now the first three lines of B. The lost lines must have concluded the second speech of the deity and given an account of the deliverance of Zakkur and his city (since the narrative is obviously a celebration of that deliverance). Unfortunately, we cannot tell whether the deliverance was portrayed as the act of the deity, or at least as a miraculous event, or whether at this point a more mundane account was given. We cannot therefore compare the deity's promise of deliverance with the narrator's account of it.

Although the discourse is brief in comparison with the duration of the events recounted in the complication, there is a quickening of the pace, both of events and of discourse. The forming of the confederation occupies the longest sentence, including the list of kings and armies (A4–9). The siege is recounted in one sentence of three clauses (A9–10). Finally, Zakkur's prayer occupies a sentence of one clause. In the beginning of the resolution, by contrast, the discourse proceeds more slowly than the time represented. Time stands still in the introductions to the speeches of the Lord of the Heavens, one of which consists of three clauses (A11–13). In the speeches themselves, of course, the discourse has a one-to-one correspondence with narrated time. The (missing) concluding account of the actual raising of the siege must then have reverted to the telescoping discourse of the complication. The increase in pace through the complication and the abrupt retardation after Zakkur's appeal have the effect of throwing great weight on the speeches of the deity.

Spelling out the composition of the forces pitted against the king and the divine promises of deliverance from those forces and then balancing the statement of divine support in the opening abstract with the promise of divine support in the first divine speech, the narrative emphasizes the king's dependence on the god and the god's support of the king. The narrator, as Zakkur, portrays the Lord of the Heavens as a patron who faithfully and effectively responded to him when he called on him in a crisis. Here is a carefully constructed and worded narrative concerning a single critical event, with a clearly developed complication and resolution, written to acknowledge the aid of the Lord of the Heavens[18] and to display Zakkur's security as the god's favorite. The contrast with the following account of building activities is patent. There the narrator monotonously lists his own achievements, including his submission of this inscribed report to Ilu-Wer— with no mention of the Lord of the Heavens.

On the most general level, the siege narrative is a story of deliverance in two basic moves: a danger to the protagonist and deliverance from the danger (cf. Culley 1976, 71–100; 1992, 63–66). But this underlying structure is here extended by reference to divine intervention. This involves two additional moves: an appeal to the deity and the deity's verbal reply. Thus the structure becomes: danger, appeal to the deity (here in the form of a gesture), divine speeches (here mediated by prophets), and deliverance. The divine speeches serve both as a response to the king's appeal and as a promise of the deliverance that is about to be accomplished—the first serving primarily as response, the second as promise. This may be represented as follows:

B. APPEAL   >   C. RESPONSE + PROMISE
A. DANGER   >   D. DELIVERANCE

In stories of this structure, B and C are variable. The appeal to the deity may be a nonverbal gesture or ritual, or there may be no appeal to the deity of any kind. In that case, C functions solely as promise, not as response, the divine speech being entirely at the deity's initiative. Then again, there may be no divine speech. An appeal to the deity may be followed directly by the deliverance, understood explicitly or implicitly as the deity's response. (Lacking any representation of the deity, the diagram allows us to recognize the broad structural similarity to that of other stories of deliverance, such as those we considered in chapter 5.)

While the danger and deliverance in stories of such general structure may take many forms, here the danger is represented concretely by a siege, and the protagonist is the king of the besieged city. Further, the narrative arises from and commemorates a particular siege, purporting to be a record of an actual event, recalled and recounted in the first person by the king himself. The story of that event would first have been told in Zakkur's court. As suggested before, the version now before us was probably composed and used in a memorial inscription prior to its incorporation in the present inscription (which cannot have been composed more than a decade or two after the original event). The theological character of the story—the king is delivered in consequence of a divine message received through prophets—is central to it. The presentation of the severity of the danger facing the king and the promise and fulfillment of the divine deliverance accomplish the inscription's aims of presenting the Lord of the Heavens as the powerful protector of the king, the one who put him on the throne in the first place and who stands by him and delivers him from any opposition. The reader is to take note: this king is the protégé of this god.

In light of an Assyrian campaign in the vicinity (according to the Eponym Chronicle) and Adad-Nerari III's establishment of the frontier between Atarshumki of Arpad and Zakkur of Hamath (according to the Antakya stela), it has been supposed that that Assyrian king intervened to save Zakkur from this siege (Hawkins 1982, 400, 403–4; *RLA* 7/1–2, 158),[19] the motivation for the siege probably being to force Zakkur to join an anti-Assyrian alliance. It has even been suggested that the Assyrians might have come at Zakkur's request, but this seems highly unlikely: the accounts of such invited intervention in the inscriptions from Zinjirli ignore the gods, explicitly acknowledge the role of Assyria, and take pride in the local king's accomplishment (see chapter 5 in this book). Zakkur, however, says he is indebted to a power beyond himself. This may be his interpretation of the abrupt departure of the besiegers at the approach of the Assyrian army—or under various other conceivable circumstances (cf. Millard 1990, 52). As with most of these stories, we are not in a position to compare different accounts of the same events or, consequently, to judge the complex realities behind them. Historians will compose their own stories based on their sense of probabilities within the larger historical conditions.

Zakkur's narrative is a good historical source of another kind, however. Its form and rhetoric display the narrative resources and the ideology of an early-eighth-century Aramaean court. One can only speculate whether the story was of sufficient ongoing significance that third-person versions were recounted in subsequent generations.

Stories of Miraculous Deliverance from a Siege in the Bible

If such a first-person account of a king's deliverance from a siege was ever inscribed in the royal court of Samaria or Jerusalem, it has not been preserved or, if preserved, recovered. Third-person narratives of such deliverances, however, are recounted in the context of the Deuteronomistic History. Thus again we have, on the one hand, a royal inscription with a first-person narrative in which narrator and protagonist are identical and represent the sponsor of the inscription and, on the other hand, third-person narratives by unknown authors writing as omniscient narrators. In this case, however, there is no question of the biblical authors' dependence on epigraphic models. Rather, the authors of both the Aramaic inscription and the Hebrew narratives have adopted a tale type with a common structure as a vehicle for their various interests. A review of a few biblical tales of miraculous deliverance from a siege will show how Israelite narrators use the same underlying structure to tell the same type of tale, how they further exploit its didactic potential, and also how they complicate the relations between king and deity and reader.

2 Kings 18:13–19:37

As is now widely recognized, 2 Kings 18:13–19:37 contains three accounts of the deliverance of Jerusalem from a siege.[20] The historical event to which all three accounts refer is the threat of a siege of Jerusalem by the Assyrian army under Sennacherib during the reign of King Hezekiah. According to the first account (2 Kgs 18:13–16) a siege was averted by Hezekiah's submission and payment of significant tribute, following Sennacherib's conquest of all the other fortified towns of Judah. The general historicity of this version is confirmed by an account in the annals of Sennacherib, who claims to have isolated Hezekiah in Jerusalem and imposed a large tribute on him, which he paid.[21] The account in 2 Kings 18:13–16 is comparable to other accounts of the same strategy also found in 2 Kings (12:18–19; 15:19–20; 17:3). The two following narratives, however, are constructed on the pattern of the divine deliverance outlined in the discussion of Zakkur's narrative: the response to the threat is not buying off the invader, but a royal appeal to the deity, followed by an oracle from a prophet and corresponding divine deliverance. As in Zakkur's inscription, danger prompts appeal, which elicits response and promise, issuing in deliverance. Most of the numerous, extensive treatments of these two accounts have concentrated on their historical value or on their use of theological traditions. Here we shall concentrate on their narrative character.

It should be stated at the outset that it is most likely that at least the first of these two narratives—which, following others, I shall refer to as narrative B—existed independently prior to its adoption into the books of Kings and Isaiah (36:1–37:38), since it is so different in character from the other materials in both books. The assumption that independent oral stories specifically about Hezekiah and prophets circulated already in the seventh to sixth centuries is supported by the reference to such a story in Jeremiah 26:18–19a. In the narrative of Jeremiah 26, some elders cite as precedent in a judicial dispute a tradition that when the prophet Micah had prophesied the desolation of Jerusalem, Hezekiah had feared Yahweh and pleaded with him, so that Yahweh changed his mind about what he was going to do to them. Although the prophecy cited has been preserved in the book of Micah (3:12), such a story is not known from any other source. It is assumed to have been familiar in oral form to the audience portrayed in Jeremiah 26, and we may assume that it was familiar to the author and hearers of that narrative. It assumes a Hezekiah who is a model of piety, as in the story of 2 Kings 20:1–6 and the third story (narrative C) of 2 Kings 18–19. Scholars are divided on whether this third narrative had an independent existence or was built from the first in its present context.[22]

2 Kings 18:[13,] 17–19:9a, 36–37   Narrative B (2 Kgs 18:[13,] 17–19:9a, 36–37 = Isa 36:[1,] 2–37:9a, 37–38)[23] is dominated by two extended, highly rhetorical speeches delivered by an Assyrian officer to the representatives of Hezekiah and the inhabitants on the walls of the city, in which he attempts to persuade them of the futility of holding out against the Assyrian king. The initial situation presupposed in 18:17 is that of v. 13: Sennacherib's invasion of Judah.[24] Whatever the original beginning of this narrative, v. 13 now focuses on Jerusalem as the one city remaining for the Assyrian king to deal with. Sennacherib sends from Lachish three officers—each identified by office—with a strong force to Hezekiah in Jerusalem. They station themselves at one of Jerusalem's sources of water, just outside the city walls (v. 17).[25] Three Judean officers, identified by name and title, go out to meet them (v. 18). This sets up a confrontation outside the city wall between three specific representatives of each monarch. The relatively detailed description of the composition of the two embassies and of the locale lends unusual concreteness to the scene.

The chief Assyrian officer, the rabshakeh, now addresses them: "Say to Hezekiah: 'Thus says the great king, the king of Assyria' " (v. 19; the contrast between the simple "Hezekiah" and the titles of the invader is patent) and launches into a long message for him (19b-25).[26] Eventually, the Judean officers interrupt to ask that in the hearing of the people on the wall the Assyrians speak to them not in Judean (Hebrew) but in (the international diplomatic language of) Aramaic, since they (the Judean officers) also understand that language (v. 26). With this, the narrator suggests their fear that the population within earshot may well be persuaded by the Assyrian arguments for surrender. The Assyrian officer rejects the request, claiming now that it is not to the king or them that his master has sent them to say these things but precisely to the people on the wall who will have to consume their own excrement (if the siege continues; v. 27). This interruption reminds the reader of the larger scene and fills in more physical detail by evoking the ranks of Judeans standing on the walls.[27]

The rabshakeh goes on to do exactly what they asked him not to do: he addresses the people loudly in Judean (vv. 28–35). But at the end of this second speech, the narrator reports: "They were silent and answered him not a word, for it was a royal order: 'Do not answer him' " (v. 36).[28] This emphasizes the people's obedience to the king and deflects our attention to him as the one who controls his people (contrast the king in 2 Kgs 6:24–30 as described later in this chapter and in chapter 2), but the people have now been exposed to the full rhetorical force of a clever enemy. This concludes the first scene.

The three Judean officers, again with full names and titles, return to Hezekiah with garments torn in desperation and report to him the rabshakeh's words (v. 37). Hezekiah's reaction is to appeal to Yahweh. He does so in two ways. First, in 19:1, he tears his garments and covers himself with sackcloth (ritual gestures anticipated by his officers).[29] He then sends his officers (again with full names and titles) and the senior priests, covered in sackcloth, to Isaiah, the prophet (19:2). They come to Isaiah in v. 5. But since their message is not mentioned there, another writer has contributed a message before this reference to their arrival.[30]

In this, they refer to the danger in graphic, metaphoric language (v. 3; see Darr 1996) and continue: "Perhaps Yahweh, your god, will hear[31] the words of the rabshakeh, whom the king of Assyria, his master, sent to insult the living God,[32] and will disprove the words which Yahweh, your god, has heard: raise a prayer on behalf of the present remnant" (v. 4). This request for Isaiah's intercession is not the same as an appeal for an oracle. Thus, it is the original ritual acts—like those of Zakkur—rather than this secondary speech that fit into the second stage of the traditional form: appeal to the deity.

After the officers come to Isaiah, he does not intercede for them (in response to the speech of v. 4) but gives them an oracle, a message from Yahweh in response to Hezekiah's ritual appeal in v. 1: "Thus shall you say to your master: 'Thus says Yahweh: "Do not be afraid of these words that you have heard, with which the king of Assyria's officers have vilified me. I am putting a spirit in him, such that when he hears a report, he will return to his land; and I will fell him by the sword in his own land'" (vv. 6–7). This constitutes the divine response and promise of deliverance. The promise includes the threefold prediction of report, return, and violent death.

There is no mention of the messengers' report back to Hezekiah or of any response by him to the rabshakeh and his colleagues. After noting the rabshakeh's return to find the Assyrian king attacking Libnah (v. 8), the narrative turns immediately to the fulfillment of Isaiah's prophecies. First, the king hears a report on Tirhakah, king of Cush: "He has set out to do battle with you" (v. 9a). Although Tirhakah did not come to the Egyptian throne until some years later, this reference draws on a historical reminiscence. Sennacherib's annals report that the leaders of Ekron had appealed to the Egyptians for help and that Sennacherib had had to face an Egyptian army at Eltekeh, where he claims to have defeated it prior to his assault on Judah. In the Hebrew narrative, the intervention of the Egyptians has been erroneously attributed to Tirhakah and, more significantly, shifted to explain the end of the siege of Jerusalem. The news of the Egyptian advance here serves as the fulfillment of the first part of the prophecy—"when he hears a report"—and as the reason for the Assyrian withdrawal.[33] This is the first of the three events that constitute the fulfillment of the divine promise and the conclusion of the narrative. The other two appear in 19:36–37, now following narrative C, which has been inserted here. The Assyrian king departs and returns to Nineveh (v. 36); while he is worshiping in the temple of his god, two of his sons cut him down with the sword and escape to Urartu ("Ararat"), and his son, Esarhaddon, succeeds him (v. 37). Verses 9a, 36–37 serve both as the fulfillment of Yahweh's promises and as the deliverance from the danger, the latter extending to the unhappy fate of the attacker.[34]

This story conforms to the full narrative pattern of divine deliverance from a siege, as observed in Zakkur's inscription: danger (expressed especially by the rhetoric and threats of the rabshakeh), appeal to the deity (here directly by ritual act and indirectly by appeal to a prophet), divine response (through a prophet) promising deliverance, and fulfillment of the promise in actual deliverance. The structure may be outlined as follows:

A. DANGER (18:[13,] 17–37)
B. APPEAL TO THE DEITY (19:1–2)
C. DIVINE RESPONSE + PROMISE (THROUGH PROPHET) (19:6–7)
D. DELIVERANCE (19:8–9a, 36–37)

The contrast with Zakkur's narrative is immediately obvious. There the divine speeches occupy more space than the danger and appeal, whereas here the divine speech is as brief as the rapid denouement of the story. Here nothing is made of the relationship between king and god; indeed, in the speech that Hezekiah is eventually given, he relies on the relationship between prophet and god, twice in his speech to Isaiah referring to "Yahweh, *your* god." In contrast with the Lord of the Heavens's statements of commitment to Zakkur, Yahweh refers to Hezekiah only in a conventional reassurance: "Do not be afraid of the things you have heard." And whereas in Zakkur's narrative the deity speaks directly to the king, the prophets being mentioned only in passing as the medium of the reply, in the biblical story Yahweh appears only in Isaiah's speech: it is the prophet who replies to the king's appeal, quoting an oracle from the deity. Thus here the prophet plays the key role in the resolution, both as the object of Hezekiah's appeal and as the giver of the oracle.

Finally, whereas in the Aramaic narrative the danger was expressed by the list of kings in the confederation and their matching of the defenders' siegeworks, here it is expressed ideologically through the elaborate, ad hominem rhetoric of the rabshakeh's extraordinarily long speeches. (Of the thirty-one verses of this narrative, the rabshakeh's speeches occupy sixteen, that is, approximately half.) These are the most striking and distinctive feature of the narrative.

The first speech, addressed to Hezekiah, questions his trust, not in Yahweh, but in fine speech (20a) and in Egypt (21, 24b).[35] If he cannot provide the riders for two hundred of the Assyrian king's horses, how can he repel one of the king's officers (23–24a)? And then—ad hominem—does he think that the Assyrian king has come to destroy this place apart from Yahweh? Yahweh told him to come against the land (25)! This speech envisages precisely the occasion disclosed in the previous account, Hezekiah's rebellion against Sennacherib (20bβ; 14; cf. 7b). It addresses the real policy options of the king—diplomacy and appeal to Egypt—as well as the belief that Judah's god is a powerful force for their defense (for the Assyrian's claim that Judah's god is *against* them, cf. Mesha's recognition of his god's anger with his land during the Israelite occupation and 2 Kgs 10:32; 13:3; etc.). Rooted as it is in the policies and beliefs of the Judean court, the speech not only addresses the audience in the narrative but also reflects and addresses the real issues facing seventh- and early-sixth-century Judah. Thus the Assyrians' arguments are representative of an opposition explicitly Assyrian within the narrative but implicitly internal to the Jerusalem of the authors. At the same time, the narrators envisage an audience in their own image, one able to appreciate the fallacy of the arguments (as pointed out by Ben Zvi 1990). The scoffing at reliance on Egyptian support (vv. 21, 24b) is both appropriate in the mouth of the Assyrians and ironically consistent with the Yahwism of the narrator (as found in prophetic literature, e.g., Isa 31:1 and Ezek 29:6–7). The challenge to match the forces of the Assyrians (vv. 23–24a) is fitting in the mouth of the Assyrians (as in that of the pragmatists in the city) but ignores the faith of those for whom Yahweh's power (not Egypt's) is more than a match for the Assyrian army. Finally, the claim that it is Yahweh who has sent the Assyrians against Judah and Jerusalem (v. 25), while a fitting claim for the Assyrians to make—and also consistent with a strain in the Isaiah tradition (10:5–11)—is absurd to those who believe that Yahweh will protect the city that is faithful to him.

The second speech appeals to a populace that will suffer as much as or more than its leaders (27b). The Assyrian king invites them to make their peace with him immediately, open up the city, and return to their homes to enjoy their supplies of food and water (31b). He urges that they not let Hezekiah deceive them or lead them astray (29a, 32b) by telling them that they can rely on Yahweh to deliver them (30, 32b). No other god has been able to save its city from the king of Assyria, so how can they hope that Yahweh can save Jerusalem from him? Hezekiah cannot save them (29b), nor can Yahweh (35b).[36] If *bṭḥ*, "trust," was the dominant motif of the first speech, *hiṣṣîl*, "deliver," is that of the second (the root occurring nine times). Hezekiah himself cannot deliver, and his appeal to trust Yahweh is deceptive because Yahweh cannot deliver either. Reliance on Hezekiah is quickly dismissed, and the argument becomes theological: since no other god has delivered its city, it is unreasonable to expect that Yahweh can deliver his.

The speech attempts to separate the people from their king, appealing positively to their self-interest and negatively to precedent. It presumes that Hezekiah calls for faith in Yahweh, claiming that Yahweh is sure to deliver the city; but belittles that claim by putting Yahweh in the same category as the gods of all the cities Assyria has already conquered. Its arguments are again plausible in the mouth of the invader, but the portrait of Hezekiah as trusting in Yahweh to deliver the city—the faith of the narrator—reveals that that stance and the arguments against it are the issues faced by the author. Inhabitants of Jerusalem continue to be vulnerable to such suggestions. On the level of the plot, the arguments are disposed of through the obedient silence of the populace, the king's appeal to Yahweh's prophet, the latter's communication of a specific promise from Yahweh, and finally Yahweh's fulfillment of this in his deliverance of the city. But in the communication of narrator with implied hearers, the arguments raise questions to which the hearers' theological traditions provide ready answers, answers that are the reverse of what the Assyrians argue: faith in Yahweh is the one thing that will save the city, and it is the Assyrian arguments that are deceptive.

Thus the author uses extensive arguments and rhetoric that have the ring of authenticity in the mouth of the Assyrians and probably correspond to the beliefs of some Judeans but are recognized by those of his own community as expressing a gross misunderstanding of the true nature of the situation. For those firmly rooted in the beliefs of that community, the irony of the speeches may extend to a level of absurdity that is humorous.

But while that readership knows that the argument is already lost, it has yet to see how people and king will respond. It is obvious that the arguments create a crisis for the court. The king turns to Yahweh's prophet, who will know what Yahweh will do or require in the situation.[37] In the event, it is the prophet who resolves the matter and is vindicated by Yahweh. For the narrator and his audience, king and prophet each play an ideal role. Hezekiah's reaction to the danger, both in his acts and in his added speech, indicates that he does not have special access to or influence on Yahweh. Isaiah's subsequent oracle is equally silent on the subject of Yahweh's support of the Judean king (in contrast with the relationship between Zakkur and the Lord of the Heavens). Hezekiah puts his faith in Isaiah as Yahweh's mouthpiece, and Isaiah's message from Yahweh, while giving conventional reassurance to the Judean king ("fear not"), addresses the insults of the Assyrian king by announcing that Yahweh will accomplish the Assyrian king's departure and death. Thus, the prophet plays a more significant religious role than the king, and his speech, like the second Assyrian speech, discloses that the fundamental conflict is between "the great king, the king of Assyria" and Yahweh. If Zakkur's narrative claims that he is to be respected because of the Lord of the Heavens's support of him, this narrative claims that Yahweh and his prophet are to be respected because of the former's general power and promises and the latter's unique access to Yahweh (and especially Yahweh's specific plans; cf. Amos 3:7).

In this story, the danger is represented not by a physical assault but by the arguments of the rabshakeh. The real issue is not so much military or political as theological: who wields the greater power, the Assyrian king or Yahweh? While the king is central to both plot and theme in Zakkur's narrative, he has become vestigial in narrative B. It is Hezekiah's officers and people who face the Assyrian envoys and their arguments; the king is not present. And it is his officers who go to Isaiah and receive his message from Yahweh; there is here not even a reference to the king's hearing of the message. Hezekiah is merely a functional link between the different parts of the story. The real confrontation is between the king of Assyria, represented by the rabshakeh, and the god of Israel, represented by the prophet.

2 Kings 19:9b–35 The third story (narrative C) is also based on the same pattern, though now more complex and layered.[38] The same initial situation—Sennacherib's isolation of Hezekiah in Jerusalem—is presupposed. Again, the extremity of Hezekiah's danger is expressed through a message that the Assyrian king sends to him via messengers, but the narrator does not otherwise set the scene (vv. 9b–10a). The message makes two arguments. The first is transposed from 18:29; now it is not a warning to the people not to let Hezekiah deceive them by claiming that they will be delivered but a warning to Hezekiah not to let Yahweh deceive him by claiming that Jerusalem will not be handed over (19:10). The second takes up that of 18:33–35: the kings of Assyria have destroyed all the lands, their gods did not deliver them, and their kings are gone, so what hope has Hezekiah (19:11–13)? These are purely theological arguments. What is at issue is Yahweh's reliability as defender of Jerusalem and power as compared with the other gods.

The appeal to the deity follows. Hezekiah takes and reads what is this time a written message, goes in person to the temple of Yahweh, lays the message before Yahweh (v. 14), and prays to him (vv. 15–19). His prayer addresses Yahweh as the only god of all the kingdoms of the earth, the maker of heaven and earth. It calls upon Yahweh to see and hear the words of Sennacherib, which he sent to insult the living God. He admits that the Assyrians have indeed laid waste the nations and burned and destroyed their gods[39] but counters that precedent with what is at once an appeal and a challenge: "Now, Yahweh, our god, deliver us from his power," with the additional, motivating clause: so that Yahweh may be universally recognized as the only god (19). Through this speech, the character of the king is both more fully drawn than in the previous narrative and more positive. Hezekiah here recognizes Yahweh as the only living god of the whole world and so can give full weight to the Assyrians' invincible record: unlike Yahweh, the gods of the other nations could be burned and destroyed. The request for deliverance is simple and direct. The king does not tear his clothes or don sackcloth, but confidently states his faith in Yahweh as the only god. He has no doubt of Yahweh's ability to save Jerusalem from the Assyrians and so concentrates on motivating him: drawing his attention to the fact that the Assyrian king has insulted him and claiming that he will be universally recognized if he does intervene.[40]

Hezekiah here addresses Yahweh himself, rather than appealing to Isaiah to intervene with his god. Nevertheless, it is Isaiah who conveys the response from Yahweh. Wildberger finds this unsettling—Isaiah now has telepathic powers (1982, 1420)! But it accords precisely with the Aramaic narrative: Zakkur "lifted [his] hands to the Lord of the Heavens, and the Lord of the Heavens spoke to [him] through seers and through prophets." The kings pray to the deity, and the deity replies through prophets. Here the role of the king is elevated once again to a more typical and central role, appealing directly to the deity himself.

The divine response and promise of deliverance follow immediately. Isaiah sends Hezekiah word of a divine oracle, beginning with a reference to Hezekiah's prayer (v. 20). In the Masoretic text, the oracle consists of a poetic address to the king of Assyria (vv. 21–28; including a quotation of a boastful speech by the king: vv. 23–24), an announcement of a sign and promise addressed to Hezekiah (vv. 29–31), and a prose oracle announcing Assyria's departure and Yahweh's protection of Jerusalem (vv. 32–34). However, only the last (originally ending with *ně'um-Yahweh*, "oracle of Yahweh," at the end of v. 33)[41] is the direct and original response to Hezekiah's prayer in this story. Beginning and ending with the promise "he will not come into this city," it is precisely the divine response and promise of deliverance. Here there is no traditional word of reassurance ("fear not") for Hezekiah. But such is unnecessary, given Hezekiah's obvious confidence.

Verse 36 again serves as the literal fulfillment of the announcement of the king's departure (v. 33). But this time the reason for the departure is provided by v. 35, in which the envoy of Yahweh spreads death through the Assyrian army.

While the previously identified structure of the story of divine deliverance from a siege is used here, it is even more remote than the previous story from the historical siege of which it speaks. Although the plot closely follows the outline charted earlier and observed in the Zakkur narrative, the interest, even more than in either the preceding narrative or the inscription, is in the speeches. The forms and themes of the speeches build on the larger literary resources of Israel from the sixth century on and are less interested in a particular event (a siege in 701 BCE) or relationship (between king and prophet) than in Yahweh's general role in the world—in relation to presumptuous conquerors, to other gods, and to his own city. The characters are even simpler and more idealized than in narrative B: Sennacherib the destroyer of nations, vilifying Yahweh; Hezekiah the pious king, trusting Yahweh; and Isaiah the dutiful prophet, receiving and passing on oracles from Yahweh.

In other narratives in the books of Kings, we have noted the contrast between the success of a king in an individual diplomatic move and the condemnation or belittling of him in the Deuteronomistic evaluation (see chapter 5). We see the reverse in 2 Kings 18. The failure of Hezekiah's rebellion against Sennacherib, reported in vv. 13–15, contrasts with the enthusiastic approval of him in the evaluation (cf. vv. 3–7). In that context, his rebellion against the king of Assyria is mentioned without any reference to its ignominious end (v. 7b). The two long narratives that follow vindicate this approval of the rebellion, trivialize the now parenthetical notice of Hezekiah's surrender and payment, and narrate models of divine deliverance that lay out the imperial power's incomprehension (in the first story) and the true Yahwist's faith (in the second). Read in their present order and context, the three stories show the increasing piety and success of the king. In the first, he is pragmatic, and there is no mention of the deity or of an Assyrian withdrawal. In the second, he appeals to the prophet to intervene with the prophet's god: the Assyrian king is now distracted but does not withdraw completely. Finally, the king appeals to God directly and in true faith—and now at last experiences complete deliverance.

2 Kings 6:24–7:20

Second Kings 6:24–7:20 is another variation on the same pattern, now elaborated not by speeches but by shifts in point of view and complication of the plot.

The present biblical form of this narrative may be outlined as follows:

Exposition: Benhadad's attack on Samaria (6:24) and the desperate siege conditions (6:25–30)
Complication: the king's confrontation of Elisha and Elisha's prophecies (6:31–7:2)
Resolution: the discovery of the Aramaeans' flight and the fulfillment of Elisha's prophecies (7:3–20)

The fulcrum of this story is Elisha's prophecy, which predicts the end of the famine. The dominant interest is the role of the prophet (6:31–7:2, 16b–20), especially his prophecies and their fulfillment: the central announcement of the reversal of the siege conditions (7:1, 16b) and the ancillary prophecy of the punishment of the king's officer for his incredulity and mockery (7:2, 17–20). In relation to the prophet, the king appears as a helpless and desperate man, frustrated at both Yahweh's and Elisha's inaction (6:31, 33; 6:27 probably also belongs here).[42] Apart from 6:27, these interests are represented in two segments of the narrative: 6:31–7:2 and 7:16b–20. They significantly affect our view of two other parts of the narrative: the divine deliverance mentioned in 7:6–7 reads as a parenthetical explanation within the arc from prophecy to fulfillment, and the king's suspicions in 7:12–14 suggest his failure to recognize the fulfillment of Elisha's prophecy, which he heard in 7:1.[43]

Despite the presence of prophetic oracles in both this story and that of Zakkur, they function in quite different ways. In the Zakkur narrative, the prophetic oracles are an immediate divine response to a royal appeal to the deity. The Israelite prophet, however, does not respond to a royal appeal to the deity but counters a royal statement of despair about the deity's attitude (6:33; foreshadowed in 6:27 and 31). In the biblical story, the prophecies do not resolve the crisis but introduce an additional complication—how can this starving, desperate city become prosperous overnight?—and their specific fulfillment is delayed until vv. 16b, 17–20, long after Yahweh's disposal of the invaders in vv. 6–7 and even after the city's slow discovery of their deliverance in vv. 3–16a.

It has been argued by Schmitt and, following him, Jones and Würthwein that composers of prophetic stories have here, as also in 2 Kings 3, reworked an earlier story (Schmitt 1972, 37–41; Jones 1984; Würthwein 1984, 309) so that it now conforms to the prophecy-fulfillment theme so prominent in the stories of Elijah and Elisha. The underlying story on which this prophetic theme has been overlaid conforms more closely to the pattern of the preceding stories of divine deliverance from a siege, though it is already developed with considerable sophistication.

This earlier version (6:24–26, 28–30; 7:3–16) portrayed the king more sympathetically than the final (prophetic) version: as deeply concerned for his people and performing ritual actions understood as an appeal to Yahweh (6:30). Yahweh's scattering of the Aramaeans, reported in 7:6–7, is understood now not as an explanatory aside between prophecy and fulfillment but as Yahweh's response to the king's appeal. The king's suspicions in 7:12 read now not as disbelief of the prophet's prediction but as an appropriately human reaction. Since he has no information from God or prophet, his precautions in 7:12–15 are perfectly appropriate and, indeed, prudent. The final reference to the comparatively low price of good food (7:16b) now expresses the reversal of the initial situation, represented in 6:25 by the high price of bad food.[44] This earlier form of the narrative may be outlined as follows:

A. THE DANGER: Benhadad's attack on Samaria (6:24) and the desperate siege conditions (6:25–26, 28–29).
B. THE APPEAL: the king's ritual appeal to Yahweh (6:30).
D. RESPONSE = DELIVERANCE: This is a case in which there is no verbal (oracular) response. The deity's actions constitute the response: Yahweh's scattering of Benhadad's army (7:6–7). However, the king's and people's recognition and enjoyment of deliverance is delayed until 7:15–16.

Würthwein argues that 7:6–7 were not in the original story, which was a purely profane tale of an unusual end to a siege. The resumptive repetition of "they came to the edge of the camp" (vv. 5b, 8a) gives away the seams of the addition. He even dates this addition after the prophetic insertions (Würthwein 1984, 310, 312, 315–16). But what type of story would such an "original" story have been? Would not hearers of such a story have cried out for an explanation of the extraordinary abandonment of the Aramaean camp? Stories of the kind currently under discussion exist precisely to explain such unusual developments. The original story must surely have been conceived already as a story of divine deliverance;

the resumptive repetition is occasioned simply by the *narrative* interruption, which takes the reader back to the time and action that had been left hanging before an analepsis.[45]

There is no need for an exposition introducing the characters: the king of Israel and the king of Aram were prominently featured in the immediately preceding story in 2 Kings 6. As in the Zakkur narrative, a brief reference to the hostilities initiated by the enemy leads directly into a crisis focusing on details of a siege that express the extremity of the situation. The Israelite defenders of Samaria face incredible prices for food and resort to cannibalism (6:25, 28–29), thus initiating their own demise.[46] As in the Aramaic narrative, the appeal to the deity is conveyed through a ritual gesture: the Israelite king wore sackcloth and tore his outer garments (like Hezekiah in 2 Kgs 19:1). In both narratives, the deliverance is expressed through a reversal of the specific crisis facing the city: in the Aramaic narrative, the attacker's wall and ditch; in the Hebrew narrative, the lack of normal food.

But there are also major differences between the two narratives. Zakkur's inscription focuses on the prophetic response to the king's appeal in quoted oracles of salvation, which are followed (presumably) by an account of the actual raising of the siege. The prebiblical Israelite narrative lacks any divine communication to the king. Yahweh delivers Samaria from the siege before, not after, the king and people know it (7:6–7), and the narrative traces in detail the slow process whereby the besieged discover their deliverance (7:3–5, 8–16). This process of discovery (7:3–16)—with no counterpart in the other narratives here considered—is more than twice as long as the rest of the story. These distinctive features of this story deserve comment.

The Aramaean narrator dwells on what he most wants his readers to appreciate: the words of support Zakkur has received from his god. The Judean narrator has no interest in divine words of support for the anonymous Israelite king. On the contrary, what the narrator wants readers to appreciate is society's blindness to the works of the deity: having disclosed to readers how Yahweh has dispelled the Aramaeans, he dwells on the long process of discovery by various members of the society. The extended depiction of the extreme conditions in the besieged city is exceeded only by the extended, slow disclosure of the deliverance of the city. This begins with the narrator's sudden abandonment of the city and king in their extremity after 6:30 and introduction of new characters in a new setting in 7:3. The lepers at the city gate have a conversation in which they analyze their own situation and interests. Unlike the king, who has no choices,[47] these new characters conclude that they do have a choice—at least one in which they have nothing to lose—and decide to go over to the Aramaeans (7:3–4). It is from the point of view of these outsiders that the reader then makes the discovery of the abandonment of the Aramaean camp ("They came to the edge of the Aramaean camp— and look [*wĕhinneh*], there was nobody there!"; v. 5).

At this point, the activity of the lepers is interrupted by another change in scene and point of view. The reader—and none of the participants—now learns what Yahweh has already done prior to the lepers' discovery: "Yahweh had caused. . . ." The reader learns that Yahweh has already responded to the king's ritual appeal and dispelled the enemy while the inhabitants of the city continue to despair, rescuing the Samarians while they still think they are perishing.

Yahweh had caused the Aramaean camp to hear the sound of a great army. As Yahweh intended, this is misinterpreted by the Aramaeans (v. 6b) to their cost (v. 7; see chapter 5). In this preprophetic form of the narrative, vv. 6–7—the narrator's disclosure of Yahweh's disposal of the enemy—are the turning point of the narrative. The reader now knows that the king's appeal is answered, and attention turns to the city's discovery of its deliverance.

With the lepers we have discovered the abandoned Aramaean camp (7:5) and apart from them have learned what Yahweh has already done (7:6–7). The city's appreciation of their deliverance then follows slowly in a series of delays and advances. The first delay is the lepers' looting (v. 8). Then there is an advance with their reconsideration of their behavior, their report to the guards at the city gate (vv. 9–10), and the communication to the palace (v. 11). Then comes the second delay: the king suspects a trap (v. 12). There follows the proposal and preparation of the exploratory mission (vv. 13–14). The full extent of the rout is now finally discovered (by readers as well as characters; v. 15a), and a confirmatory report is made to the king (v. 15b). Only after all this do the people pour out to enjoy the goods of the abandoned enemy camp (v. 16).

The lepers' discovery of the Aramaeans' departure is an unintended consequence of their judgment that while they probably faced death whatever they did, there might be a chance of survival around the Aramaean camp. It is then only their fear of punishment that finally persuades them to report their discovery to the city. Their selfish plundering of the site is a comic absurdity under the circumstances that functions not unlike the comic subplots in the tragedies or histories of Shakespeare. Indeed, their rationalism, greed, and fear of punishment in time of war are specifically reminiscent of Falstaff.[48]

If the Aramaeans are deluded by Yahweh in v. 6, the results of this delusion are then also misinterpreted by the king in v. 12. Now it is only the courtier's proposal of an exploratory mission that discloses what we know to be the king's misprision. From lepers to king, all proceed in ignorance, and the discovery of the actual deliverance depends on the decisions of the lepers pursuing their own self-interest and the proposal of a single courtier.

This complicated process of discovery is the peculiar contribution of this narrative. In the stories discussed here, prophets reveal in advance to king and reader what the deity is going to do. Here, no prophets give anyone advance knowledge. Rather, the narrator reveals to the reader what the deity *has already done*—and this *is never learned by the king (or other characters)*. The king learns—after the lepers and the exploratory party—of the Aramaeans' flight but not what caused it. By revealing Yahweh's activity to the reader early in this process, the narrator shows the reader the limitations of sublunary human understanding, dwelling on the characters' ignorant pursuit of what they think are their own interests, which stands in ironic contrast with the freedom Yahweh has already given them. The traditional role of prophet and king in such stories has been displaced by the role of narrator and reader—not with respect to a current historical crisis but with respect to a narrative of human behavior. The narrator gives the reader a revelation inaccessible to all the participants in the narrative and hence, by implication, a perspective on human behavior not generally recognized.

Aramaic sieges of Samaria may well have taken place during the latter part of the ninth century. Stories of miraculous deliverances may have been told shortly afterwards, roughly contemporary with the briefer history of the narrative of Zakkur's deliverance. That the prebiblical story we have just examined stands at some social and cultural distance from such political and literary phenomena is suggested by the anonymity of the king, the sophistication of the narrative techniques, and the specific theological use of those techniques. It may be thought that there is Judean mockery of Israelites here—"they don't even recognize it when Yahweh does something for them"—but particular Israelite or Samarian features are not emphasized. The story presents a broader picture of Yahweh's free activity apart from human mediation or observation, of the accidents that allow humans to benefit from that activity, and of continuing human ignorance of the activity itself—apart from those like the narrator with eyes to see.

The further complication of the story by the introduction of the prophetic material deserves some comment. First, the king's response in v. 27 suggests a reading of the woman's words in v. 26 as an appeal representing the whole population in its present extreme danger. It anticipates and complicates the king's approach to Elisha, which should be an appeal for help but is, in fact, a reproach (v. 33b) following the threat in v. 31 (cf. v. 32b). As noted previously, the story now shifts the interest to Elisha's prophecies. The main one predicts the imminent abundance. What follows now gradually discloses to the reader—again with stops and starts—how that prediction will be fulfilled. Verses 6–7 are now reduced in significance to an aside to the reader in the trajectory from prophecy to fulfillment: the prophecy, not Yahweh's action of 7:6, is the divine response to the king, and v. 16b, not v. 6, is the fulfillment of the prophecy. The king's conclusion in 7:12 now appears to be a deafness to, or lack of faith in, the prophetic word. This is reinforced by the second prophetic oracle delivered to the skeptical officer in v. 2, an oracle which depends on the reliability of the first; in effect, "you will see this for yourself, but you won't benefit from it." The degree to which the prophetic theme overshadows the story is illustrated by the addition of the last four verses, which spell out laboriously the fulfillment of this second oracle: as Elisha's first oracle was fulfilled to the letter, so the oracle against the man who doubted it is also fulfilled. Elisha's credibility is now the concluding, if not the central, point of the story, and the reader is given a monitory object lesson about the danger of questioning the prophetic word. The revelation that the narrator shares with the reader in the earlier version of the story has been overshadowed by a tale reinstating the revelatory authority of the prophet and his word.

2 Kings 3:4–27

At the end of 2 Kings 3, there is an extraordinary account of a siege from which a king is miraculously delivered—as told from the point of view of the invaders.

Defeated in battle by Israel (vv. 24–25a), the Moabites take refuge in Kirhareseth, which the Israelite slingers surround and pelt with stones (v. 25b). The king of Moab sees that the battle is going against him and tries to break out with a force of swordsmen but is unsuccessful (v. 26).[49] Finally, "he took his first-born son, who was to rule after him, and offered him up as a burnt offering on the wall; and there was great wrath against Israel, so that they moved off from him and returned to their land" (v. 27).

Here clearly is another example of a siege narrative structured according to the pattern defined previously. As in 2 Kings 7, however, there is no oracular divine response or promise preceding the deliverance:

    A. THE DANGER (vv. 24–26)
    B. THE APPEAL (v. 27aα; here again in the form of a ritual act)
    D. THE RESPONSE = DELIVERANCE (v. 27aβ).

The obscure feature of this story is the nature of the deliverance. At issue is the significance of the term "wrath" (qeṣep). Normally, it is used of divine anger, especially in the expression "there was wrath against. . . ." Everywhere else in the Bible, the god in question is indubitably Yahweh. But the king of Moab certainly does not sacrifice to his enemy's god in this hour of need. The sacrifice is directed to Chemosh. But then Yahweh is not going to respond to a sacrifice offered to some other god. Thus the divine wrath here must be that of Chemosh, who responds to Mesha's sacrifice by expressing his wrath against Israel. How he does this is undefined (as often in the case of Yahweh's wrath).[50]

It is remarkable that the people represented by the unsuccessful attackers preserve and tell the story of the divine deliverance of their enemy. The manner in which they do this is notable. The omniscient narrator expresses at length the extremity of the Moabite king's position, initially by reference to the king's own point of view ("he saw that the battle was too much for him," v. 26a), then by his military response (the attempt to break out of the siege, 26b), and finally by his religious response (the appeal to his god in the form of the public sacrifice of his heir; v. 27aα). The character of this last act is emphatically elaborated. The narrator refers to the king's son by three expressions: "his son, his firstborn, who was to rule after him" (cf. the four expressions in a better-known story of human sacrifice—"your son, your only child, whom you love, Isaac," Gen 22:2; also Jdg 11:34), and refers directly not only to the sacrifice of the son but also to its public location: "on the (city) wall." With the last phrase, the king's desperation and the terrible nature of his appeal are exposed, not only to the reader but also to both attackers and defenders. The modern reader may decline to speculate on the effects of this on Chemosh but can scarcely refrain from imagining the psychological and social repercussions on the observers.[51] While certainly sympathizing with the observers, however, the ancient reader, for whom sacrifice was a central religious act, would also have considered the power and effects of the act on the actor's god.

The narrator now shifts from the clear and defined to the shadowy and suggestive. The reference to the divine response and the deliverance of the city is brief and cryptic: the theological term "wrath" at once implies divine action and obscures for the reader the particular form that action took. This stands in sharp contrast with the narrator's account of the divine intervention in the siege of

Samaria in 2 Kings 7:6, where the readers, but not the besieged, know precisely the divine role in the departure of the attackers. Here, though the besieged and attackers may be quite clear about the nature of the divine intervention, the reader is not. We know only the final result: the withdrawal of the allies. The matter-of-fact conclusion—"they took off . . . and returned"—is similar to that of the previous stories treated above concerning the siege of Jerusalem (2 Kgs 19:36). The brevity of the treatment of the actual deliverance is typical of these biblical stories but especially appropriate here, where it slights the success of the enemy and the role of the enemy's god.

As a story of the enemy's deliverance from a siege, this is, of course, only the conclusion of, or an appendix to, a story of a generally successful military campaign by Israel and Judah (3:4–9a, 20–25a).[52] In this extended story, the allied victory in the field (vv. 24–25a) leads into the danger faced by the now besieged Moabite king (v. 25b). The allies' success is then dampened by their final failure to take the king and the city in which he holds out. This more complex story, told by those who identify with the attackers, begins with the motivation for the campaign—Moab's rebellion against Israel—and Israel's engagement of Judean support, in which the unanimity of the two kings is emphasized (v. 7). They journey through Edom for seven days (v. 9a). In the morning, the land is full of water (v. 20). In v. 21 there is an analepsis: the Moabites had heard of the allies' attack, prepared themselves for battle, and stationed themselves at the border. With their rising in the morning, we are brought back to the present, for they see the water in the sunrise. The significance of the allies' journey through Edom is now disclosed: the water looks red to the Moabites (the Hebrew word for "red," 'ādōm, is a play on the name Edom, 'ĕdôm). Their misinterpretation of this "red" water as the blood of the allies' armies leads to their defeat in battle. The allies march through the land destroying everything, while the Moabite forces by implication flee and secure themselves in Kir-hareseth (v. 25). The story we have already discussed now provides the conclusion to this campaign: Mesha holds out successfully, and the king of Israel fails in his mission to reimpose tributary vassal status on him. As in 2 Kings 18–19, the rebellion of a vassal leads to a punitive campaign in which the rebel king is isolated in his city, appeals to his god, and is miraculously delivered. But where that story is told by a narrator sympathizing with the besieged, here the narrator sympathizes with the attackers.

Yahweh still plays no role in this story, and the concluding reference to "wrath against Israel" remains an appropriately imprecise allusion to the traditional theological explanation for failure to take a city. Most striking in this story is its placement of the reader in the enemy camp (and mind) in two substantial sections: vv. 21–23 and 26–27. These serve to preserve the Moabite viewpoint in a story now generally told from the point of view of an observer of the Israelites campaigning against them.

In vv. 9b–19, a prophetic episode has been introduced into the earlier narrative. These verses now have us linger over a consultation by the two kings, so that after their seven-day journey through Edom (v. 9a) there is a long delay before the encounter with the enemy. In this scene, the crisis en route is resolved by the sudden appearance of Elisha: the troops' lack of water in the Edomite wilderness

(v. 9b) now leads to Elisha's transmission of an announcement from Yahweh that great quantities of water will appear from nowhere (vv. 16–17). To this is added a promise of victory (v. 18) and instructions on what to do to Moab (v. 19).[53] Thus, the water in which the Edomites later think they see the blood of the invaders is now used for two quite different purposes: initially, to satisfy the thirst of the invaders and so fulfill the prophecy of Elisha (this fulfillment is not actually mentioned) and, later, to delude the defenders (the delusion not prophesied but now also by implication caused by Yahweh). The initial victory and subsequent scorched-earth policy of the Israelites are now also the fulfillment of the prophet's words (vv. 18–19; though the promise of victory is compromised by the final failure to take Kir-hareseth).

This middle section also contrasts the piety of Jehoshaphat and the faithlessness of Jehoram (vv. 10–14; contrast their unanimity expressed in v.7). While the army's success in vv. 24–25a may be seen as reflecting the prophet's favor for Jehoshaphat, the reader may now understand the final failure of the troops to capture Kir-hareseth as explained by the disfavor in which the prophet holds Jehoram (v. 13a). Jehoram's faithless belief that "Yahweh has called up these three kings to hand them over to Moab" (vv. 10b, 13b) both justifies and foreshadows the final turn of events, suggesting that Yahweh allowed the wrath of Moab's god to drive the Israelites off. In this final reading, Israel's ultimate failure was both ordained by Yahweh and deserved, and the role of Chemosh is further diminished.

It is not surprising that the outcome of the siege is passed over so quickly. What is surprising is that it was mentioned at all. Tales of how "our" god delivered us from "our" enemies were common to Israelites and their neighbors and to many other societies. Tales of how "our" enemy's god delivered them from us are rare anywhere. Admittedly, there is no direct statement that "Chemosh drove Israel off." That is the kind of statement we would expect to find in Mesha's version of the war between Israel and Moab (cf. ll. 18–19 of the Moabite stone). Even mention of Chemosh is here carefully avoided. At the same time, the details of the sacrifice and the pregnant phrase "there was great wrath against Israel" would have been understood by the ancient reader as clear indication that the sacrificial piety of the other king was effective and that his god had protected him and instigated Israel's withdrawal. This explanation for Israel's failure to take the city is produced by the author's use of the type of story to which this chapter is devoted.

Summary

To conclude, stories of miraculous deliverance from a siege, while based on a simple, standard pattern, are developed and used in very different ways in the inscription of Zakkur and in several biblical contexts.

The early-eighth-century Aramaean king of Hamath, Zakkur, uses such a story to display his support by the god who made him king ("the Lord of the Heavens"). While it may originally have been told in his court or on a memorial inscription, it has now been incorporated into an inscription dedicated to and placed before another god (Ilu-Wer). This story is introduced by a statement of the narrator-protagonist's piety and the Lord of the Heavens's support of him. The narrative moves rapidly from forming a confederation against Zakkur and listing of the kings involved to overcoming his city's defenses and his appeal to the deity. The god's reply comes via prophets in two speeches giving his assurance of support and promise of deliverance. The remainder of the narrative would have recounted the king's actual deliverance (in the missing lines before the following list of Zakkur's building activities). The divine speeches dominate that part of the story that is preserved. In the first, the god echoes—and so justifies—the claims made by the narrator-protagonist in his introductory statement about the god's support of him. The story illustrates these promises and claims about the relationship between Zakkur and his god and, while formally the king's acknowledgment of the deity's support, is functionally his demonstration to the reader of the king's secure and protected position.

The two stories of divine deliverance in 2 Kings 18–19 (Isa 36–37) are both patterned after the same basic structure. In the first story, three officers of the invading Assyrian king and of the defending Israelite king, Hezekiah, meet outside the city walls. This scene is dominated by the long speeches of the rabshakeh, one of the Assyrian officers. He makes a series of ad hominem arguments to the king and the people, the first criticizing actual royal policies and the second faith in king or Yahweh. Their clothes torn, the officers go to the king, who expresses his anxiety with the same gesture (tearing his clothes). He sends to the prophet Isaiah. The prophet replies with an oracle reassuring the king and announcing the fate of the invader. The prophecy is immediately fulfilled. In this story, the conflict is primarily verbal: the major threat is the rabshakeh's "words," occupying half the story: it is on these that the prophet offers reassurance. Since the Assyrian's arguments are not explicitly countered (the Judeans remain silent, as ordered by the king) and the prophet refers to them as vilifying Yahweh, the reader is expected to recognize their falsity and offensiveness. Faith in Yahweh, the god of the prophet, rather than the theology expressed by the Assyrians, is vindicated by Yahweh's quick dismissal of the invading army. Here the story of deliverance from a siege is used to attack particular policies and a particular theology—put in the mouth of the enemy—and to reinforce an alternative, implicit theology, which is best represented not by the king but by the prophet. The story is addressed to and appeals to the reader who recognizes and embraces this particular theology. Such a reader will enjoy recognizing the fallacy of the rabshakeh's arguments, will feel superior to the despairing Judean king and his officers, and will appreciate the role of the prophet as appropriately representing Yahweh in his characterization of the Assyrian's speeches and correct prediction of his end.

The second story about Isaiah is formally similar but different in the explicitness and social locus of its theology. The rabshakeh gives only a short speech, adapting two of the arguments used in the previous story. Hezekiah himself makes a direct appeal to Yahweh, not only laying the Assyrian arguments before Yahweh (physically in the form of the tablets on which Sennacherib's message has been written) but also praying to him (where previously he had appealed to Isaiah).

The narrator's faith in Yahweh finds expression in the king's prayer (rather than in the prophet's oracle). The following oracle (vastly expanded over time by various elements) consists basically of a simple statement that the invader will not do a thing to the city but will return to where he came from. The deliverance then comes in the form of a nocturnal visitation on the Assyrian army by Yahweh's envoy, with the result that in the morning they are all corpses. Here the central exhibit is the piety of the king. The king both models the appropriate response to the enemy's threat and expresses the beliefs that expose the fallacy of the enemy's arguments. The prophet's brief oracle guaranteeing Jerusalem's complete security and the divine envoy's decimation of the Assyrian army shows the effectiveness of Hezekiah's prayer and the validity of his beliefs. Here, the appreciative reader will embrace the king's faith and acknowledge the central role of the king (rather than the prophet) as bearer of that faith. In this respect, this story is closer in function to that of Zakkur. But while Zakkur's story is in part propaganda for his own rule, the authors of narrative C in 2 Kings 19 are idealizing a king of the remote past as a model for present leadership. Both the stories in 2 Kings 18–19 (Isa 36–37) are didactic, the former less aggressively so, since it appeals primarily to the in-group, and the latter asserting explicitly the specific beliefs to be held.

The original story of the siege of Samaria in 2 Kings 6–7, which may in part reflect Judean attitudes toward the north, displays the terrible conditions prevailing during the siege and the king's despair (again expressed through torn garments, as well as the wearing of sackcloth). There is no oral communication from the deity, and the deity's intervention is performed beyond the ken of the besieged. The city's deliverance is then discovered incidentally by outsiders (lepers), who only after some time think of reporting what they have found back to the city. Even then, the king believes that the invaders are trying to trick him, and only the idea of a courtier prompts further investigation, which finally leads to the recognition and enjoyment of the city's deliverance. But the narrator has shown the reader (alone) early on what the deity has done. The narrator thus serves as prophet in relation to the reader, disclosing a realm of divine activity unseen by others. With this superior knowledge, the reader is able to enjoy the comic irony of the behavior of the characters through the second half of the story.

This is suppressed in the prophetic supplementation of this story by the explicit and dogmatic assertion of prophetic revelation. The prophetic word and the challenge to it come as the crisis of the story between desperate siege and discovery of relief, and the story now concludes with an emphatic and prolix statement of fulfillment both of the original prophecy and of the prophecy of punishment for the challenger. Yahweh's activity is, as it were, bracketed by the word given to the prophet and its fulfillment, these focusing not on divine activity but on human experiences. The central importance of the prophet's word is underlined by the punishment of the one who doubts that word. While still sharing with the reader a privileged view of divine activity in the world, the narrator now insists that the prophet tells the audience and readership what they need to know, which is knowledge, not of past divine activity, but of future outcomes.

The story of the siege of Kir-hareseth is very different. Formally, it resembles the same basic structure, but uniquely the narrator's sympathies here lie with the besieging forces. He moves into the enemy camp and thinking to describe the desperate military situation, then has the besieged king sacrifice his only son on the city wall (thus in the sight of attackers and defenders). The divine response and means of deliverance are described cryptically in the pregnant clause "there was great wrath against Israel," and then the Israelites depart. The ancient Israelite listener would have understood this to refer to the wrath of the Moabites' god, though the biblical text avoids referring to Chemosh directly. The story nevertheless implicitly gives a traditional theological explanation for a failed siege, now concluding a longer story of a previously successful military campaign and field battle.

Here, too, a prophetic passage has been added to the story, in which a prophet's predictions and instructions anticipate the subsequent victory. The prophet expresses his favor toward the Judean king (thus justifying the favorable oracle) and his disfavor toward the Israelite king. Elisha's charge that the latter did not share his commitments may now be taken to suggest a reason for the armies' failure in the final siege: Yahweh's disapproval of the Israelite king was ultimately behind the wrath following Mesha's sacrifice.

Although the narrators of the two stories in 2 Kings 18–19 go beyond Zakkur in their exploitation of the didactic possibilities of the traditional form, the last two stories show the more surprising creativity of Israelite narrators in their elevation of the reader above the characters in 2 Kings 7 and in their transfer of the divine deliverance to their enemies in 2 Kings 3.

Conclusion

The Roles of the Stories and the Role of the Deity

While each of the preceding chapters may be read as a separate study, together they shed light on three general topics. This comparison of epigraphic and biblical narratives contributes to our appreciation of the literary character of each; to our reconstruction of the transmission of certain stories and types of stories; and to our recognition of the role of the deity in different kinds of stories. This concluding chapter addresses these three topics in turn.

The Literary Character of the Stories

In the case of the petitionary narrative, it was possible to define a narrative genre on the basis of its social setting (it is recounted by a person in need to an authority with the power to address the need), purpose (to persuade the authority to intervene in the speaker's favor), and certain narratological features (the narrator is the central character, the story is told from that person's point of view, the plot takes him or her into a dire situation, at which point the narrative ends). Examples of this genre in the Bible, though written, disclose that such petitionary narratives were always oral products, hence the extraordinary written form of the field-worker's petition in the Mesad Hashavyahu inscription must be the consequence of the inaccessibility of the officer in question. This inscription is, nevertheless, a record of a real petition to a local authority. The Bible preserves several literary versions of the genre, some adapted with considerable sophistication and subtlety to a more complex situation. While one (in 1 Kgs 3:16–27) demonstrates the superior wisdom and judgment of the monarch, others expose the limits of his power or the failings of his judgment (2 Sam 14:1–20; 1 Kgs 20:38–42; 2 Sam 12:1–7). Such virtuosity in the use of the genre contrasts with the simplicity and clumsiness of the field-worker's narrative. The two categories of this one genre represent the opposite extremes of quotidian and creative literary narration within Israel.

The story of the construction of the Siloam tunnel was first recorded in an inscription within the tunnel itself. The only characters are the excavators, and the plot focuses on the final stages of the excavation (in which the two work parties meet in the middle) and leads to the measurements of the completed project. These features, together with the anonymity of the inscription and the obscurity of its location, suggests that it was an unofficial record sponsored by the project manager. By contrast, biblical accounts of the making of the tunnel give the king sole credit for the project. The earliest of these, 2 Kings 20:20, reflects the interests and point of view of the court. The later versions in Chronicles and Ben Sirach appear to depend on the account in Kings, continuing exclusive attribution of the project to the monarch. The biblical accounts have the bare, official character of a building inscription or chronicle, until enlivened by Sirach's poetic imagination.

The inscriptions from outside Israel are all royal products. The king is the narrator and speaks of events in his own life or, in the case of Bir-Rākib, in his father's life. All the corresponding biblical narratives (except Deut 23:5–6) are third-person accounts, finally part of the Deuteronomistic History.

In the inscription of King Mesha of Moab, a general account of his recovery of Israelite territory is followed by four stories of particular campaigns. These stories, though varied in detail, generally refer initially to Israel's occupation of a territory and then recount Mesha's reconquest of it and the administrative measures he undertook to incorporate it into his state. After a section treating in more detail of his construction in Dibon and more generally of his administration of his land, another campaign story following the earlier pattern brings us to the end of the preserved text. The Aramaic inscription from Tel Dan appears to recount another story of the same type, and a transposition to the theological plane appears in the stipulations of the Sefire treaty. Of two comparable stories in 2 Kings 13, the first (vv. 1–7) is of complex literary origin and laden with biblical phraseology and theology; the second (vv. 22–25), apart from the wording of v. 23, is quite similar in several respects to the stories of Mesha and the Tel Dan inscription. Since these are the only two royal memorial inscriptions from Israel's immediate vicinity and both proclaim recovery of territory from a neighbor, it may well be that Israel's king also erected a memorial to his recovery of territory occupied by Aram—and that the Deuteronomistic historian made use of this account. But it may also be simply modeled on such royal epigraphic accounts. While the summary account of David's campaigns in 2 Samuel 8 may reflect awareness of inscriptions such as Mesha's, the summary of Joshua's campaigns in Joshua 10 is too monotonous and the individual campaign narratives too restricted in scope to be related in any way to the preserved Northwest Semitic royal inscriptions. The exiguity of similar material in the Deuteronomistic History strongly suggests that the historian did not in general use royal inscriptions as a source.

Two monuments from Sam'al and several biblical narratives tell the story of a king or claimant to the throne who appeals to a more powerful monarch to intervene against a local ruler who threatens him. Kilamuwa, in a minimal story, boasts of "hiring" the king of Assyria against the king of the Danunians and of the economic benefits his people derived from the Assyrian intervention. Three stories in the Bible use the same word for "hire" in three similar situations but from the point of view of those against whom the third force has been engaged or of a narrator sympathetic to them. These have artistic and religious rather than political motives. The first story, part of a longer literary narrative, appears in a brief speech in which the initial aggressors misinterpret what they perceive (2 Kgs 7:6). Yahweh causes the Aramaeans besieging Samaria to hear noises, on the basis of which they construct for themselves a story explaining these sounds (the king of Israel has hired Egyptian and Hittite kings against them), abandon their camp, and flee. The narrator thus explains the cause (unknown to the Israelites in the narrative) of the abandonment of the Aramaean camp by recounting to the reader this divine activity and Aramaean misapprehension. In another occurrence, also a brief incident in a longer literary narrative (2 Sam 10), the Ammonites hire Aramaeans to assist them in battle against Israel, whom they have provoked. The narrator concludes the story with the subjection of the Aramaeans to Israel; the defeat of those hired against Israel is more thorough and permanent than that of the hirers, who retreat into their city and are left alone. The third occurrence is in a summary story cited to support a law. The account of the story of Balak's hiring of Balaam against Israel in Deuteronomy 23 involves a transposition of the normal plot to the religious sphere; Balak of Moab appeals, not to a military power, but to the religious power of Balaam, and Yahweh responds in kind on Israel's behalf. The story is told with Yahweh and Israel in the first and second persons, respectively. The narrator motivates us to exclude Moabites from the convocation of Yahweh by telling us, the hearers, that they hired a religious force against us that Yahweh, out of his great love for us, turned to our advantage.

The inscription of Bir-Rākib preserves a fuller account of this type of story. It spells out the details of the threat to Panamuwa and his people before his appeal to Assyria and the benefits and achievements of his reign afterward. At the center of the narrative, Panamuwa takes a present to the Assyrian king, who then establishes him as king, kills his antagonist, and releases political prisoners. Two biblical narratives recount the siege of a Judean king in Jerusalem, the king's message and gift to a more powerful king, and the latter's invasion of the attacker. The symmetrically structured story of Asa in 1 Kings 15 gives the fuller account, with some evocation of the larger social world as in the story of Panamuwa. The story of Ahaz in 2 Kings 16 is more roughly composed. It appears to incorporate discrete historical reminiscences, and its present narrative structure may have been influenced by the common structure of such stories. In any case, the numerous commonalities between the two stories in Kings at once distinguish them from the Samalian inscriptions and make clear that they both come from the same social and cultural context in Judah. Neither has the broad scope of the Samalian inscription, its interest in the general economy or welfare, or its personal rhetoric. Instead, their economic interests focus on disbursements from the temple and palace treasuries, their diplomatic interests include the wording of the message that accompanies the present, and they maintain an impersonal, matter-of-fact style and tone quite unlike the personal and political rhetoric of either of the Samalian royal inscriptions. While both claim an achievement by the Judean king in question, the context belittles that achievement (Asa) or condemns the king in general (Ahaz). It seems clear that these two stories were composed neither in the courts of the two kings nor by the Deuteronomistic historian. They appear to have originated in the Judean court some time after the reigns of the kings in question and before the composition of the Deuteronomistic History.

Other stories tell of more miraculous deliverance from military threats, specifically sieges. Under siege, the king appeals to the deity, the deity responds (sometimes through prophets), and the city is delivered. All these stories are much more obviously didactic. The story of the siege of Hadrach in the inscription of Zakkur is so told as to display compellingly the god's support of Zakkur. Again, the political function of this story contrasts with the theological purposes of most of the stories of the same type in the Bible.

Two such stories appear in 2 Kings 18–19 (Isa 36–37). In the first, the threat is expressed especially through the lengthy ad hominem arguments of the Assyrian envoy. The king tears his clothes and appeals to a prophet. The prophet gives a divine message: words of reassurance, promising the attacker's departure. The prophecy is then fulfilled. Whereas Zakkur's story elevates him in relation to his god (and so in relation to his people), this story relegates the king to a simple functional role. He refers the matter to Isaiah, and the prophet is elevated. Speaking for Yahweh, Isaiah ignores the Assyrian rhetoric and, while giving the conventional reassurance "fear not," simply and authoritatively announces the departure and fate of the Assyrian king. Isaiah's address to the king's messengers is followed, not by notification of the king, but by immediate fulfillment of the prophecy. The Assyrian arguments have a certain plausibility in the context of contemporary beliefs about the gods and Israel's political and military position and may represent the views of many in the author's Jerusalem. For the narrator and implied audience, however, they are specious because they misrepresent Yahweh. The reader is expected to perceive the falsity of the theology put in the mouth of the Assyrians and so to anticipate the actual role of Yahweh through his prophet.

The second story is of similar structure but different emphasis. The Assyrian envoys' message is quite short, reiterating the final argument from the Assyrian speech in the previous story. The king, by contrast, utters a lengthy prayer to Yahweh, countering the Assyrian arguments with the truth about the gods. Yahweh is not just another god. He is the maker of the universe, and the other gods are not gods at all. The following prophetic oracle again announces the invaders' departure, though this has been expanded with various other elements. Yahweh's envoy then smites the Assyrian army. Here the king is a model of true piety and spokesman for the truth—vindicated by the following oracle and devastation of the enemy. The centrality of the king brings this story closer to that of Zakkur.

But Zakkur was telling the story of a unique event in his own life and aiming to affect the readers' relationship to him through the display of his relationship to his god. Both Hebrew stories are literary creations concerned with theological arguments and ideal roles rather than individual relationships or a unique occasion. They aim to influence the reader's beliefs and loyalty to particular cultural institutions. (The historical events on which they build took a very different course, as reflected in the brief narrative preceding the first story [2 Kgs 18:13–15]: Hezekiah bought off the Assyrians by submitting and paying a massive tribute.)

In the original story of 2 Kings 6–7, the simple structure of these stories is complicated: the narrator informs the reader how the city has been delivered soon after the final display of its desperation, but its own discovery of its deliverance is delayed by several devices. Thus the reader is quickly relieved of the tension created by the description of the desperate siege conditions and then entertained as the ignorance and self-interest of various characters now advance and now delay the city's enjoyment of its deliverance. A revision of this story introduces the prophet as predictor of specific events and insists on his reliability and the fate of those who doubt him. The authority of prophetic knowledge now subordinates the authority of the narrator as revealer of divine action.

The same structure is used in 2 Kings 3, but here the narrator's sympathies are with the attackers, not the defenders. Formally, the last verses of the chapter correspond closely to the standard pattern of such stories, so that it is implicitly Chemosh who discomfits the Israelites in response to the Moabite king's desperate appeal. This story appears to explain Israel's failure to take the Moabite city. The prophetic passage now included in the earlier part of the story suggests that the Israelites' final failure may be due in part to Jehoram's not sharing Elisha's commitment to Yahweh.

The Transmission of the Stories

The narratives in royal inscriptions are doubtless renditions of stories told in one form or another in the court of the named author of the inscription and then consigned to writing probably late in the reign of that king. In two cases, the inscription we have recovered is probably not the original written version of the story. Zakkur's deliverance from the siege of Hadrach by the Lord of the Heavens was probably first written down in a memorial inscription commemorating that major event and Zakkur's subsequent building activity in Hadrach. This was later incorporated into the dedicatory inscription for Ilu-Wer, set up before his image in his temple in Apish after Zakkur had completed further building projects in that city. The inscription of Mesha probably also had an earlier edition, celebrating the victories over Israel and comprising the stories of the campaigns for the recovery of northern territory and the account of the following building activities. The later campaign to the south—for Horonaim—led to the production of a second edition in which the story of that campaign was appended to the preceding material. We know that the story of Panamuwa was told after his death, since it is only then that his successor put his story into writing. In general, however, it is questionable how long such stories would have been transmitted orally or in writing after the first generation.

Neither of the two Hebrew epigraphic narratives relates to the court. The narrative in the Siloam tunnel inscription is introduced with the words "This was the account," referring to a story that the author had received. This too must have been an oral story and can have originated only with those working at the rock face. The author has incorporated their account into his inscription. Again, it is doubtful that this story would have been told beyond the generation of those involved. Like all genuine petitionary narratives, that in the Mesad Hashavyahu inscription is essentially oral and ephemeral, written down only out of circumstantial necessity. It is the expression of the field-worker, modified only so far as the scribe saw fit.

All of the other Israelite stories reviewed are now components of literary works—especially the Deuteronomistic History—which are, in turn, part of the Bible, that body of literature that comes to us through centuries of written transmission, selection, and supplementation by a succession of Jewish communities. Many of the stories, particularly some of those discussed in chapters 2 and 6, are literary in a narrower sense; that is, they are (part of) sophisticated narratives that, whatever their oral prehistory, are the work of artistic scribes. Others, particularly several reviewed in chapters 3, 4, and 5, are either didactic, theological narratives or simple, factual accounts of little human or artistic interest. The form of minimal narratives about construction projects is generally similar in the royal inscriptions and in the books of Kings, so that it remains a possibility that Judean kings produced building inscriptions which were later used as a source by the historian. Close similarity between stories of military campaigns in the royal inscriptions and in Kings occasionally suggests that one or two of the latter may have been influenced by Israelite royal inscriptions. But the stories of military success in Kings lack any trace of royal rhetoric, so that it remains unlikely that they made direct use of inscriptions, and the rarity of such stories in Kings argues against their use in general. It is, of course, possible that narratives, both of building and military activity, were more closely related to a Judean chronicle, but we have no example of a Northwest Semitic chronicle with which to compare them.

Whereas in modern society an author publishes a fixed text on a specific date under copyright, in the ancient societies of Syria-Palestine, literature, whether written or not, was unstable until it "died"—either from lack of interest and significance to the (oral) community or because the physical objects on which it was written were damaged, lost, or buried (like the various inscriptions we have recovered). The shaping and reshaping of an oral story were affected not only by the competence of the performer but also by the occasion on which the story was told and the nature of the audience. (In the case of the inscriptions, we have some limited access to these factors; in biblical literature almost none, except so far as the occasion was the writing of a larger work of which the story in question was part.) As the passage of time significantly affects people's views of past events, whether in their individual lives or in their communal history, so also it affects their views of events and explanations in stories. As stories shift synchronically from one social setting to another or diachronically from one set of social conditions to a succeeding one, actors, events, and explanations may also shift. Stories told at the town gate may be rather different from the same stories as told in the royal court, and stories told at the courts of Samaria and Jerusalem may become rather different when recounted by literati of the Babylonian exile or religious authorities in the Persian province of Judah.

We can see something of such changes of perspective both in the inscriptions and in the Hebrew literature. The long story of Panamuwa's political, diplomatic, and military activities, written down on Bir-Rākib's inscription dedicated to his father (ll. 2–19) but presumably long familiar at court, is oblivious to any role of the gods in those events, never referring to any divine act or word. In the context of his own immediate goals, however, Bir-Rākib's opening thematic statement on the inscription (ll. 1–2) claims that the gods saved and supported Panamuwa. The effect of this opening acknowledgment is to confer a theological perspective on the following narrative. Similarly, two Judean diplomatic stories recounting the achievement of a particular king and presumably transmitted in the Judean court in subsequent generations, have been incorporated in the Deuteronomistic History in contexts that in one case belittle that achievement and in the other condemn the king from a distinct, theological point of view. Or again, some Judean stories of military campaigns or miraculous deliverance have been reshaped and reinterpreted by the superimposition or insertion of stories of prophecies and their fulfillment, thus reiterating one of the themes of the present books of Kings.[1] Finally, we have in the two versions of the story of Balaam—the brief story (in the second person) in Deuteronomy 23:5–6 and the more prolix and complex version (in the third person) in Numbers 22–24—an example of how a traditional tale may be summarized and recast in the second person in a particular didactic context (as the motivation for a law) or elaborated into a complex work with its own theological and rhetorical character and aims.

The Role of the Deity in the Stories

Some recent studies of biblical prose narrative place considerable emphasis on monotheism as the factor distinguishing it from narrative elsewhere in the ancient Near East. Thus Robert Alter writes: "What is crucial for the literary understanding of the Bible is that [the] reflex away from the polytheistic genre had powerfully constructive consequences in the new medium which the ancient Hebrew writers fashioned for their monotheistic purposes" (1981, 29). According to Alter, the monotheistic Hebrew writers abandoned "the polytheistic genre" to shape "the new medium" of prose narrative. Despite his explicit commitment to a synchronic criticism of the Bible, Alter's comparative statement is diachronic—and quite misleading. First, Alter confuses literary categories (genre) and theological categories (monotheism, polytheism). Certainly, many ancient Near Eastern narratives are polytheistic in their depiction of the world, most famously the great poems in the mythic-epic tradition, but in many others, especially prose narratives, only one god or no gods appear. This suggests that the Hebrew writers did not shape a new medium but exploited and developed a well-established one. Second, although the Bible has been generally received since its compilation and closure as a monotheistic book, "the ancient Hebrew writers" were by no means all monotheists.[2] Our literary understanding of the Bible as a whole may depend on our appreciation of its monotheism and the "monotheistic purposes" of those who determined its final shape, but our literary understanding of the work of the "ancient Hebrew writers," writing long before that later momentous transformation of their material into a religious canon, requires that we recognize sometimes a complete disregard of the divine realm and other times the nuances of the relations among and the kind of reality accorded a variety of divine beings. In other words, ancient Near Eastern narrative cannot be lumped together under the term "polytheistic genre," and ancient Hebrew writers did not fashion "a new medium" for "monotheistic purposes."

Comparisons in the preceding chapters authorize some specific observations about the role of the divine realm in ancient Hebrew narratives (whether or not they were included in the Bible) and narratives recovered from elsewhere in Syria-Palestine.

The two Israelite narratives from outside the Bible allow us to correct the tendency to characterize Hebrew narrative on the basis of our general view of the Bible. The petitionary narrative in the Mesad Hashavyahu inscription and the several such narratives in the Deuteronomistic History neither refer nor allude to the existence of the divine realm. The epigraphic document and the literary exemplars demonstrate that in narratives composed to explain and justify a petition to the authorities—whether in reality or in art—it was neither necessary nor appropriate to give the deity any role at all. Consequently, there is no trace of monotheism or any other theism in these narratives. The petitionary narrative is simply a nonreligious genre.

The story of the completion of the Siloam tunnel found inscribed within the tunnel, distinctive among building inscriptions in the ancient Near East, makes no mention of the deity. The biblical accounts of the same project likewise ignore the deity. Again, there is no trace of monotheism or any other theism either in the unofficial account in the tunnel or in the official or poetic accounts preserved in the Bible. Further, no deity appears anywhere in the building sections of the royal inscriptions we have considered. Only in the far north (under Assyrian influence?) is there clear reference to a divine role in royal construction. In the eighth-century inscription of Azatiwada from Karatepe, the king says that he built his city "because Baal and Resheph of the Goats[3] had comissioned me to build it" (A ii 10–11), and in an eighth-century inscription on a statue of the god Hadad, Panamuwa says that the god "summoned me to build" (l. 13). In no other Syro-Palestinian inscription does the deity perform such a role.[4] In general, then, the one nonroyal building inscription from Israel, the minimal accounts of Israelite monarchs' building activities in Kings, and the stories of building projects in Syro-Palestinian inscriptions south of the modern Turkish border give the deity no role.[5] Here again is a nonreligious genre shared by Israel and its neighbors for which the terms "polytheistic" and "monotheistic" are simply irrelevant.

Thus, two genres of Hebrew narrative attested both epigraphically and in the literature preserved in the Bible are neither monotheistic nor religious in any way, and only a "canonical" reading can make them so. In the case of these two genres, we may contrast Hebrew literary and epigraphic narratives with "biblical narrative," where the latter term refers to literary narratives as read in their final canonical context by early Jews and Christians and by church and synagogue since. To appreciate the various Israelite narratives as composed by their Hebrew authors, we must read them on their own terms and in light of their prebiblical environment, remembering that none of them became "biblical" until there was a Bible—long after most of them were composed. It need scarcely be added that there are many other narratives preserved in the Bible (without analogues among the recovered Northwest Semitic inscriptions) which similarly disregard the divine realm.

Like the the two genres just mentioned, one of those found in the royal inscriptions from outside Israel also lacks any divine role—the diplomatic narratives of Kilamuwa and Bir-Rākib (and indeed the whole series of minimal narratives concerned with Kilamuwa's establishment of the security, peace, and prosperity of his realm and the whole narrative of the life of Panamuwa recounted by Bir-Rākib). The disposal of an immediate military threat by the diplomatic engagement of a superior force is recounted in both these inscriptions and in several narratives in the Bible without any reference to the deity. The exception that proves the rule is the Deuteronomist's story of Balaam, in which the king of Moab appeals not to a superior military force, but to what he believes is a superior religious force, to intervene against Israel. Precisely because of the substitution of a religious power for the standard military power, the narrative is transposed onto another plane in which it is "natural" for the deity to appear. Consequently, Israel's God intervenes to counter the threat posed by Balaam. This is not a story of ordinary diplomacy but of a conflict between religious powers.

To summarize thus far, the divine realm is completely absent from the petitionary narratives, stories of building projects, and stories of diplomatic initiatives reviewed here. This is true regardless of whether the story is recorded in an inscription or a literary text, in Israel or in one of the other states of Syria-Palestine. Thus, Israelite prose narratives of several genres preserved in the Bible are not monotheistic and, indeed, are in no sense theological or religious.

Other narratives in Northwest Semitic inscriptions from outside Israel feature a deity very prominently. In King Mesha's narratives of campaigns to recover occupied territory, the narrator variously tells us what Chemosh did, quotes Chemosh telling the protagonist what to do, and recounts what the protagonist did to acknowledge Chemosh's role. The narrator of the Tel Dan stela in a comparable narrative similarly recounts the actions of Hadad on behalf of the protagonist. In two analogues to these stories in 2 Kings 13, the narrator portrays Yahweh favoring the king of the occupied territory. Where a summary series of campaigns is narrated in 2 Samuel 8 and Joshua 10, Yahweh similarly gives the ruler victory over the enemies to whose land he lays claim. Thus the roles of Chemosh, Hadad, and Yahweh are essentially alike in the Moabite, Aramaic, and Hebrew narratives of successful military campaigns. Finally, stories of miraculous deliverance from a siege depict the deity in a major role: as the Lord of the Heavens responds to Zakkur's appeal in a crisis, so Yahweh responds to the king of Judah in 2 Kings 18–19 (Isa 36–37) and to the king of Israel in 2 Kings 7, and (tacitly) Chemosh responds to the king of Moab in 2 Kings 3.

The type of story and the author's purpose determine whether the deity has a role.[6] Where military conflicts are concerned, stories of successful campaigns of conquest recognize the role of the god in directing and giving success to the king, thus justifying the king's action. On the defensive side, stories of diplomatic initiatives ignore the divine realm. Diplomacy is a human skill, and those who practice it may claim credit or be held responsible for its success or failure. Finally, when those besieged by superior forces are delivered after all human resources have failed, that deliverance can be attributed only to the deity.[7]

None of the narratives from Israel's ancient environment reviewed in this book is polytheistic. In all those stories in which there is a divine role, one deity alone occupies that role. Again, there is no distinction between Israel and its neighbors. Were the Moabites, Aramaeans, and Israelites all monotheists? All the evidence suggests that most of these states were officially henotheistic. Each had its national, official deity, who normally figured in the literature produced by the court and elite of the capital city. But in each state other deities also were recognized— at the local level and, for some purposes, at the center. So some of our inscriptions, when they move from narrative to blessings or curses, refer to various deities. Bir-Rākib concludes his inscription with a prayer for the blessing of all the gods, including several mentioned by name. Kilamuwa ends his inscription, which previously made no reference to any god, by invoking various gods to curse anyone damaging it (each god significantly identified with a previous individual ruler or dynasty). Similarly, the latter part of Zakkur's inscription invokes various gods to punish anyone damaging the inscription. In a word, curses and blessings invite the listing of any divine powers likely to be recognized by a potential violator. So Israelite inscriptions from Khirbet el-Qom and Kuntillet ʿAjrud reveal that Israelites could invoke more deities than the one Yahweh when pronouncing blessings (Yahweh of Teman, Yahweh of Samaria, Asherah). Thus, inside as well as outside Israel, several deities may appear together in certain types of expression having purposes quite different from the narratives.

Of the stories we have reviewed, some types have no role for a deity, other types have a role for one deity only. Yet other types of stories featured several deities or the collectivity of the gods. Unfortunately, we have almost none of ancient Syria-Palestine's belles lettres. However, the narrative in the partially re-covered Balaam text from Deir ʿAllā has the gods come to Balaam by night and speak to him in a vision. He then tells his people what the gods are doing: they assemble in council and address a particular deity whose name is unfortunately not preserved. A prophetic narrative such as 1 Kings 22 also has a prophet describing a vision in which he sees the assembled divine beings (there identified as "spirits") participating in a council with Yahweh (22:19–22), and Zechariah 3:1–7 recounts a prophetic vision in which two divine beings, one representing and one opposing Yahweh's will, are actors, along with the high priest. Both Micaiah's audience within the narrative of 1 Kings 22 and the implied readers of both that narrative and Zechariah 3:1–7 accept such multiple divine beings as appropriate in a vision report; that is, vision reports may introduce multiple divine characters in both Israel and its vicinity. If we had Northwest Semitic poetic narratives about the divine world or poetic epics such as are well known from Mesopotamia, we would also expect to find several divine characters in them—as we do in the few brief samples of such genres that have survived in Biblical Hebrew poetry (e.g., Ps 82; Deut 32:8–9; cf. Job 1–2).[8] In sum, a contrast between monotheistic Hebrew narrative and the polytheistic narratives of its neighbors is misleading. Both Israel and its neighbors produced narratives in which there were many gods, one god, or no gods. The distinctions are not between Israel and its neighbors but between narratives of different types and purposes.

None of this is very surprising. Indeed, what has here been claimed with respect to narratives in these Syro-Palestinian cultures accords with the more general observations of a social scientist.

> Faith and skepticism and various degrees of reliance on mystical or non-mystical comforts are functions of situations and circumstances. A complete inventory of the explanatory beliefs (mystical and nonmystical) available in a given culture is thus meaningless unless accompanied by a minutely detailed exposition of their deployment in actual situations, sufficiently well specified to permit rigorous comparison in other cultures. The detachment of beliefs from their ambient circumstances produces gross distortion and misunderstanding. . . . Again, . . . the passage of time is another critical variable affecting explanations of the same event (as it is reevaluated) by the same [I would add: or other] actors in the same culture at different stages in the unfolding social drama. (Lewis 1986, 20–21)

On the basis of the few types of stories reviewed in this book, it seems that the absence or presence of the deity or the number of divine beings in a narrative depends upon the kind of narrative, and the kind of narrative depends on the purpose of the author. Different kinds of narratives have different purposes and use different means to achieve them. The theological character of a story is determined not by whether it comes from a monotheistic Israel or a polytheistic neighbor but by what kind of story is being told for what purpose in any of these societies. For every type of story, there is general consistency among the exemplars attested with respect to the presence or absence of the deity (or number of deities). It is immaterial whether the narrative is written in Hebrew, Moabite, Aramaic, Phoenician, or Samalian. The prose narratives of Israel and of its Syro-Palestinian neighbors reviewed here are to this extent alike. Our understanding and appreciation of Hebrew narratives preserved in the Bible depend, in part, on our recognizing that monotheism is often quite irrelevant.

We have looked in some detail at the few narratives in Northwest Semitic inscriptions that have analogues in narratives preserved in the Bible, often commenting on the specific linguistic and rhetorical means employed and the general social context implied. This has frequently led to a larger historical field: the different social and literary contexts through which stories have passed and the different purposes they have served. Study of the inscriptions informed and stimulated analysis of the comparable stories preserved in the Bible and sometimes led to suggestions concerning their social and literary contexts and development. We were able in some cases to clarify aspects of the literary productivity of the Judean court and of the Deuteronomistic historian's use of sources. We were also able to show that, throughout the Syro-Palestinian world, including Israel and Judah, the presence or absence of one or more gods in a story is a function of the type and purpose of story, not of whether the story is in Hebrew prose. The ongoing comparison of biblical narratives with the most closely related congeners recovered from their vicinity can only further illumine Israelite storytelling and historiography.

Notes

1. Using techniques now generally known as source criticism, form criticism (genre criticism), tradition criticism, transmission criticism, and redaction criticism.

2. See, for example, Davies 1992 and Thompson 1992. Archaeologists, by contrast, engaged in increasingly sophisticated interpretation of material remains, are contributing significantly to the reconstruction of the material and social history of the two kingdoms. See, for example, Stager 1985 and the summary of recent work on particular periods and topics in Dever 1990.

3. Some of these transmute the Bible's traditional status as a Jewish or Christian canon of divinely revealed religious truth into a literary canon of reader-produced secular wisdom. Having discarded the religious faith that the Bible qua Bible has sustained and by which it has been sustained for so many centuries, these critics still cling to the literary consequences of the religious judgments that made of the literature a Bible.

4. Note the titles, as well as the content, of Berlin 1983, Sternberg 1985, and Brichto 1992. Ironically, despite their large claims for biblical narrative as a whole, such critics focus their attention on specific narrative chefs d'oeuvre in the Bible, not on the rather mixed quality of the mass of narrative material now combined there. Thus, Sternberg generalizes about the monotheistic and historiographic character of the (rather less artistic) whole but concentrates his detailed studies on selected discrete narratives of exceptional artistry and sophistication. Other introductions to biblical narrative art include Alter 1981, Bar-Efrat 1989, and Gunn and Fewell 1993.

5. A basic principle of semantics is that "understanding an utterance necessarily involves the receiver's recognition of the sender's communicative intention" (Lyons 1977, 33). It is also worth noting here that, as the sender's meaning involves choices made on the

basis of intention, the receiver's meaning involves choices made on the basis of value or significance (Lyons 1977, 33).

6. Compare Levinson 1991, Barr 1995, and the concluding reflections of Rogerson 1995.

7. The former produce "histories" that retell the stories in the literature, while the latter produce histories that ignore the richest material for reconstructing Israel's mental and social world. Some recent studies that in different ways have attempted to come to grips with both the literary and the historical dimensions of individual biblical narratives include Levenson 1978, Damrosch 1987, Brettler 1991, and Carr 1993.

8. Comparisons with more universally attested narratives—typologically, rather than culturally related—have been similarly fruitful. See, for instance, Ben-Amos (1992), which has a useful bibliography.

9. The book of Revelation contains much narrative material that both differs significantly from that of the first five books of the New Testament and is slightly more comparable to ancient myth because narrative in the apocalyptic genre recounts events on a cosmic scale and draws on old mythical material. Similarly, there is material in the Hebrew Bible, especially in the poetic books, which is more closely related to the Near Eastern mythic-epic tradition than to most of the prose narratives. In both cases, biblical material undermines attempts to draw an absolute contrast between monotheistic Bible and polytheistic myth.

10. See especially Genesis 6:1–2 and various scenes featuring the old divine assembly, such as Job 1–2 and 1 Kings 22:19b–22. See Parker 1995a and 1995b. On Genesis 1–11, see Damrosch 1987, 88–143, and on the transformations of the "combat myth" in the ancient Near East, the Aegean, the Hebrew Bible, and later Jewish and Christian literature, Forsyth 1987. In an earlier book, I compared selected biblical stories with episodes in two Ugaritic narrative poems, chiefly to suggest that common oral tales had been taken up and adapted in very different ways in the two different traditions (Parker 1989).

11. The major exception is the epic of Erra.

12. Two inscriptions on stone found in Jerusalem and one in Samaria—all three only small fragments—could possibly come from royal memorial inscriptions. In 1978, Millard and Pardee both suggested that Hebrew inscription 88 from Arad might be a draft or copy of a royal inscription, but both also mentioned the possibility that it might be part of a literary text. Millard notes that since we seem to have the beginning of this inscription, and it is unlike the beginning of any other royal inscription, it could only be an extract from such a source (Millard 1978). However, after identifying himself and referring to the length of his father's reign, Mesha of Moab continues his memorial inscription (see chapter 4): *w'nk mlkty* "and I ruled . . ."; and Arad 88 begins: *'ny mlkty bk* ["I ruled over a[ll?]. . . ." Is it possible that the writer would in this context begin with such a statement, omitting the king's self-identification as obvious and ignoring the length of the previous king's reign (which is unique to the Mesha inscription)?

Because the Siloam tunnel inscription is in the third person and does not even mention the king (see chapter 3), Eissfeldt concluded that first-person royal inscriptions were less common in Israel than in its environment (1965, 51–52). Naveh has argued that the apparent lack of a distinct lapidary script in Israel "may indicate that there was little occasion for developing such a style in Israel: there was no widespread custom of erecting stelae by the king and offering votive inscriptions to the deity" (1968, 71; similarly 1982, 69–70).

13. For estimates of the population of ancient Israel, see Shiloh 1980 and Broshi and Finkelstein 1992.

14. See Jamieson-Drake 1991, especially 147–48. Compare the critical review in Lemaire 1992.

15. This is my conclusion based on the epigraphic evidence alone. It is not inconsistent with the evidence of the relevant biblical texts, though it would require more space than is available here to demonstrate this. For a brief overview of the epigraphic evidence see Mazar 1990, 514–20, and for a fairly comprehensive collection of Hebrew inscriptions (in transcription) see Davies 1991. Of the inscribed seals in particular, Mazar writes that they "belonged to dignitaries, members of the royal family, and other prestigious personalities" (1990, 518). The forty-one inscribed bullae (clay seal impressions) from a house of the late preexilic period in Jerusalem are almost all from unrelated individuals—clear evidence that the original documents belonged, not to a family, but to an official archive (Shiloh 1986, 37; Shiloh and Tarler 1986, 208).

Some, such as Millard 1985 and Demsky 1990 (with bibliography), wax enthusiastic about the extent of literacy in ancient Israel. But see the salutary considerations introduced already by Warner 1980. It is generally estimated that in ancient Near Eastern societies less than 1 percent of the population would have been fully literate and perhaps close to 10 percent able to read and write simple administrative lists and notes. See Whitt 1995, 2395–96 with bibliography on 2397.

For a more probing exploration of the relations between orality and literacy in ancient Israel and Judah and in biblical literature, see Niditch 1996.

16. Hoftijzer and van der Kooij 1976 and 1991. The much better preserved Ahiqar papyrus is from a fifth-century Aramaic-speaking community in Elephantine in southern Egypt. The narrative of Ahiqar was probably composed in Mesopotamia during the later seventh or sixth centuries BCE (Lindenberger 1983, 19–20; 1985, 482). A new edition of the text has been published in Porten and Yardeni 1993, 22–53 (and foldouts 1–9). Both Lindenberger (1985) and Porten and Yardeni (1993) offer English translations. The tale of Ḥor from the same period and place is very fragmentary (Porten and Yardeni 1993, 54–57). While a detailed comparison of Ahiqar with several biblical narratives is desirable, the Persian period has not yet yielded enough Northwest Semitic narrative material to allow a broader study such as those undertaken in this book.

17. On the ancient understanding of certain kinds of writing apart from reading ability, see Whitt 1995, 2395 with bibliography on 2397.

18. For us, too, storytelling is primarily oral: we tell oral stories at work, at home, and at parties; in speeches, sermons, and newscasts; in law courts, classrooms, and restaurants; in comedy clubs, in therapy, and in song; and elsewhere. Compare J. Miller 1990, 66.

19. On the continuities between oral and literary forms of expression, see Halverson 1992 and Collins 1995, especially pp. 78–80 (with bibliography).

20. On this and the larger subject of literary exegesis or interpretation within biblical literature, see Fishbane 1985.

21. Which cannot have been before the last century BCE, since the Qumran scrolls attest to several different text forms. On the text of the Hebrew Bible and the overlap between text criticism, and literary criticism, see Tov 1992, especially chapter 7.

22. In some cases, we will find evidence of an earlier edition here, too—earlier, however, by only a few years.

23. For these and other narratological terms, see Prince 1987.

24. Compare Culley's remarks on condensation and summarization (1992, 112–13).

25. This is so worded as to win fairly wide assent, I think, despite the remarks concerning the uncertain date of composition of most biblical texts. It is doubtful that any biblical literature was written to be part of the Bible—or that much biblical literature was written to be part of one of the present biblical "books."

26. Only within one religious community can we actually speak of *the* canon, since there are historically different canons: for example, among Christians, the Greek Ortho-

dox, Roman Catholic, Protestant, and other canons; among Jews, the Masoretic Text— but the Septuagint for many Jews during the first centuries of its existence—and among Samaritans, the Pentateuch alone.

27. For recent reviews of modern scholarship on the Deuteronomistic History, see Knoppers 1993, 1–56 and McKenzie 1992.

CHAPTER TWO

1. The *mishpāḥâ*—usually, but not very satisfactorily, translated "clan"—appears to have been an endogamous association of families, often coextensive with a village or small town. It was evidently the most significant unit of social life beyond the family for most Israelites.

2. On 2 Chronicles 19:4–11 (judicial reform attributed to Jehoshaphat), see now Knoppers 1994. Albertz still argues for the establishment of a Jerusalem supreme court of priests and elders by Jehoshaphat (1994 [German original 1992] 183–84.

3. This would include, of course, the deity. In that case, however, we would classify the petition as a prayer. On some analogies between petition and prayer, see Greenberg 1983, 20–22.

4. Characterized as a "judicial plea" by Pardee (1978; 1982, 17–24) or as a "petition on the grounds of *gzl*" ("abuse of power") by Westbrook (1988, 35, n. 128), who is followed by Dobbs-Allsopp ("an extrajudicial petition for justice"; 1994, esp. p. 52).

In the following translation (and in others in this book) square brackets enclose parts of the text that have been damaged or worn away.

5. Some would take this word (*'āmēn*) with the preceding clause: "will testify for me, 'it is true.' "

6. Following Westbrook's specific genre designation and a previous suggestion of Delekat, Dobbs-Allsopp proposes to restore *[(w)h' gzl 't]* "He unjustly took (my garment)" (1994, 52). This fits the context nicely. However, as Dobbs-Allsopp notes, previously the speaker had used the simple verb *lqḥ*, "took" (twice), so that *[(w)h' lqḥ 't]* "He took (my garment)" would be a less creative restoration. Either restoration would resume an element of the narrative when the speaker has moved on to another rhetorical genre. In the one petition in the Bible that extends beyond the narrative (in 2 Sam 14), there is a clean distinction between the two sections.

7. Dobbs-Allsopp proposes to understand *'m l'* ("if not") as an asseverative: "Surely it is . . ." (1994, 52–53). But, as he notes, the asseverative usage of these two words derives from the oath formula (as in "May God do this to me, if . . . not . . ."), and a hypothetical oath normally makes sense before *'m l'*—but not here. *'m l'* is also used in another syntactic context, following imperatives or cohortatives, where the sense seems to be "and see if . . . not . . ." Significantly, in neither of these cases is the clause introduced by the copula *w* "and, but"—as the present clause is. It seems better to take this clause and those following as expressing alternatives: the officer may act out of duty or out of mercy.

8. For a convenient transcription and bibliography, see Pardee 1982, 20. A more recent valuable contribution to the understanding of several linguistic features of the text is Booij 1986.

9. Compare the five parts Smelik sees (Smelik 1992b). His parts two and three correspond to the two parts of the narrative which I discuss later. After distinguishing the "initial plea" (ll. 1–2), Pardee (1982, 23) treats everything else through line 12 as the "basis" of the plea (ll. 2–12) and designates ll. 12–15 the "request for return of garment" (ll. 12–15)—my part four. In this, he is anticipated by Dion, who speaks of the "exposé du cas" (ll. 2–12) and the "demande du plaignant" (ll. 12–15; Dion 1979, 577). Weippert and

Weippert offer a more detailed breakdown into eight parts (1989, 147–49). Similarly, Renz 1995, 320. (Unfortunately, the latter work arrived too late for me to incorporate its treatment of the Mesad Hashavyahu and Siloam inscriptions [on pp. 315–29 and 178–89, respectively] into this and the following chapters.)

10. See Dick 1979. (I am grateful to Professor Greenstein for reference to this article.)

11. Here I disagree with Dick, who makes two assumptions—that Hosha'yahu has accused the peasant of neglecting his corvée labor and that he has taken the garment as a pledge—and concludes that the ostracon "is a written appeal for an official adjudication (12–14)" (Dick 1979, 43–44). But what is striking about the text is that it does *not* suggest any rationale for Hosha'yahu's behavior and that the final appeal is not for adjudication but simply for the return of the garment!

12. In light of the repetitive features of the text as a whole, this seems preferable to other solutions, such as making two separate clauses out of these words, such as, "Your servant is working at the harvest. Your servant was in Hasar-Asam" (Pardee 1978 and 1982, 20–21). The best study of the syntax of these words is that of Hoftijzer (1986), who points out that in biblical Hebrew, clauses such as '*bdk qsr* have present or future reference, while those such as *qsr hyh 'bdk* not only refer to the past but also are typically used to give introductory information about the speaker at the beginning of a speech. Comparing 1 Samuel 17:34, Judges 12:2, and Deuteronomy 6:21, Hoftijzer construes the first word of the inscription—"your servant"—as a *casus pendens* (extraposition or nominative absolute). But all of the parallels cited by Hoftijzer have a special reason for using a *pendens:* its modification by a relative clause, the corresponding noun serving as object, or the nouns being synonymous rather than identical. In our sentence, however, there is no good reason for a *pendens.* While Hoftijzer's analysis may be grammatically correct, in the context of the repetitive style of this document, the double use of "your servant" is perhaps more suitably characterized as pleonasm. In other words, it is another indication of the colloquial repetitiveness of the speaker—as reflected in the English translation used here.

13. Compare the comments by A. Finet on the distinctions among letters found at Mari between those composed by scribes and those dictated directly (Hecker and Sommerfeld 1986, 15). In our case, we should not expect the style of this inscription to correspond to that of literary Hebrew (such as we find in the Bible) or even to the epistolary Hebrew of officials, as found in the correspondence from Lachish or Arad. Contrast the claim that this is "a well-composed piece of prose with certain literary virtues" (Kuyt and Weselius 1991). Young's attempts to characterize the language of the inscription are based on his discomfort with the number of narrative verb forms, unusual for the Hebrew of the inscriptions (1990), but Young fails to recognize the dominant genre of this inscription (narrative, in which a high frequency of converted imperfects would be expected) as contrasted with most others.

14. It seems to me that those who believe that this text illumines or illustrates some aspect of Israelite legal practice ignore the total silence of the text about a range of pertinent circumstances and motives. Crucially, it conveys only one, partial view of the situation—partial in both senses: it expresses the interests of one party, and it omits information indispensable for an informed judgment on the case. We cannot, for example, classify this case with that of Exodus 22:26 (Heb. 22:25; cf. Deut 24:12–13), since there is no suggestion here that the garment was taken as a pledge or kept beyond sundown (though others understand "for days" as "a few days ago").

15. The peasant would doubtless be flattered to learn how persuasive his case has been with most modern scholars. Smelik, for example, writes: "The author succeeds in making the readers see the case from his point of view, compelling them to accept his solution . . . as the only logical one. . . . it seems unnecessary to ask Hoshaiah why he took [the

garment], or to investigate whether the main character finished his task" (Smelik 1992b, 61).

16. This is not to say that none of them could have originated in traditional tales or even in historical petitions, but that, as presented to us in the biblical text, they are composed by the authors of those texts.

17. As noted previously, in cases in which the hearer knows the parties involved—the petitions of Esther, for example (Esther 5–7)—petitions may lack any significant narrative component.

18. This translation still seems appropriate, despite Meier's argument against Boyce (see n. 20) that the use of the verb *ṣ'q* to introduce a dialogue in which subsequent speeches are followed by forms of *'mr* is simply an old northern convention unrelated to the more common meaning "cry out (for assistance)" (Meier 1992, 188–95). The dialogue in some of the passages he cites is a sequence of speeches between which other actions and so lapses of time occur (e.g., 2 Kgs 4:40; 6:6–7, 30–31), and in the first two of those cases the two speeches are by the same person. Thus, it is questionable whether all the speeches in question can be called parts of dialogues (or "interchanges of speech"). Meier also claims that the Bible uses other verbs besides *ṣ'q* to introduce the "cry of the legally marginal" (Meier 1992, 189 and notes 3–6). But the passages he cites are not petitions, as defined here, but rebukes or complaints (Exod 16:2–3; 17:3; Jdg 15:18), requests that some-one not do something (that is, opposing an initiative by another party: 2 Sam 13:12; 19:18–19), a speech to oneself (Gen 21:16), a warning (Jdg 9:7), a vow (1 Sam 1:11), or a general prayer for strength (Jdg 16:28). On 2 Samuel 14:4, see later. Then again, of the four cases of *ṣ'q* that Meier dismisses as irrelevant to his study (Meier 1992, 188), one introduces a request for permission to do something (Exod 5:8), one is part of an expression describing a wail of despair but introduces an appeal or request (Gen 27:34)—thus both related to its use to introduce petitions, though here between parties of ongoing relationships—and two introduce prayers (Exod 17:4 and Num 12:13). (While many prayers may be character-ized as petitions to a deity, the deity is usually assumed to know the circumstances of the petitioner, so that a petitionary narrative is often absent.)

19. The references to the king's enquiry and the woman's account are ambiguous: the king may also be asking for a first-person account of the story that Gehazi was in the process of telling. This may be the reader's first assumption following the immediately preceding speech of Gehazi. But, as just noted, the Hebrew *wayiš'al hammelek lā'iššā,* "the king enquired of the woman," may well refer to the standard response to an appeal: *ma-llāk,* "What is the matter?" In any case, the king's following speech leads the reader to the conclusion that the woman has recounted the story of her house and land. (If vv. 4–5 were a secondary addition to a much simpler story of the woman appealing to the king for her estate [Würthwein 1984, 317], then the verb "enquired" would originally have referred unambiguously to her petitionary narrative.)

20. Boyce limits his investigation of the parties in an appeal to the socially marginal and the king, emphasizing the distance between the two (Boyce 1988, 28–33; Cogan and Tadmor 1988, 79 see *ṣ'q* as the legal term for appeal specifically to the king.) Boyce is correct that it would be counterproductive for petitioners to suggest in any way that they posed a threat to the official they approached. But many officials besides the king were—presumably more frequently—the objects of petitions, and anyone who felt wronged might bring such a petition to an appropriate official, as in the Mesad Hashavyahu inscrip-tion. Presumably, only the most difficult or desperate cases came to the king. But that does not mean that petitioners might not themselves be relatively powerful and privileged. Nor does it mean that the weakest would not prefer to have their petition presented by a more influential person—it is assumed that Elisha would perform such a service (cf. 2 Kgs

4:13). (Similarly, in the divine sphere, the people would like to rely on individuals whom they believed to be especially influential with Yahweh to present their petitions to him; see 1 Sam 7:7–8; 12:19; Jer 15:1–2; Ps 99:6–8.)

21. Schmitt (1972, 99), followed by Würthwein (1984, 288), thinks this is an addition by a theological reviser. In any case, it perfectly suits the character of the petition and is not out of place in the speaker's mouth.

22. Note that the same may be true—mutatis mutandis—of the situation and petition of the field worker. That he is pleading for a *legal* judgment is a pure assumption.

23. This narrative may be based on a traditional tale with several later avatars in various cultures of Asia and Europe (Gressman 1907; Gunkel 1921, 35–36 = 1987, 54–55).

24. The women are identified as prostitutes. This piece of information serves to explain how in ancient Israelite society two women with babies come to be living together on their own, rather than in their husbands' or fathers' houses. The house they share may have been where they plied their trade (cf. Josh 2:1b). Another consequence of their identification as prostitutes may be that they are "women whose word cannot be trusted. For the harlot is characterized in the ruling stereotype as a woman of smooth and self-serving speech" (Bird 1989, 132). In the words of Lear's fool: "He's mad that trusts in the tameness of a wolf, a horse's health, a boy's love, or a whore's oath."

25. On the social function of *by 'dny,* see Hoftijzer 1970, 427–28.

26. As in the narrative of the field-worker, the opening statement is a verbless clause using a participle.

27. I follow the Masoretic text. The Septuagint lacks the first "in the house" in v. 18 and the parenthetical "your maidservant was asleep" in v. 20. Both could be oral or scribal variants. The omissions make for smoother reading, but the additions may better reflect the speech of the prostitute. The repetition of "in the house" (which also occurs twice in the preceding v. 17) is reminiscent of the field-worker's style. The note that she was asleep, while it might be a scribe's explanatory addition, is entirely in character with a speech in which both the speaker and the narrator wish to make a watertight case.

28. The second woman's speech and its introduction are not present in the Septuagint. Again, the Septuagint is more economical; the Masoretic text uses repetition for greater emphasis.

29. On the simultaneity of the two speeches, expressed through the use of the participle to introduce the second, see Weippert and Weippert 1989, 142–43. This is completely missed by van Wolde, who is puzzled that the second woman would propose going ahead with the division of the baby after the first woman has given it up (1995, 639)!

30. Using the same words as those used by the real mother, and affirming the relationship: "She is his mother" (van Wolde 1995, 639). But van Wolde thinks the king's two commands mean that he changes his mind, not that he uses a deliberate strategy. His "wise" decision is then simply the obvious conclusion to be drawn from the real mother's unanticipated decision to give up her child, and her decision, rather than his, is the focus of the story (van Wolde 1995, 639–41).

31. If anything, Sternberg is inclined to see the first woman as the fraud and the second as a woman of simple honesty. See also now Leibowitz and Leibowitz 1988–89.

32. As Sternberg himself observes elsewhere, "literary judgment sits in a court of conscience" that is not identical with a court of justice (1985, 441).

33. According to Cogan and Tadmor, in both cases "the proceedings follow formal rules of address" (1988, 79).

34. So Schmitt 1972, 41, followed by Jones 1984, 2:430 and Würthwein 1984, 311. See further chapter 6.

35. In this respect, I would compare the whole narrative of 2 Kings 6:24–7:20 with a work such as Shakespeare's *A Winter's Tale,* which begins with an apparently tragic exposition but proceeds into comedy and a happy ending.

36. And—in the present form of the story—his initial protestation to the woman: "If Yahweh cannot save you, how can I?"

37. For the analogies between the two cases, as well as the broader legal context of the episode, see Bellefontaine 1987, 62–63.

38. For the arguments see Budde 1902, 267, and McCarter 1984, 345–46. Hertzberg's and Hoftijzer's attempts to defend the present position of vv. 15–17 must be judged unsuccessful (Hertzberg 1964, 332–33; Hoftijzer 1970, 442–44). In this and the following two cases, once the (fictitious) petitionary narrative has achieved its purpose, it is inevitably exposed as a trick and is, unlike a parable, of no further use. Hence, in their present position vv. 15–17 are vacuous. As part of the initial petition, however, they fit perfectly into the genre as we characterized it at the beginning of this chapter. On the difficult vv. 13–14, see now Caquot 1991.

39. I follow the Syriac, with Joüon (1928, 310–11) and McCarter (1984). This clause nicely parallels the following one. The MT has "and that we may destroy . . . ," incorporating this clause (and a selfish motive) into the clan's speech and thus blurring the contrast between the two social goods here in conflict.

40. Presumably levirate marriage is out of the question, as the woman had sons when her husband died.

The demand that she hand over her son suggests that she has hidden her son somewhere. This, in turn, confirms that the society is operating according to traditional clan justice. There are not yet any "cities of refuge" established by the state where unintentional killers might flee the "avenger of blood" pending an independent inquiry (Num 35:12; Deut 19:1–7; Josh 20:6). Hence, her only recourse beyond the *mišpāḥâ* is the king.

41. But not in Genesis 4 (the story of Cain and Abel), which is often cited in this connection.

42. It seems to me that Camp and Nicol, respectively, exaggerate and underestimate the role of the woman (Camp 1981; Nicol 1982).

43. The word *'am* obviously has a specialized meaning here. The use of the singular "the man" in v. 16 (and "the vindicator of blood" in v. 11) tends to favor the interpretation of *'am* as referring to one particular person. See McCarter (1984, 346), who is followed by T. Lewis (1991, 611).

44. For the "ancestral estate," see T. Lewis 1991.

45. There is an interesting analogue in the Egyptian story of Horus and Seth, preserved in a manuscript of the twelfth century BCE. Here Isis disguises herself as a young woman, is accosted by Seth (who is seeking to disinherit her son, Horus), and proceeds to tell him that she is a widow with one son whom a stranger is now trying to throw out and displace. She concludes by saying she would like Seth to champion the son. Seth asserts the right of the son. Then Isis casts off her disguise and announces his own mouth has condemned him. For translations see Lichtheim 1976, 214–23, especially 217–18, and Simpson 1973, 108–126, especially 115–16. Hagan compares this with 2 Samuel 12:1–4 (1979, 306–7; on 2 Sam 12:1–4 see later).

46. The "looking around" of the Septuagint and Lucian probably render an original *š'h.* The Targum's and Peshitta's "turning, going" may be an interpretation of the masoretic text's *'šh* (construct!)—if it is not a reflex of a Hebrew *pnh.*

47. Could the payment of a talent of silver have originally been the reward for guarding the man? As it stands, it is an alternative *punishment* for losing the man, but it would make better sense as a reward for the alternative *behavior.* The later corresponding sentence

of the king concerns only "life for life" and does not envisage any pecuniary alternative (v. 42b). Material blessing, however, would have been understood to follow from obedience to Yahweh's demands.

48. Literally, "the man of my net." See Stern 1990, 45, who, however, sees this meaning as secondary, the primary meaning being the usual: "the man I had demanded be devoted to me by destruction." But, as Stern demonstrates, there is no reason for thinking that Yahweh had demanded or the king had promised such devotion to destruction (Stern 1990, 44). As with the contract between soldier and prophet, the captive was simply to be kept under guard. The penalty in both cases for letting the captive go was death—extended in the case of the king to the death of his army.

49. The three have been grouped together under the genre "juridical parables" (Simon 1967; followed by Long 1984, 1991). Others have designated 2 Samuel 12:1–4 a "melodrama" (Lasine 1984) or a "fable" in contrast to the "anecdote" of 2 Samuel 14:5–7 (Coats 1981).

50. For the form, compare *yšlm šnym* "he shall compensate twofold" (Exod 22:6, 8). Several Greek witnesses have "sevenfold" here, which fits well with the literary character of this narrative and is adopted by many commentators, including Carlson 1964, Simon 1967 and McCarter 1984. Even though the judgment appears in formal, legal language, a proverbial punishment (cf. Prov 6:30–31) is more fitting in this context than a legal one. The Masoretic text's "fourfold" is probably an accomodation of David's pronouncement to the Torah; for fourfold compensation in the case of someone stealing a sheep for slaughter or sale, see Exodus 21:37. It might also have been influenced by the recognition that eventually David will lose four of his sons. For the intertextual relations and the literary consequences of the reading "sevenfold," see Carlson 1964, 152–57, and of "fourfold" see Ackerman 1990, 49–50.

51. Many commentators read *lô* for *lô'* and translate: "and had compunction about his own." But while this matches the sentiment mentioned in v. 4a, the translation is strained. Besides, the traditional reading prepares the ground much better for the immediately following condemnation.

52. This first pronouncement—*Ḥy-Yhwh ky bn-mwt h'yš h'šh z't*—is not a legal judgment but a moral categorization, which is sometimes as revealing of the speaker as of the person so categorized. The same language appears in David's taunt to Abner and his men for not protecting Saul from a potential killer: "What you have done is not good. *Ḥy-Yhwh ky bny-mwt 'tm*—by the life of Yahweh, you are minions of Death" (1 Sam 26:16). David has no judicial authority to pronounce sentence here but is expressing his personal moral judgment of Abner and his men. Or again, when Saul rages against Jonathan at the news that David had asked permission to be absent from the table in order to attend a family celebration, he orders him to bring David to him, *ky bn-mwt hw'*, "because he is a minion of Death" (1 Sam 20:31). This certainly not a legal sentence for a capital crime! Rather, the phrase expresses an emotional condemnation of someone who, *from the speaker's point of view*, is as undesirable a character as an agent of Death. (That the expression may nevertheless be interpreted by an anxious hearer as "someone who *should* be consigned to Death's domain" is clear from Jonathan's response in v. 32.) Again, in 2 Samuel 19:29 Mephibosheth says, "All my father's family were nothing but agents of Death (*'nšy-mwt*) to my lord, the king; yet you set your servant among those eating at your table." The point is not that Mephibosheth's family were deserving of death, but that they treated David badly, so that Mephibosheth in turn deserved to be treated badly by David—hence his great appreciation of David's kindness. Compare McCarter's (1984) "a fiend of hell" and English "hellcat," "hellion" (though neither of these words was originally related to the word "hell").

53. One student of this passage can write: "The picture of David as royal guardian of right is implied in Nathan's turning to him with the parable" (Roth 1977, 11) without perceiving the dissonance between parable and judicial response.

54. So striking are the discrepancies that Daube is led to reconstruct a speculative prehistory of the story, tracing its origin to political propaganda against Saul (Daube 1982). Simon, however, suggests that the taking of the poor man's ewe was tantamount to taking his life (Simon 1967, 230, n. 2)—thus an analogy to David's taking of Uriah's life.

55. But then it may be argued that it is a parable that David interrupts before its completion. That would certainly heighten the irony of David's response—rushing to a judgment that will be turned against himself. But it also undermines the significance of the alleged parable, which, on this interpretation, is never completed and therefore never becomes an appropriate object of interpretation. Furthermore, to argue that David interrupts Nathan's story entails interpreting Nathan's response also as ad hoc. This works against the point of the larger story, which puts Nathan—and ultimately Yahweh (v. 1)— in complete control.

56. Whether this is an original reading (so McCarter 1984, 294) or a later interpretation is immaterial.

57. Thus Hagan is correct in stating that "Nathan approaches David . . . by appealing to the king as judge, as one who can discern right from wrong" (1979, 307). Whether the melodramatic features of the story, first noted by Hagan (1979, 306), were common in such exercises we cannot know, but their particular appropriateness in this context is well expounded by Lasine (1984).

CHAPTER THREE

This chapter is an expanded and refocused version of Simon Parker, 1994, "Siloam Inscription Memorializes Engineering Achievement" from *Biblical Archaeology Review* 20(4):36–38.

1. See, for example, Wenning and Zenger 1982.

2. For an overview of Israel's underground water systems, see Shiloh 1987.

3. The first thorough study of the inscription was Guthe 1882 (with a photograph of his plaster cast taken in July 1881). The most recent study, with extensive bibliography, is Younger 1994.

4. The etymology and meaning of this word (*zdh*) are still disputed. Puech's helpful analysis of the situation referred to in the inscription does not seem to me to dispose of the meaning "cavity, fissure" or the like; his own proposal ("resonance") is scarcely justified by his proposed etymology (Puech 1974). A relationship with Ugaritic *dd,* as proposed by Del Olmo Lete (1978, 43–44), is quite possible. While *dd* is also without secure etymology or precise denotation, the Ugaritic context favors something like "grotto," which has an obvious semantic relationship to "cavity." Gill's study (1994) lends material support to the meaning "cavity." For other proposals and bibliography, see Hoftijzer and Jongeling 1995, 306.

5. I am grateful to Ivan Kaufman for letting me see his photographs of the inscription.

6. The latest dictionary of ancient Hebrew prefers the translation "manner" for *dbr* here (*DCH,* vol. 2, 406b), while the latest dictionary of Northwest Semitic inscriptions favors "story" (Hoftijzer and Jongeling 1995, 240).

7. Or could this be a case of the "epistolary perfect"—the use of the perfect verb to refer to something that, though in the present for the writer, will be in the past for the reader? But here no verb is strictly necessary: the biblical passages referred to consist of nominal sentences. Hence the use of the perfect insists on something that would not otherwise be expressed.

8. Abells and Arbit have noted that the construction of a wall to raise the water level at the spring so that it would flow along the Siloam Channel would have allowed water also to pass through the karstic system to the rock above the Siloam pool; they have suggested that this would have given the excavators of the tunnel "complete confidence that the project would conclude with the successful meeting of the two work crews" (1995, 6). It seems to me that, in view of the unprecedented length of the proposed tunnel, reasonable hope would be more likely than "complete confidence." Abells and Arbit suppose that such confidence in the successful meeting of the two parties would be necessary because time was of the essence: "the Assyrians were about to attack Jerusalem and had already conquered some fifty cities in Judah and Israel." The latter statement comes from the authors' imagination. There is no evidence anywhere that even hints at the timing of the construction in relation to contemporary events.

9. All of these facts argue against its being "an official inscription," as claimed by Cogan and Tadmor 1988, 221, and, with reservations, by Israel 1984, 85. The official account appears rather to be reflected in the biblical texts reviewed later.

10. But not necessarily of the same project. However, even if 2 Kings 20:20a refers to a project other than the Siloam tunnel, that account is clearly interpreted later by Chronicles and Sirach as referring to the Siloam tunnel. In any case, the contrast drawn later between the palatine perspective and that of the author of the tunnel inscription would presumably hold for any major construction project.

It is not certain what project is referred to in the poetic oracle of Isaiah 22:9–11 ("you [plural] collected the water of the lower pool . . . and made a basin between the two walls for the water of the old pool"), which, in any case, is scarcely in narrative form. (The two lines may be in synonymous parallelism.) Unlike any of the sources discussed here, the oracle attributes the construction to the undefined (plural) addressees (the inhabitants of Jerusalem, its elite . . . ?), and is expressed by a voice critical of the project. For further poetic use of such construction, see Isaiah 51:1b and Janzen 1986 (I owe this reference to Katheryn Pfisterer Darr): Janzen links the language of this poetic line with that of the Siloam inscription.

11. It is true that in the context of the account of the reign of Hezekiah in 2 Kings this reference "may be neutral, a piece of archival information" (Ackroyd 1987, 183), but, in relation to the other source of information that we have in the tunnel inscription, it clearly elevates the role of the king to the exclusion of all other participants.

12. Cf. also ll. 25–26: "And it was I who cut channels for Qarho with Israelite prisoners." See further chapter 4.

13. See the discussion in Van Seters 1983, 292–302, especially 298–99. Contrast the suggestion that such chronicles may have been the source of the tunnel inscription (Levi Della Vida 1968, 162–66). Levi Della Vida has to suppose that the inscription was produced long after the event, and that chronicles were unofficial writings (since he recognizes the unofficial character of the inscription)!

Garbini, however, thinks that Levi Della Vida's hypothesis "gives a fully satisfying explanation of the peculiar structure of the inscription" (*spiega in maniera pienamente soddisfacente la singolare struttura dell'iscrizione*) and further claims, on the basis of the material common to the inscription and the passages from Kings, Chronicles, and Sirach (see later), that "it is not possible to deny their substantial stylistic and literary unity" (*non è possibile negare la loro sostanziale unità stilistica e letteraria*)—explained by their common source in "the chronicles of the kings of Judah" (1969). The little common material which he identifies is primarily lexical. But since the four texts all speak of a similar project, it would be surprising *not* to find some common vocabulary, even if they were all completely independent.

14. As earlier proposed by Noth (1987, 57).

15. Thus Welten (1973, 196) writes of "a welcome supplementation of the other information about the Siloam tunnel."

16. For "bronze," the Greek version reads "iron." "Water" follows the Greek; the Hebrew text has *hrym*, "hills," which may be an error for *hmym*, "the water."

CHAPTER FOUR

1. Most of the royal inscriptions we have refer to wars the king fought, and the Bible suggests the frequency of Israel's and Judah's experience of warfare. The Assyrian annals display the Assyrian army's annual military campaigns and the frequency with which particular regions on Assyria's borders were attacked. Compare the observations on warfare in the classical world in Finley 1985, 67–87.

2. See the bibliography and detailed reconstruction of these events in M. P. Graham, "The Discovery and Reconstruction of the Mesha Inscription" in Dearman 1989, 41–92.

3. Lemaire reports that he is now preparing such an edition (1994a, 32). Meanwhile, for a large, readable photograph of the inscription, see Dussaud 1912, vii.

4. For details, see Andersen 1966, 85–88, and more recently Niccacci 1994. For de Moor, these strokes are sufficient to categorize the inscription as "narrative poetry." On this basis, he structures the text into verses (groups of cola), strophes, and canticles (de Moor 1988, 150–60). This reflects the Kampen School of Theology's view of Northwest Semitic poetry, applied in the same article to the inscriptions of Kilamuwa (166–71; see chapter 5 in this book) and Zakkur (160–65; see chapter 6). But the "poetic" structure here includes "cola" of one, two, three, or four words, and the strophes and canticles sometimes cut across narrative units to no purpose. Rather than trying to force these inscriptions into some poetic schema, it is better to recognize in them a formal, often parallelistic prose, sometimes comparable to formal biblical prose. (In fact, prose and poetry are our categories, not those of the ancient literatures. We would do better to observe and describe the discriminations of the ancient scribes, and the grammatical [syntactic] and semantic [topical] structures of their texts, rather than to impose on those texts complex structures taken from other literatures.)

5. This is largely in accord with the analysis of Smelik 1990 and 1992a, 59–92 (though he would see another major section similar to B in ll. 28–31) and Niccacci 1994 (though he begins D in l. 30). On the specific character of lines 28–31 and their relation to the rest of the inscription, see the discussion later.

6. These often correspond to Andersen's "paragraphs" (1966, 114–16).

7. Because this clause ends with a vertical stroke, Niccacci combines it with the preceding clause—and then has to resort to strained historical explanations to make sense of the two (1994, 236). His syntactic analysis ignores significant syntactic differences among what he alleges are parallel sentences. As he admits, the decision in such cases "depends on the interpretation, not on the syntax" (1994, 239; cf. 241).

8. The reading *hyt*, instead of the older *ryt*, was proposed in Lemaire 1987, 205–207. For his English translation, see Lemaire 1994a, 33.

9. Lemaire relates *grm, grt* to Hebrew *gûr* "lion-cub," seeing here a metaphor for "child," and understands *rḥmt* as "pregnant women." The list would then include male and female adults, male and female children, and pregnant women (Lemaire 1987, 207–8; followed by Niccacci 1994, 229; Margalit 1994, 273).

10. This may refer to plantings similar to those mentioned by Assyrian kings—or-

chards as well as gardens, from the Middle Assyrian as well as the Neo-Assyrian periods. Compare Ecclesiastes 2:5–6, where the Hebrew cognate is used. But Eshel (1993) has recently suggested that the reference here may be to a building similar to the "House of the Forest of Lebanon" in the account of Solomon's building activities (1 Kgs 7:2–6; 10:17, 21; cf. Isa 22:8).

11. As *mšm't* in 1 Samuel 22:14 and 2 Samuel 23:23 (= 1 Chr 11:25) and in the Ugaritic letter CAT 2.72:11. In the present context, the meaning "subject(ed)," as in Isaiah 11:14, would produce a statement of the obvious.

12. Like others, I take the vertical stroke here to be misplaced (as in ll. 3–4 and 16)— or at least to be used differently from elsewhere, that is, to mark a juncture within a sentence. Niccacci takes it to be separating two clauses, so he translates "Now, as for Beth-Baal-Meon, there I brought . . ." and sees this as beginning section D. But nowhere else in the inscription do we find a clause beginning *w* + noun + *w* + prefixing verb, and the topic is completely unrelated to that of D (Niccacci himself admits that "no narrative proper accompanies the mention of Beth-Baal-Meon"). See Niccacci 1994, 231 and 235.

13. The reading *bt[d]wd* has recently been proposed in Puech 1994 and Lemaire 1994a and 1994b. See especially the photographs in 1994a (p. 35). The phrase would have been written as one word, as in the Tel Dan inscription, to be discussed later in this chapter. Margalit restores differently and supplies a reference to the Edomites in the following gap—which is historically and geographically plausible, though without any textual basis (1994, 275–6).

14. As restored in Lemaire 1987, 210. Compare lines 11, 14–16.

15. There has been little serious literary criticism of the inscription, but on the first nine lines, see the analysis in Schweizer 1974, 91–102; on the literary form of the whole, see Smelik 1990, 1992a, 59–92; and on its larger literary character, Müller 1994.

16. This statement even includes Garbini, who questions the value of the Deuteronomistic History at this point. He surmises that the historian has taken the names of Jehoram and Ahaziah of Judah (Jehoram being a son-in-law of Ahab of Israel) and made of them two successors of Ahab (in reverse order). The original sources would have had Jehu following Ahab. This means that Omri could have reigned close to forty years, as suggested by the Mesha inscription. See Garbini 1988, 36–37. His reconstruction assumes that the language of the inscription is to be interpreted literally, that the conquest of the land of Medeba is related to Mesha's "rebellion" against Israel, and that that rebellion took place soon after the death of Ahab (i.e., that 2 Kgs 3:5 contains historically reliable data). If Biran and Naveh's reconstruction is correct (1995), the Tel Dan inscription would attest to the historicity of Jehoram of Israel (see later in this chapter).

17. As we shall see, the actual recovery of territory is at the center of all these stories, which provides additional support for the reading and interpretation *wyšbh*, "he returned it" (as against *wyš[b] bh* "he dwelt in it"). See P. D. Miller 1969. Smelik notes the wordplay: *yšb—yšb* "(Omri) occupied it—(Chemosh) returned it" (1990, 1992a).

18. For the possibility that the expression refers to a person rather than a thing, see Blau 1979–80.

19. Compare the boast of Tiglath-Pileser I that he "conquered their fortified city Murattash within the first third of the day from sunrise" (AKA 58 iii 100; Grayson 1976, 11 [par. 25]). These royal boasts are echoed in the narrative of 1 Samuel 11, which has Saul's army enter the Ammonite camp "in the morning watch" and beat the Ammonites "until the heat of the day" (1 Sam 11:11).

20. The listing of aliens (*grm, grt*) suggests that the town was a major trading center, crowded with many more than the native population. The word here translated

"[slave-girls" (*rḥmt*) is the same as that used by the attendants of Sisera's mother, imagining what Sisera and his soldiers are up to following their defeat of Israelite tribes (Jdg 5:30). (But note Lemaire's interpretation in n. 8 here).

21. Stern claims no such prior commitment was made (1991, 19). This assumes that the perfect verb in the dependent causal clause refers to the same time (and, indeed, the same action) as that of the verb in the preceding main clause. I take such perfect verbs in dependent clauses as having a pluperfect sense, as in biblical Hebrew.

22. Grammatically a *casus pendens* or nominative absolute (or extraposition).

23. See n. 13.

24. The wordplay of ll. 7–9 is repeated here (see n. 17).

25. See further Andersen 1966, 116–18 (extending the initial observations of Segert 1961, 236) and recently Müller 1994, 383–86.

26. As surmised already by Segert (1961, 237). Smelik (1990 and 1992a) now considers ll. 28–31 to be the conclusion of the inscription and terms ll. 31 to the end an appendix.

27. With ll. 28–29 compare 2 Samuel 8:15, which concludes the summary narratives of David's campaigns (see later). For other inscriptions which seem to combine an earlier inscription with supplementary material, compare the Zakkur inscription (see chapter 6) and the Hadad-yith'i inscription from Tell Fekherye (Abou-Assaf, Bordreuil, and Millard 1982, 61–68).

28. In the original circumstances, the divine directions may well have been given in response to oracular inquiries—as frequently in the stories in the books of Samuel.

29. A glance at the maps in Dearman 1989 (esp. p. 382) or Smelik 1992a, 75—even allowing for some uncertainty about the site of Jahaz—will make this evident. Smelik's historical reconstruction of the order of the campaigns is based on strategic considerations.

30. The fragments from Tel Dan have already generated a large bibliography, which it is unnecessary to list here. Some of the commentary on the first find was understandably rendered at least partially obsolete by the discovery and publication of the second and third fragments. Nevertheless, both before and after that publication, strong arguments have been made for quite different interpretations. Unfortunately, scholarship on these three scraps has radiated as much heat as light, with political and personal passions discernible in the language of the participants. It will be desirable in the near future to have a monograph that reviews all the evidence and all the arguments from a less engaged perspective.

31. I accept the claim of the publishers of the fragments that these are from the same inscription. Thompson (1995) and Cryer (1995) have argued that the second and third fragments are not related to the first. To my mind, while their arguments have some merit, they are not altogether persuasive. But see the following note.

32. I put in italics the rendering of the second and third fragments, so that, if it is proved that they belong to a different inscription, the first can be read alone.

33. The reading *ml[k]* is clearly superior to that of the editio princeps. See Puech 1994, 224–25. A. Yardeni has further identified the shaft of the final *n* of the word on fragment A and suggested the reconstruction translated here (Biran and Naveh 1995, 16).

34. This is perhaps the most controversial term, some arguing that it should be translated "temple of (the god) Dod" (e.g. Knauf, de Pury, and Römer 1994).

35. I have followed the careful reading of fragment A by Puech, without adopting his hypothetical reconstructions (Puech 1994) and the treatment of all three fragments in Biran and Naveh 1995, without following all their reconstructions, and with attention to the still valid comments of other publications on the first fragment.

36. "Kings" in this time and place is an inflated title of local tribal and city chiefs.

37. See Parpola and Watanabe 1988, xxvii–xxviii and lv, n. 10 for the arguments.

38. On "prestige" and "interest," compare Liverani 1990. Lemaire and Durand (1984) have argued that Bir-Ga'yah was Shamshi-ilu, the Assyrian governor in Til-Barsip (near Carchemish on the Euphrates), a hypothesis that, despite strong criticism of it by, for example, Fales 1986, Ikeda has attempted to sustain by identifying KTK as an acronym of Kummukh, Til-Barsip and Carchemish (the initial letter of which is identical with that of Kummukh in Aramaic; Ikeda 1983).

39. The usual restoration: *[byth 'd] 'lm* "his house for (ever)": (1) does not seem quite sufficient to fill the space and (2) entails a future reference ("belongs to . . . for ever"). I restore *[byt aby m]'lm* which (1) seems to fill the space better, (2) is stylistically more consistent with the context (which always uses the expression "my father's house," never "his house"), and (3) provides an appropriate antecedent situation for the event and the time described in the following clauses—and so accords with the first stage of the narrative pattern we are tracing. (Mesha's use of *m'lm* "for ages" [l. 10], is a concession to the occupying enemy, rather than a claim of Moabite occupation.)

40. See the gods listed in Sefire IA, ll. 7–14 and the Akkadian version VI 6–26 (Parpola and Watanabe 1988, 13).

41. The narrative in the Sefire treaty is distinctive, cast as the background for a treaty stipulation, and so transposed to a thoroughly theological plane. The relation between inscription and previous oral narration is less clear in this case.

42. For the history of Damascus in this period, see conveniently Pitard 1987, 160–75.

43. Contrast the lengthy narratives in 1 Kings 20 and 22.

44. The conclusion to Jehoash's reign is repeated in 14:15–16, following Jehoash's appearance in a narrative about Amaziah of Judah (14:8–14).

45. Or with the Aramaic narrative from Tel Dan (although we do not know whether the text recovered so far was followed by references to administrative arrangements).

46. Compare also the second narrative: "Omri took possession of the land of Medeba, and he lived in it during his time and half the time of his son . . . but Chemosh returned it in my time" (ll. 7–9).

47. Compare also the second narrative; see previous note. In the inscription from Tel Dan, it is the succession of the liberating king that marks the end of the oppression.

48. This is located after v. 7 in the Lucianic version. Burney argues that this was its original location (Burney 1970, Part 2, 316).

49. It is related thematically (though not in phraseology) to vv. 4b–5 and especially to 14:26–27.

50. Could it have replaced a more traditional court notice of divine favor or intervention on behalf of the oppressed king, more like what we read in Mesha's inscription (ll. 4, 8–9) or the Tal'aym narrative?

51. However, as noted before, there is a further narrative about Jehoash in 14:8–14, after which the notice of the conclusion of his reign is repeated (14:15–16; cf. 13:12–13). All this is presented within the account of the reign of Amaziah of Judah (14:1–20), the initiator of the war recounted in vv. 8–14.

52. Other scholars take v. 25b to be inserted by the composer of vv. 18–19. But it is remarkable that there is nothing negative about v. 25b in itself. It can be read negatively only when preceded by vv. 18–19. It thus seems to me likely that a "prophetic" editor, who wished to take from Jehoash's glory, added vv. 18–19, at once building on the prophetic narrative of vv. 14–17 and subverting the reference to three victories in v. 25b.

53. Briend characterized v. 5 as a "relecture largement postérieure aux faits et même aux premières rédactions des livres des Rois" (1981). Thus guesses at what historical individual is intended are futile. (For such guesses, see the list in Cogan and Tadmor 1988, 143.)

54. Recognized already by Montgomery (1951, 434). According to the wording of this narrative, the oppression continued under Benhadad, while according to that of 13:24–25 the Israelite recovery began under Benhadad. Perhaps Mesha's "half the time of his son" suggests how the two may be compatible.

55. The Hebrew word is ʾābad, here used in a transitive form: "for the king of Aram had finished them off." The cognate appears in line 7 of the Moabite inscription: "Israel had finally disappeared (been finished off) for ever." This language probably has its origin in common royal bombast.

56. David presents the transliterated Hebrew text of the six campaigns in parallel columns that nicely disclose the common material and the variations (1990, 212–13).

57. Less significant variations include the additional mention in some cases of the king of the city and of its subordinate towns and the displacement of some phrases from the standard order.

58. See Grayson 1976, 84 and references there.

59. These and other examples are listed on pp. 212–14 of David 1990.

60. This earlier form may be discerned by reading the present verses in the order 38–39, 36–37, 34–35, 31–32, 29–30 (omitting v. 28 as redactional and v. 33 as a later addition). The only substantive change required would be in the identity of the previous city in the phrases "from (previous city)" and "just as he had done to (previous city)"—reversing what the historian must have done to adapt his source to its new role.

61. See the various suggestions listed in Stoebe 1994, 242.

62. Compare also the claim that, after David's defeat of the Philistines in 2 Samuel 5:20, "they abandoned their idols there, and David and his men carried them off" (v. 21).

63. McCarter notes that this practice is not attested elsewhere (1984, 247). Stoebe observes that it is hard to imagine it being an extract from annals (1994, 247). For a possible parallel in a curse, however, see the inscription of Idrimi (an Akkadian inscription from Late Bronze Alalakh in North Syria) l. 95: if *ebla limdudūšū* may be read as a discrete clause, it will mean "(may the gods) measure him off by line"—that is, have him executed (so Greenstein and Marcus 1976, 66, 68, 94–95). (I owe this reference to Professor Greenstein.)

64. With the LXX and 1 Chronicles 18:4 (*epistēsai, lĕḥaṣṣîb*). The MT has *lĕhāšîb* "to restore," which McCarter would revocalize as *lĕhôṣîb* "to set down" (1984, 243).

65. So now Stoebe 1994, 243, 249–50.

66. Related to the preceding topically, but not literarily (Stoebe 1994, 250).

67. On the redactional connectives of vv. 11 and 12, see Stoebe, 1994, 251.

68. This is a translation of the MT. The word *yād* (v. 3), which I translate "monument," presumably acquires that meaning by the resemblance of the typical stela to the rough outline of a hand ("hand" being the most common and literal meaning of the word) and so may refer to any such monument, whatever its function, and whether uninscribed or bearing an inscription of any genre (see Delcor 1967, 230–34). The word *šēm* (here translated "memorial"), by contrast, acquires that meaning by an extension of its more usual range of meaning: "name, reputation, memory (as in 'his memory lingers on')," and so would seem to imply a monument with an inscription that commemorates (ensures the memory or reputation of) someone. Thus, in Isaiah 56:5 the *yād wāšēm* "monument and memorial," that Yahweh promises the eunuchs moves from the general to the particular. The particular is "an everlasting memorial that cannot be cut off" (v. 5b)—unlike descendants, for which it is a substitute.

69. The first and third of the three consonants of the words are identical and the second (*d/r*) is easily confused at many stages of the evolution of the Hebrew script. For details on the textual problems here, see McCarter 1984, 246.

70. And in the summary of the gifts and booty dedicated to him in the supplementary material following the Aramaean campaign (v. 11).

71. So, for instance McCarter 1984, 253 and such recent translations as NRSV, JPSV, and REB. Stoebe sees it as a redactional connective that may be read as the conclusion of the preceding or the introduction of the following, though he considers the latter more likely (1994, 254).

72. For example, those of Kilamuwa (see chapter 5) and Azatiwada (*KAI* 26 = *TSSI* 3:15), both of which give more space to the king's internal administration of his realm than to his external conquests or building activities.

73. Stoebe also notes that two of the verbs it uses (*hkny* and *kbš*; vv. 1 and 11) are attested almost exclusively in postexilic writings (Stoebe 1994, 242, 245). The judgment that the whole text is relatively late (postmonarchic) is probably sound (246).

74. The first hypothesis, which depreciates the literary character and relations of the two stories in favor of an assumption of their historicity, now usually involves the additional hypothesis that the campaign behind chapter 8 followed the campaign behind chapter 10. See Pitard 1987, 93 and nn. 39 and 40 for further bibliography.

75. Of course, this says nothing about the possible role of chronicles in the Deuteronomistic History, since they are a quite different genre. If the Jerusalem court produced chronicles similar to the Babylonian chronicle series, these would presumably have been a late development. The earliest year mentioned in the surviving Babylonian chronicles is 745. The earliest date of composition of a chronicle must obviously have been somewhat later. (On the Babylonian chronicles, see Grayson 1975, Brinkman 1990, and the collection of French translations with extensive introduction in Glassner 1993.) The direct influence of Babylonian literature on Judah was certainly much later—not before the sixth century.

CHAPTER FIVE

A much abbreviated version of this chapter was published in Simon Parker, 1996, "Appeals for Military Intervention: Stories from Zinjirli and the Bible," *Biblical Archaeologist* 59: 213–24.© American Schools of Oriental Research.

1. On the Assyrians' policy and practice of besieging cities, see Eph'al 1983, 91–95.

2. In the other account (2 Kgs 12:18–19), the invader is Hazael of Damascus. This probably reflects a time when Damascus was the strongest power in the west, and Assyria was unable or unwilling to venture west for such a mission.

3. Akkadian text (RS 17.340) in Nougayrol 1956, 48–50; English translation in Beckman 1996, 30–31.

4. There is now a good treatment of all the Semitic inscriptions from Zinjirli in Tropper 1993. For a plan of the excavated city, see von Luschan 1911, 262; for plans of the palace, see Tafeln 49 and 50; and for a photograph of the gateway, see Tafel 52.

5. The text reads *Y'DY*, the non-Semitic name for the state. For the sake of readability, I have consistently translated this by the Semitic name, Sam'al, the vowels of which are known from Assyrian inscriptions.

6. According to convention, uppercase letters are used for names with unknown vowels.

7. The reading is the only one permitted by the remaining traces of the letters, according to Tropper 1993, 33. The best explanation for a reference to a second parent is that offered by Gibson 1982, 36: Kilamuwa here identifies himself by his mother to distinguish himself from his brother, presumably born of a different mother.

8. Tropper nicely compares the opening of the Akkadian inscription of Kapara of

Guzan: "I am Kapara son of Ḥadiyānu. What my father and my grandfather [   ] did not accomplish, I did accomplish" (1993, 35; the Akkadian verb is *epēšu*). Elsewhere, Tropper compares the use of Phoenician *p'l* here with the common Aramaic *'bd* (1993, 31). It is worth noting, however, that in a comparable passage in a later, Aramaic inscription from Zinjirli, one of Bir-Rākib's, the verb *'ml* is used, arguably with a comparable meaning: "My father's house accomplished *('ml)* more than any" (*KAI* 216; Gibson 1982, 15; Tropper 1993, B1:7–8).

9. *l(h)lḥm*. The *h* is restored from immediately above where it was erroneously inserted into *hlpny(h)m*.

10. The comparative sense of *'l* (in the first sentence), well known in the Akkadian cognate, *eli*, is uncharacteristic of Northwest Semitic but found in the Phoenician of neighboring Karatepe (Azatiwada *KAI* 26:A III 2–4; Gibson 1982, 41–64). See Held 1961, 24 (with some similar Hebrew constructions).

Liverani surmises that in the second sentence the same word in the phrase "hired against" may have another sense, attested in Hebrew (as in Gen 30:28) as well as Akkadian, namely, "at the expense of" (Liverani 1991, 180–81). But this seems inapposite and unnecessary. The hiring is in the first instance "at the expense" of Kilamuwa, even though he ultimately benefits economically from the work of the hired king. The purpose of the hiring is that the Assyrian king might turn "against" the Danunian king.

11. Sperling objects that the word "garment" (*swt*) refers to a royal mantle (since it is mentioned as being worn by a deceased queen in the Batno'am inscription *KAI* 11:1) or indeed to a temple veil (in *KAI* 76 A 4). He proposes that *swt* is here related to an Akkadian word for a type of groats and then interprets the word for "sheep" (*š'*) and Samalian Aramaic *š'* as cognate with Akkadian *še'u* "barley" (Sperling 1988, 333). But the use of a *swt* by a dead queen does not entail that all *swt*s were fit for royalty—a "dress" is worn by poor women as well as queens—and the word *swt* in *KAI* 76 A 4 has no immediate context, so nothing can be said about its particular meaning there. Further, it might be objected that if the price were measured in grain, an indication of quantity would be stated. When the native words make sense, it is unnecessary to resort to Akkadian loanwords.

Hebrew apparently offers a cognate in Genesis 49:11 where *lĕbûšô* is parallel to *sûtōh*, both meaning roughly "his garment." Also in favor of this translation is the economic language of the rest of the inscription, which the present line anticipates, as we shall see.

The meaning of the verbal root of the word *gbr* (usually translated "man" in Hebrew) is "be strong," and slaves are bought especially for their physical strength. My English translation "boy" ("girl") is intended to imply both the youth and the servile role of these traded people. The youth of a *gbr* is certainly in the mind of the author of Job 3:3, which uses the Hebrew cognate in the phrase *hōrâ geber* "a boy has been conceived." It is worth noting that in Ge'ez (Classical Ethiopic) the cognate verb is commonly used for "act, do, work, make, labor," and the like, and the noun *gabr* has developed the specific meaning "slave, servant, bondsman, vassal" (Leslau 1991, 178).

12. A double bar is inscribed here in place of the single bar that separates the other lines of the text.

13. One segment of the population, presumably the earlier non-Semitic stratum, subjected by the Aramaean invaders but now cultivated by Kilamuwa, whose name comes from their language.

14. For this reading and understanding, see now Tropper 1993, 39–41; 1994.

15. Restoration on the basis of parallelism; compare Sperling 1988, 335.

16. In this section of the inscription, the parallel contrasts between the former state

and the latter disallow the other proposed translation, "linen," which is too close to the material of the new state. The counterpart of someone who had never even seen the face of a sheep or an ox is someone who had never even seen a tunic. Thus *ktn* must have a meaning similar to that of Hebrew *ktnt* (a meaning also attested of Official Aramaic *ktn*).

17. Compare the equally hyperbolic claim in David's poetic lament over Saul and Jonathan (there addressing the women of Israel and speaking of Saul): "who clothed you with scarlet and fineries, who set ornaments of gold on your clothes" (2 Sam 1:24).

18. For this understanding of the last sentence, see Zevit 1990.

19. The image seems eminently suitable, so that it is unnecessary to look for other ways of construing the words (for which see O'Connor 1977, 19, 21; Fales 1979:10–15).

20. Text in Piepkorn 1933, 82; translation in Reiner 1985, 25.

21. As in the famine brought on by a siege. See the Assyrian and Babylonian documents presented and discussed in Oppenheim 1955 or, indeed, in conditions of starvation for whatever reason—see Nehemiah 5:2–5. In these cases, however, the children are in effect mortgaged into slavery, with the possibility of being redeemed. In the cuneiform documents, it is also sometimes expressly stated that one purpose of the transaction is to keep the children alive, the new owner having responsibility for feeding them. For people selling themselves into slavery in order to survive during a famine, see now Hurowitz 1994. A Babylonian omen apodosis predicts a natural famine and adds: "There will be a famine in the land. People will sell their children for silver."

22. Could the feeding and survival of the children also be involved, as in the cuneiform documents mentioned in the preceding note?

23. The prices in several of these cases is given not in the common medium of exchange (silver shekels) but in terms of other goods or services (barter).

24. The text is KBo I 11, Rev. ll. 30–32, for which see Güterbock 1938, 124–25 and the more recent translation of Kempinski 1983, 37.

25. Some commentators have found Kilamuwa's statement so unrealistic that they have strained to elicit other meanings from the text; see the references in Tropper 1993, 37. But the statement is at once descriptive of the transaction and revealing of Kilamuwa's viewpoint. Compare the use of the term "hired" by those against whom the transaction is directed in 2 Kings 7:6 (see later in this chapter).

26. The attack is assumed in the word "hired," which entails a job undertaken for pay, pace O'Connor 1977. If the Assyrian king had not attacked the Danunians, Kilamuwa would not have been able to claim that he had "hired" him. Compare the Hebrew uses of the verb *śkr* later in this chapter.

27. Presumably, visiting Assyrian officials would not have been able to read the West Semitic script in the ninth century. The king of Sikan (on the upper Khabur) designated himself "governor" in the Akkadian but was able to call himself "king" in the Aramaic version of the bilingual Tell Fekheriye inscription also (ninth century). The rulers of the Syro-Hittite states at this time could use their own script to express their role with respect to their subjects (for the benefit of the literate members of the court), whatever their role with respect to the Assyrian overlord.

28. This Assyrian expedition probably corresponds to one of Shalmaneser III's campaigns against Que (north of the Gulf of Iskenderun) in the 830s.

29. For a photograph of the statue, see von Luschan 1893, 54.

30. Tropper's edition serves as the basis of the following translation. For a very different reading (with extensive restorations), see Margalit 1994, 303–13.

31. *šḥt 'zh hwt bbyt abwh*. Compare the language describing the first event in the

story of Idrimi: *ina Ḫalab bīt abiya mašiktu ittabši,* "A terrible thing occurred in Ḫalab, my father's house" (ll. 2–3).

32. Tropper (1993) cautiously suggests: "and a cursed fellow(?) stole(?) his throne(?), . . ." Clearly the enemy is the subject of the next verbs.

33. The word for "seventy" is followed by seven dots.

34. Compare Idrimi's departure from Emar (inscription of Idrimi, ll. 13–15). This clause suggests the motif of the departure of the hero with only his essential equipment or personnel, after which he passes through alien territory and eventually assumes the throne. For the motif, see Liverani 1972, and compare the reference to Panamuwa's flight and n. 33 below. At the end of the line Tropper (1993) allows: ". . . master . . . pierced . . . Panamuwa(?)"

35. The singular suffix must refer to a plurality of people—the rest of Panamuwa's "father's house"? Clearly, the subject is again the enemy.

36. Tropper sees the possibility of reading "and Panamuwa . . ." or ". . . [Panamuwa] son of QRL. . . ." In any case, Panamuwa I, not Bir-Rākib's father, seems to be speaking next. Compare the Hadad inscription of Panamuwa I, ll. 24–27 (Tropper 1993, H 24–27).

37. Or "disappeared from the land." The verb *'bdt/w* is feminine singular or masculine plural, according to Tropper (1993), who translates "musste(n) . . . umherirren(?)" For my translation, compare *ḫalqānu,* "we fled," in Idrimi l. 4. Was the subject the family or staff of Panamuwa? The missing word(s) at the beginning of the sentence read(s) *'--tt.*

38. Tropper (1993) (followed by Margalit) restores *šy,* used of an offering to Hadad in line 5 of the inscription dedicated to that deity by Panamuwa I (the son of QRL) and of gifts to Yahweh in Isaiah 18:7; Psalms 68:30; 76:12. Although Tropper claims that there is probably insufficient room for any word longer than *šy,* it is tempting to suggest a cognate of Hebrew *šḥd,* used in the two biblical passages discussed later in precisely the sense required here, and Old Aramaic *šḥd* (Sefire III *[KAI* 224] 28), where, although the immediate context is broken, it also seems to refer to the sending of gifts by the vassal to engage another king to attack the overlord.

39. Tropper (1993) sees *šʿr* as a possible reading and suggests the translations: "drove out" or "the evil."

40. This theology is virtually identical with that found in the Aramaic inscription of Zakkur (early eighth century): "The Lord of the Heavens delivered me and stood by me" (ll. 2–3). In Zakkur's inscription, this corresponds with the oracle he receives from the Lord of the Heavens in the following story (see chapter 6).

41. A comparison of l. 6 with the Kilamuwa inscription ll. 7–8 appears in Liverani 1991, 182–83.

42. In almost the same language, Bir-Rākib will boast in his own memorial inscription of his palace's superiority to those of his rivals: "I took my father's house and made it better than the houses of any of the great kings" (*KAI* 216 [Tropper B1]: 11–14).

43. See the recent review of these lines in Greenfield 1991, 122.

44. Similarly in his own independent memorial inscription, *KAI* 216 (Tropper B1): 4–7.

45. As in the siege of Jericho (Josh 6:1). It seems strained in such contexts to insist that the phrase "go out and in" refers to waging war successfully (van der Lingen 1992). A city under military threat is more concerned with getting in and out (especially for diplomatic communications and food) and disposing of the invader by whatever means than with waging war.

46. In the present context, this alludes to the previous depletion of the treasury by Shishak (Sheshonk), king of Egypt (1 Kgs 14:25–26). This link demonstrates that the

present wording of the story is that of a continuous historical narrative, rather than any isolated source on Asa. The reference to Asa's dedications in 15:15 may be from a later Deuteronomistic author concerned to demonstrate Asa's devotion to Yahweh (although a continuous reading of the present text suggests that Asa's gifts were not significant enough to replace the treasures plundered by Shishak).

47. Similarly Weinfeld 1988, 347 (but using the present tense). I owe this reference to David C. Hopkins. The common translation "Let there be a treaty . . ." founders on the inapplicability of the volitive to the previous two kings ("my father . . . your father") and on the lack of anything in the Hebrew text as we have it to justify in translation the insertion of "as there was" before the reference to the fathers. However, Rudolph 1951, 206, and Würthwein 1977, 188, conjecture that a *kě* "as" has been lost [by haplography] from before the second *bên* "between." The expression here would then be similar to the proposal of Burnaburiash II of Babylon to Amenophis IV of Egypt: *kī abbūni itti aḫāmiš ṭābū nīnu lū ṭābānu* "as our fathers were on good terms with each other, let us be on good terms" (EA 8:11–12).

48. So Würthwein 1977, 189.

49. *BDB* gives "bribe" as the general meaning, and Tadmor and Cogan claim that *šoḥad* is "rooted in legal parlance" and "bears negative connotations" (Tadmor and Cogan 1979, 499, 503, followed by Na'aman 1995). *HAL* distinguishes "present" in two of the passages discussed later, as well as in the two narratives now under review. Recently, Hocherman has argued that the term refers to a gift of appeasement, which may be used positively as well as negatively (1990–91). Compare Weinfeld 1988, 347, with further bibliography on ancient Near Eastern and Greek terms for "gift/bribe."

50. The cognate Aramaic verb appears once in the stipulations of the Aramaic treaty recorded on the Sefire stelae (from around the middle of the eighth century BCE): ". . . and they give presents to any king at all who . . ." (Sefire III 28; the context is lost). Apparently this clause must have forbidden the vassal to engage the assistance of any other king in a venture opposing the overlord's will. Certainly, the envisaged act was viewed negatively in this context, in which the overlord is the speaker.

51. The noun is also used by Jews in Elephantine of gifts given by Egyptians to official investigators—an action in a judicial context, again, clearly condemned; Porten and Yardeni 1986, 56–57 (A 4.2, l. 4).

52. His speech and gift are analogous to the prayers and sacrifices made in a special appeal (as distinct from regular offerings) to the deity. Indeed, they function similarly to those prayers which remind Yahweh of his special, long-standing relationship with the petitioner.

53. Compare the similar use of subject and perfect verb for brief notices of construction in 2 Kings 14:22a; 15:35b; of widespread cultic destruction in 2 Kings 18:4; and of large-scale military operations in 2 Kings 14:7, 25; 18:8.

54. This was the efficient way to conduct a successful siege (see Eph'al 1983, 91–97). But a prolonged siege was a worsening crisis for the defenders. The text certainly does not intend the reader to understand, with Na'aman, that "no real danger threatened [Ahaz's] city" (1995, 42); Ahaz's speech in v. 7b would then make no sense. Also, pace Na'aman, the phrase "besieged Ahaz" (rather than the city) does not imply that his response was more self-serving than that of any other king. Since the king was finally responsible for the policy to which besieging kings took exception, the besieged king was always the chief object of attack. If he were replaced by a ruler whose policies pleased the attackers, there would be no siege. It is precisely such a realignment and replacement of the king that Isaiah 7:6 envisages, even though there it is the city rather than the ruler that is the express object of the verbs.

55. The "Aramaeans" of the first half of the verse (and in some traditions the second half also) is certainly a mistake for "Edomites," the result of the confusion of two very similar Hebrew letters (resh and daleth), aided by the present context (see also chapter 3, n. 69). After this confusion, the name of the king, Rezin, was introduced from the preceding verse. See the recent summary of the arguments in Tadmor and Cogan 1979, 496. This brief account of the Edomite reoccupation of Elath and expulsion of Judeans from that city is (as emended) probably no earlier than the late seventh century, according to Tadmor and Cogan 1979, 496–98.

56. 'āz and bā'ēt hahi' correspond to the common Akkadian expressions ina tarṣi "in the time of (king so-and-so)" and ina ūmēšuma "at that time" used in royal inscriptions and chronicles. All four terms lack a precise chronological reference and serve rather to introduce a new subject pertaining to the general period under review (Tadmor and Cogan 1979, 493–96). In contrast with the 'āz of 2 Kings 16:5, Isaiah 7:1 begins: "In the days of Ahaz, son of Jotham, son of Uzziah, king of Judah. . . ." This, as well as the adoption of the rest of 2 Kings 16:5, accords with the general tendency of the editors of the prophetic books to place prophetic material in the historical framework of the books of Kings (Wildberger 1972, 265, 268–69).

57. Redford thinks it may have been taken from Isaiah 7:1 (1992, 329–30), but see n. 56 and Wildberger 1972.

58. But Ahaz, like Asa, exhibits effective stewardship of the royal treasury—in contrast with Hezekiah, whose rash display of all his treasures to the Babylonian king, Merodach-baladan, in 2 Kings 20:12–19 earns Yahweh's strong condemnation through the prophet Isaiah. (However, the latter passage is probably a post-Deuteronomistic addition, as argued in McKenzie 1991, 107–8.)

59. The Assyrian passages cited by Tadmor and Cogan certainly refer to the same circumstances as the two Hebrew passages: to the sending of gifts by one king to another to induce him to attack a third. But the word ṭātu, used by the Assyrians to refer to such gifts, does not seem inherently to express condemnation, as argued by Tadmor and Cogan (1979, 500, n. 34). The entry for this word in *AHw* (published the same year as Tadmor and Cogan's article) discloses an even wider range of meanings than *šoḥad*. It is not the word ṭātu but the point of view of the author that confers a negative evaluation on the act—no less negative when the word is translated "gifts." Neither word in these circumstances refers to a perversion of justice ("bribe").

60. Naaman's (1995) article argues that both 1 Kings 15:17–22 and 2 Kings 16:5–9 express the Deuteronomist's disapproval of the two kings. However, read apart from their immediate context, in light of the other references in the history to the diplomatic use of temple and palace treasures, and in light of the use of the pertinent vocabulary elsewhere in the Bible and in other Syro-Palestinian literature, the two stories are devoid of criticism of the Judean kings, as argued previously (and as already maintained by Würthwein [1984, 87–89]).

61. But compare the negative judgment of Ahaz's actions in Isaiah 7. Verse 20 threatens that Yahweh will take from beyond the river (Euphrates) a "hired" (śĕkîrâ) razor (glossed as the king of Assyria), which will shave off the hair.

62. Compare Panamuwa's action in the line following the story analyzed previously: 'ḥz.bknp.m[r]' h.mlk.'šr "he grasped the skirt of his lord, the king of Assyria" (l. 11).

63. References to Tiglath-Pileser's inscriptions are given according to their designation and page number in the new edition of Tadmor 1994.

64. For which see Tiglath-Pileser's annals 18:3'–7' and 24:3'–11' (Tadmor 1994, 80–83) and summary inscriptions 4:15'–18' (Tadmor 1994, 140–41) and 9: rev. 9 (Tadmor 1994, 188–89).

65. See the references listed in Tadmor 1994, 292 (s.v. Panammū).

66. And at the same time, in the fullest inscription preserved, of his association with the best kings in Tiglath-Pileser's service and of his superiority to any other king (Tropper 1993, 163:B1).

67. The following account of his cultic reform in vv. 10–16 may also be more positive than has generally been admitted (see Nelson 1986). Na'aman argues contra (1995, 46–48). A more positive assessment of Ahaz's political and religious activities (taken without the Deuteronomistic evaluations) is also suggested in Ackroyd 1987, 181–92.

68. It has been claimed that the story of Ahaz is modeled on the account of Asa's appeal to Benhadad when threatened by Baasha. The author would have known of Ahaz's payment of tribute to Tiglath-Pileser and of the fall of Damascus, and linked these two by the assumption of a causal connection between them, fleshing this out on the model of 1 Kings 15:17–22 (Irvine 1990, 88–89). But it is more likely that the latter is modeled on the former. Ahaz was a contemporary of Panamuwa, so that the account of his appeal to Tiglath-Pileser is historically plausible. The separate mention of his appeal and gift may indeed reflect two different stages in his communications with Assyria (cf. Hezekiah's delivery of tribute to Sennacherib after the latter's withdrawal from Jerusalem and return to Assyria). The historical facts were not conducive to the creation of a coherent story but were juxtaposed in a loose account claiming that the king's actions were effective. The more carefully constructed, literary story about the remoter past—the time of Asa, Baasha and Benhadad—integrates and elaborates the same elements into a nicely finished narrative.

69. Liverani, noting that the Hittites were not a great power in the Iron Age, thinks that the pair, Hittites-Egypt, may reflect a traditional, proverbial saying from the Late Bronze age, when these were the two most powerful states dominating the Levant (1991). However, the use of the plural, "kings," suggests a confederation of smaller states, which would be true of neither the Hittites nor the Egyptians in the Late Bronze age. In the eighth century, however, "kings" would reflect political conditions in Egypt (see Redford, 1992, 335), as well as among the neo-Hittite states of north Syria.

70. Realistic—but perhaps also exaggerated. There is an element of mockery in this presentation of the Aramaeans. They do not wait to confirm their suspicions, but flee, abandoning everything. (Contrast the subsequent caution of the Israelite king in vv. 12–14.)

71. Compare the discussion of this narrative at the end of chapter 4.

72. The verb "hired" again summarizes concisely a transaction that in other contexts might be recounted at length as of interest in itself. The version of the story in Chronicles expands "sent off and hired" to "sent one thousand talents of silver to hire for themselves" (1 Chr 19:6). This is partially reflected in a Qumran fragment of 2 Samuel (McCarter 1984, 268).

73. Verses 4–6 are resumed in abbreviated form in Nehemiah 13:1b–2 in the context of a reading of the law of Moses. For the pertinence of these verses—including the reference to "hiring"—for the context in Nehemiah, see Fishbane 1985, 126–27.

74. And reflects two different redactional levels. The first half, concerning failure to provide the Israelites with food and drink, has plural references to both parties, while the second half concerning Balaam uses the singular to refer to both Moab and Israel. (Nehemiah preserves the distinction in number for Moab, while shifting to the third person to speak of Israel.)

75. Other Balaam traditions have come to light in inscriptions found at Tell Deir 'Alla in Transjordan and have been published in Hoftijzer and van der Kooij 1976.

CHAPTER SIX

1. On siege warfare in ancient Israel and its environment, see de Vaux 1961, 236–38; Hobbs 1989, 177–81; and, as practiced by the eastern empires, especially Assyria, Eph'al 1983.

2. The storm god, Haddu, is normally addressed and spoken of by the title "Lord" (*b'l*), as later Yahweh was also called "Lord" (Hebrew *'Adonay* [literally "my Lord"], Greek *kyrios*).

3. The text is CAT 1.119:26–36. For the reading *[h]m* "if" in line 28, see the report of Pardee's collation in Miller 1988, 141.

4. The actual site of the find was revealed only in Dussaud 1922.

5. If the stela continued down below what has been recovered, then there would be more lines missing both at the bottom of the front and of the left side.

6. For the description and estimates of what is missing, see the editio princeps: Pognon 1907, 156–58. Photographs of the inscription appear on plates 9–10 and hand copies on plates 35–36.

7. For the definition of the dedicatory and the memorial inscription, see M. Miller 1974. Miller already notes that the Zakkur stela combines both genres. The more recently discovered bilingual (Aramaic and Akkadian) inscription from Tell Fekheriya is a dedicatory inscription concluding with curses. But this is normal in the dedicatory inscriptions of Assyrian kings, and this inscription is heavily influenced by Assyrian models.

8. An alternative possible restoration would parallel the following clause: "And who [ever   ]s what I have accomplished."

9. On the use of one military account in different building inscriptions of Sennacherib, see Reade 1975 and Levine 1983, 63.

10. Miller ignores this significant distinction. He writes: "the stela was supposedly dedicated" in response to the Lord of the Heavens's deliverance of Zakkur from the siege. "He dedicated the stela to the gods because of the support they had given him in the past . . ." (M. Miller 1974, 11, 12). But Zakkur dedicated the present stela to *Ilu-Wer*, even though *the Lord of the Heavens* had given him support and delivered him in the past! Dussaud, noting the distinction, imagined that Zakkur chased the allies to Afis, where he then erected the stela, confessing his debt to his own god while dedicating it to the local god (1922).

11. Compare the building section of Mesha's inscription (see chapter 4). Although that is broadly similar to this section of Zakkur's inscription, the sentences are more varied in length and syntax, and there is a minimal narrative in the middle, including a speech.

12. Admittedly, it contains a list of kings, each "with his army." The elements of the list are in apposition to the object of the verb of the first sentence, "sixteen kings," and spell out the composition of the confederacy that King Bir-Hadad has put together.

13. Compare the biblical song of thanksgiving and Greenfield 1969, 174–91.

14. Following the arguments of Greenfield 1969, 178–80, and Tawil 1974, 51–55. However, Zakkur's failure to use a patronymic, the meaning of the root '*nh* in the later Aramaic of Ahiqar and Daniel, and the use of perfect verb forms following the nominal sentence, *'š 'nh 'nh*, still support those who would argue for the translation "I was a poor man."

15. On the restoration, see note 17.

16. For the language of the divine oracle, see Greenfield 1969 and Ross 1970. On the victory oracle in general, see van der Toorn 1987.

17. If the missing verb in A 2–3 is restored *[ḥṣln]y* "(The Lord of the Heavens) delivered me" (so, e.g., Greenfield 1969, 184; Gibson 1975, 8, 13; Lipinski 1975, 22), the three

verbs in the oracle correspond in inverse order to the three of the epigraph. Such a correspondence in a carefully composed text is an argument for the validity of the restoration.

18. In this short narrative, the god's full title is used seven times. Even in successive clauses in which he is the subject, the title is repeated with each verb (except for one verb in l. 3).

19. But Na'aman argues for a slightly earlier date in 804 (1991, 84–86).

20. The major studies of these chapters are Childs 1967; Clements 1980; Gonçalves 1986; Vogt 1986; Dion 1988.

21. OIP 2 33 iii (translation in *ANET* 288a). There are various differences of detail between the two accounts, reflecting the different interests of the two sources.

22. For the first view, see Wildberger 1982, 1374; for the second, see Childs 1967, 97–98; Gonçalves 1986, 478–79; and Dion 1988, 10–11. On the textual relations of the 2 Kings and Isaiah versions and the textual history of the stories, see Konkel 1993. Smelik (1986, 70–93) and Seitz (1991) argued for the priority of the Isaiah setting for both. More remarkably, they treated the two stories as one. Seitz, for example, claimed that "the report of a second embassy to Jerusalem . . . (19:9b–13) is not a repetition signalling a second source, but a literary continuation consistent with the logic of the story"! Seitz's interest in the dating and function of these stories in his reconstruction of the compilation of the book of Isaiah evidently prevents him from seeing the precise duplication of two stories with a common plot: the danger represented by the rabshakeh's speech, the king's appeal to Yahweh or his prophet, Yahweh's response and prediction through the prophet, and the fulfillment of the prediction. Even if with Seitz we were to deny the first story an independent conclusion in the fulfillment of the prediction (but see later), there is no narrative logic compelling a continuation of the story in a second representation of danger, appeal, and response. This is not to say, of course, that it is not now *possible* to read the whole of chapters 18–19 continuously, or even that those who juxtaposed the various stories did not intend them to be read continuously.

23. The two Hebrew versions in the MT are conveniently juxtaposed in Wildberger 1982, 1484–90.

24. Thus the Isaiah version, which lacks most of the historical narrative—Hezekiah's capitulation—still uses the equivalent of v. 13 (Isa 36:1). That v. 13 was not the original beginning of narrative B is suggested by the claim in v. 13 that Sennacherib took all Judah's fortified cities, and the assumption in 19:8 (Isa 37:8) that Libnah, as well as Jerusalem, had not yet been conquered by the Assyrians. Then again, as Seitz has pointed out, v. 13 uses the expression "king Hezekiah," as does 19:1, 5, while vv. 14–16 use three times the term "Hezekiah king of Judah," which never appears in the two following stories (1991, 56).

25. The same spot at which Isaiah is said to have confronted Ahaz (Isa 7:3). The specification of this locale invites a comparison between the two situations. For the larger thematic significance of the relation between the Ahaz and Hezekiah chapters in the book of Isaiah, see Seitz 1991.

26. Verse 22 is a later supplement: it is addressed to a plural audience (changed to the singular in Isaiah to suit its context) and speaks of Hezekiah in the third person. Like 2 Chronicles 29–31, it attributes to Hezekiah a Josianic reform.

27. Würthwein sees the two speeches of the rabshakeh as two separate traditions, the address to the people being the older. The address to the officers would have been originally a quiet person-to-person conversation. Its placement before the other speech entails the following interruption, which serves to combine the two speeches (1984, 415–22).

28. According to Würthwein, the address to the people would have been followed by simply "the people were silent," and the rest of v. 36 would originally have had the three Judean officers as subject, describing their obedience to the king's instructions (1984, 415–22).

29. The text also has him going into Yahweh's temple, but, as Wildberger points out, this must be an intrusion from the second story, which presents Hezekiah as praying to Yahweh in the temple. Here it does not sit well with Hezekiah's message to Isaiah, which calls on Isaiah to call to *his* god (Wildberger 1982, 1389).

30. Wildberger 1982, 1389; Würthwein 1984, 424.

31. Or "will have heard." Compare Joüon and Muraoka 1991, §113*b*.

32. The phrase: "to insult the living God" is probably taken from the second narrative (19:16), the only other place where the phrase occurs (Wildberger 1982, 1389). (Note also the contrast between "insult" *[ḥerep]* here and in 19:6 and "vilified" *[giddĕpû]* in Isaiah's following oracle [v. 6].) Such a phrase in Hezekiah's mouth is less fitting here, where he hopes that "Yahweh, *your* [i.e., Isaiah's] god" will have heard the rabshakeh's words and appeals to Isaiah to pray to "Yahweh, *your* god."

33. Compare the similar development recounted in Jeremiah 37:5. It has been suggested that most of 2 Kings 18–19 was an attempt to influence royal policy in the crisis of 588 (Hardmeier 1990, followed by Albertz 1994).

34. It is possible that vv. 36–37 were originally the conclusion of 18:13–16. There is again some correlation with Assyrian records and hence with historical events. Further, like 18:13, v. 36 speaks of Sennacherib by name, whereas in 18:17–19:9a the enemy is identified only and always as "the king of Assyria." Verses 36–37 would thus have been the source of some of the content of Isaiah's oracle in 19:6–7. In the present form of these chapters, 18:17–19:35 minimizes the significance of Hezekiah's offer and payment of tribute in 18:14–16 and supersedes it with other explanations of Sennacherib's departure in 19:36–37.

35. The root *bṭḥ* ("trust") is used six times in these verses but never of trust in Yahweh.

36. Verse 32a anticipates a later deportation to a desirable land—scarcely a telling argument in this context, reflecting rather the views of those like Jeremiah, who saw surrender and exile as wiser than defiance.

37. Compare the account of Josiah's reaction to the alarming document found in the temple in 22:11–14.

38. See, for example, Wildberger 1982, 1420–22, and Würthwein 1984, 425–32.

39. "For they are not gods, but the work of human hands, wood and stone" is a later comment, interrupting "put their gods in fire and destroyed them" (v. 18).

40. On Hezekiah's Deuteronomistic faith, see Weinfeld 1972, 32–45; Gonçalves 1986, 463–70; and McKenzie 1991, 105–6.

41. See Wildberger 1982, 1436–37.

42. Schweizer and Würthwein are probably correct in seeing vv. 31 and 32b as later additions (which heighten the conflict between king and prophet), resulting in the textual confusion now present in vv. 32b and 33a (Schweizer 1974, 313–15; Würthwein 1984, 314).

43. And, as Würthwein writes, why did he not think of consulting Elisha again (1984, 314)?

44. Assuming that 7:16b was not part of the prophetic reworking, as concluded by Jones and Würthwein, but part of the original story, used by the later prophetic writers as the basis for the prophecy of 7:1. For the composition of prophecies on the basis of later elements in a story, compare 2 Kings 3 (see later) and the previous suggestion concerning 2 Kings 19:36–37. The pairing of high and low prices during and after a period of military oppression appears in the Panamuwa inscription (see chapter 5). On the particular foods of 6:25 and the motifs of high and low food prices generally, see Cogan and Tadmor 1988, 79 and 81, and Greenfield 1991. On the basis of 7:6 and the Kilamuwa and Panamuwa inscriptions, Liverani links the hiring of a great king against an enemy with booty enough to significantly lower prices (Liverani 1991; see chapter 5).

45. So Long 1987, 393–94.

46. For a detailed analysis of the narrative character and function of the mother's appeal to the king, see chapter 2.

47. As is shown by the woman's petition in 6:28–29 and the king's response in v. 30.

48. The fact that nothing further is made of the lepers' hiding of booty for themselves (v. 8) shows that this is not significant for the plot. It is significant for the temporal extension of the action, characterization, and irony.

49. For a story of a successful breakout (prompted by a prophetic oracle) and the rout of the besiegers, see 1 Kings 20:1–21.

50. In the present form of the text, the source of the wrath is delicately left unstated, so that it is possible to read the phrase, as many readers do, as a reference to the God of the present narrator (or the Deuteronomistic historians). One recent statement of the arguments for this reading may be found in Stern 1993, 11–13: negatively, the biblical writers would not acknowledge the effectiveness of another god than Yahweh; positively, Yahweh is punishing the Israelites for attacking land he had given to Moab (Deut 2:9; see Stern 1991, 53) and, disapproving of Jehoram from the start, is further angered by Jehoram's forcing Mesha to kill his innocent son! But the negative argument does not recognize that elsewhere in the Bible the effectiveness of other deities is admitted, either by direct statement or implication (e.g., Gen 6:2, 4; Ps 82:2–4, 6; Jdg 11:24). (To recognize this is not, pace Stern, to admit that the Israelites venerated the deities referred to!) The positive arguments seem to me to be strained. While Moses may report that Yahweh had forbidden him to attack Moab (in Deut 2:9), in the present story Elisha has just announced that Yahweh "has given Moab into your power" (2 Kgs 3:18b). No voice in the story counters this understanding of Yahweh's role. The one literary argument—that v. 27b reflects an orderly return journey rather than a rout—can be countered by reference to 2 Kings 19:36, in which Sennacherib makes a similarly "orderly" journey back to Nineveh after Yahweh's disposal of his threat to Jerusalem.

A reading of the text in its present context that appreciates the ambiguity of the reference (Nelson 1987, 168–70) is certainly admissible. The ambiguity may be resolved by defining the readership. By the time of classical Judaism (and early Christianity), there would have been no question that the reference could be to any god other than the one God. In earlier Israel, however, knowledge of the relations among gods and peoples and of the role of sacrifice in those relations, as well as familiarity with the standard literary structure of appeal and response in the context of danger and deliverance, would have eliminated any thought that Yahweh might have responded to Mesha's sacrifice. For another recent defense of this interpretation, see Burns 1990.

51. At least one scholar equates his view of Israel's psychological reaction with the "great wrath on Israel": Margalit understands *qeṣep* as referring to "psychological breakdown or trauma," "mass hysteria" (1986).

52. Compare Bartlett 1983, 145 (although he includes all of v. 25 in the story of the successful campaign and does not recognize the difference between the account of the military campaign and the prophetic insertion [for which see later]). Compare the analysis of Schmitt 1972, who thinks of a literary process. The criticisms of Timm (1982, 177–79) presuppose a purely literary tradition.

53. Würthwein considers these two verses a later addition (1984, 280–81, 287).

CHAPTER SEVEN

1. Compare further the history of 1 Samuel 17–18 reconstructed on the basis of the texts attested in the Masoretic Text and the Septuagint in Tov 1985.

2. For one survey of the biblical evidence, see Sawyer 1984.

3. For the association of the god Resheph with horned animals, see Cornelius 1994, 112–22 and plates 30–31 (photographs RM 21–40). RM 40 (a Late Bronze amethyst scaraboid) has two caprids: one beside the deity, the other held aloft in the deity's hand.

4. With the possible exception of the Amman Citadel inscription (Ammonite). Its incomplete first line reads: *]lkm.bnh.lk.mb' t.sbbt[*. If the first word is taken to be the last part of the divine name Milcom, the following could be a command from that god ("build yourself entrances around"—comparable to David's command to Shimei: *bnh lk byt byrwšlm* "build yourself a house in Jerusalem" 2 Kgs 2:36). The surviving text does not spell out what kind of building is envisaged.

5. Then again, in a literary topic investigated by Hurowitz—the account of the building of a temple, which is found in genres as diverse as royal inscriptions, hymns, myths, and epics in Mesopotamia, as well as in Ugaritic myth and the Bible (the lengthy accounts of the building of the tabernacle and the temple)—a deity frequently instigates or approves the project (Hurowitz 1992).

6. Compare the conclusion of Cogan in a study of Assyrian historiographic texts: "The choice of a particular actor, the royal or the divine, or their combined appearance, was likely determined by the focus of the composition; prayers and dedicatory texts hailed the action of the gods, annals that of the human agent(s)" (1991, 126).

7. The significance of the author's purpose is well illustrated in two particular contexts. First, the story of Panamuwa's diplomatic success, like all such stories, is told as an achievement of that king without reference to the divine sphere. When his son, for his own rather different pious and political purposes, recounts that initial success in the context of the story of his father's life, he introduces it with a statement concerning the gods' deliverance and support of Panamuwa. In 2 Kings 18–19, the court author of 18:13–15 tells the story of Hezekiah's successful diplomatic offer to an invader. The deity has no role in such a story. The authors of the following two stories ostensibly about the same occasion choose, for their own quite different, didactic purposes, to tell stories of a divine deliverance.

8. On Psalm 82, see Parker 1995c.

Bibliography

Abells, Z., and A. Arbit. 1995. Some New Thoughts on Jerusalem's Ancient Water Systems. *Palestine Exploration Quarterly* 127:2–7.

Abou-Assaf, A., P. Bordreuil, and A. R. Millard. 1982. *La statue de Tell Fekherye et son inscription bilingue assyro-araméeene.* Paris: Editions Recherche sur les Civilisations.

Ackerman, J. S. 1990. Knowing Good and Evil: A Literary Analysis of the Court History in 2 Samuel 9–20 and 1 Kings 1–2. *Journal of Biblical Literature* 109:41–60.

Ackroyd, P. R. 1987. *Studies in the Religious Tradition of the Old Testament.* London: SCM.

Albertz, R. 1994. *A History of Israelite Religion in the Old Testament Period.* 2 vols. Louisville: Westminster/John Knox.

Alter, R. 1981. *The Art of Biblical Narrative.* New York: Basic Books.

Andersen, F. I. 1966. Moabite Syntax. *Orientalia* 35:81–120.

Bar-Efrat, S. 1989. *Narrative Art in the Bible.* Bible and Literature Series 17. Sheffield: Almond.

Barr, J. 1995. The Synchronic, the Diachronic and the Historical: A Triangular Relationship? In de Moor 1995, 1–14.

Bartlett, J. R. 1983. The 'United' Campaign against Moab in 2 Kings 3:4–27. In *Midian, Moab and Edom. The History and Archaeology of Late Bronze and Iron Age Jordan and North-West Arabia,* edited by J.F.A. Sawyer and D.J.A. Clines, 135–45. Journal for the Study of the Old Testament Supplement Series 24. Sheffield: JSOT Press.

Bauman, R. 1986. *Story, Performance, and Event: Contextual Studies of Oral Narrative.* Cambridge: Cambridge University Press.

Beckman, G. 1996. *Hittite Diplomatic Texts.* Writings from the Ancient World. Atlanta: Scholars Press.

Bellefontaine, E. 1987. Customary Law and Chieftainship: Judicial Aspects of 2 Samuel 14.4–21. *Journal for the Study of the Old Testament* 38:47–72.

Ben-Amos, D. 1992. Folklore in the Ancient Near East. In Freedman, 2:818–28.

Ben Zvi, E. 1990. Who Wrote the Speech of Rabshakeh and When? *Journal of Biblical Literature* 109:79–92.

Berlin, A. 1983. *Poetics and Interpretation of Biblical Narrative.* Sheffield: Almond.

Biran, A., and J. Naveh. 1993. An Aramaic Stele Fragment from Tel Dan. *Israel Exploration Journal* 43:81–98.

———. 1995. The Tel Dan Inscription: A New Fragment. *Israel Exploration Journal* 45:1–18.

Bird, P. A. 1989. The Harlot as Heroine: Narrative Art and Social Presupposition in Three Old Testament Texts. *Semeia* 46:119–39.

Blau, J. 1979–80. Short Philological Notes on the Inscription of Mesha‘. *Maarav* 2:143–57.

Bloch, M. 1953. *The Historian's Craft.* New York: Knopf.

Booij, T. 1986. The Yavneh-Yam Ostracon and Hebrew Consecutive Imperfect. *Bibliotheca Orientalis* 43:642–47.

Boyce, R. N. 1988. *The Cry to God in the Old Testament.* Society of Biblical Literature Dissertation Series 103. Atlanta: Scholars Press.

Brettler, M. 1991. Never the Twain Shall Meet? The Ehud Story as History and Literature. *Hebrew Union College Annual* 62:285–304.

Brichto, H. C. 1992. *Toward a Grammar of Biblical Poetics. Tales of the Prophets.* New York and Oxford: Oxford University Press.

Briend, J. 1981. Jéroboam II, sauveur d'Israel. In *Mélanges bibliques et orientaux en l'honneur de M. Henri Cazelles,* edited by A. Caquot and M. Delcor, 41–49. Kevelaer: Butzon and Bercker; Neukirchen-Vluyn: Neukirchener Verlag.

Brinkman, J. A. 1990. The Babylonian Chronicle Revisited. In *Lingering over Words: Studies in Ancient Near Eastern Literature in Honor of William L. Moran,* edited by A. Abusch, J. Huehnergard, and P. Steinkeller, 73–104. Atlanta: Scholars Press.

Broshi, M. and I. Finkelstein. 1992. The Population of Palestine in Iron Age II. *Bulletin of the American Schools of Oriental Research* 287:47–60.

Budde, K. 1902. *Die Bücher Samuel erklärt.* Kurzer Handkommentar zum Alten Testament 8. Tübingen: Mohr.

Burney, C. F. 1970. *The Book of Judges and Notes on the Hebrew Text of the Books of Kings.* The Library of Biblical Studies. New York: Ktav.

Burns, J. B. 1990. Why Did the Besieging Army Withdraw? (II Reg 3,27). *Zeitschrift für die Alttestamentliche Wissenschaft* 102:187–94.

Camp, C. V. 1981. The Wise Woman of 2 Samuel: A Role Model for Women in Early Israel? *Catholic Biblical Quarterly* 43:14–29.

Campbell, A. F. 1989. The Reported Story: Midway Between Oral Performance and Literary Art. In *Semeia* 46:77–85.

Caquot, A. 1991. Un point difficile du discours de la Téqoïte (II Samuel 14,13–15). In Garrone and Israel, 15–30.

Carlson, R. A. 1964. *David, the Chosen King: A Traditio-Historical Approach to the Second Book of Samuel.* Stockholm: Almqvist and Wiksell.

Carr, D. 1993. The Politics of Textual Subversion: A Diachronic Perspective on the Garden of Eden Story. *Journal of Biblical Literature* 112:577–95.

Childs, B. S. 1967. *Isaiah and the Assyrian Crisis.* Studies in Biblical Theology (series 2), 3. Naperville, Ill.: Allenson.

Clements, R. E. 1980. *Isaiah and the Deliverance of Jerusalem.* Journal for the Study of the Old Testament Supplement Series 13. Sheffield: JSOT Press.

Coats, G. W. 1981. Parable, Fable, and Anecdote. Storytelling in the Succession Narrative. *Interpretation* 35:368–82.

Cogan, M. 1991. A Plaidoyer on Behalf of the Royal Scribes. In Cogan and Ephʿal, 121–28.

Cogan, M., and I. Ephʿal, eds. 1991. *Ah, Assyria . . . Studies in History and Ancient Near Eastern Historiography Presented to Hayim Tadmor.* Scripta Hierosolymitana 33. Jerusalem: Magnes.

Cogan, M., and H. Tadmor. 1988. *II Kings.* Anchor Bible 11. New York: Doubleday.

Collins, J. 1995. Literacy and Literacies. *Annual Review of Anthropology* 24:75–93.

Collins, T. 1971. The Kilamuwa Inscription—A Phoenician Poem. *Welt des Orients* 6: 183–88.

Cornelius, I. 1994. *The Iconography of the Canaanite Gods Reshef and Baʿal: Late Bronze and Iron Age 1 Periods (c. 1500–1000 BCE).* Orbis Biblicus et Orientalis 140. Fribourg: University Press; Göttingen: Vandenhoeck & Ruprecht.

Cryer, F. H. 1995. King Hadad. *Scandinavian Journal of the Old Testament* 9:223–35.

Culley, R. C. 1976. *Studies in the Structure of Hebrew Narrative.* Semeia Supplements. Philadelphia: Fortress; Missoula, Mont.: Scholars.

———. 1992. *Themes and Variations: A Study of Action in Biblical Narrative.* Semeia Studies. Atlanta: Scholars.

Damrosch, D. 1987. *The Narrative Covenant. Transformations of Genre in the Growth of Biblical Literature.* Ithaca: Cornell University Press.

Darr, K. P. 1996. No Strength to Deliver: A Contextual Analysis of Hezekiah's Proverb in Isaiah 37.3b. In *New Visions of Isaiah,* ed. R. F. Melugin and M. A. Sweeney, 219–56. Sheffield: Sheffield Academic Press.

Daube, D. 1982. Nathan's Parable. *Novum Testamentum* 24:275–88.

David, R. 1990. Jos 10,28–39, témoin d'une conquête de la Palestine par le sud? *Science et Esprit* 42:209–22.

Davies, G. I. 1991. *Ancient Hebrew Inscriptions: Corpus and Concordance.* Cambridge: Cambridge University Press.

Davies, P. R. 1992. *In Search of Ancient Israel.* Journal for the Study of the Old Testament Supplement Series 110. Sheffield: JSOT.

Dearman, A., ed. 1989. *Studies in the Mesha Inscription and Moab.* Archaeology and Biblical Studies 2. Scholars Press: Atlanta.

Delcor, M. 1967. Two Special Meanings of the Word יד in Biblical Hebrew. *Journal of Semitic Studies* 12:230–240.

Del Olmo Lete, G. 1978. Notes on Ugaritic Semantics IV. *Ugarit-Forschungen* 10:37–46.

Demsky, A. 1990. Writing in Ancient Israel and Early Judaism. Part One: The Biblical Period. In *Mikra,* ed. M. J. Mulder, 2–20. Assen: Van Gorcum; Minneapolis: Fortress.

Dever, W. G. 1990. *Recent Archaeological Discoveries and Biblical Research.* Seattle: University of Washington Press.

Dick, M. B. 1979. The Legal Metaphor in Job 31. *Catholic Biblical Quarterly* 41:37–50.

Dion, P.-E. 1979. Les types épistolaires hébréo-araméens jusqu'au temps de Bar-Kokhbah. *Revue Biblique* 86:544–79.

———. 1988. Sennacherib's Expedition to Palestine. *Bulletin of the Canadian Society of Biblical Studies* 48:3–25.

Dobbs-Allsopp, F. W. 1994. The Genre of the Meṣad Ḥashavyahu Ostracon. *Bulletin of the American Schools of Oriental Research* 295:49–55.

Dussaud, R. 1912. *Les Monuments palestiniens et judaïques.* Paris: Leroux.

———. 1922. La stèle araméenne de Zakir au Musée du Louvre. *Syria* 3:175–76.

Eissfeldt, E. 1965. *The Old Testament: An Introduction.* New York: Harper.

Ephʿal, I. 1983. On Warfare and Military Control in the Ancient Near Eastern Empires: A Research Outline. In Tadmor and Weinfeld, 88–106.

Ephʿal, I., and J. Naveh. 1989. Hazael's Booty Inscriptions. *Israel Exploration Journal* 39:192–200 and plates 24–25.

Eshel, H. 1993. The QRḤH and the Wall of the Ya'aran in the Mesha Stele. *Eretz Israel* 24:31–33.

Fales, F. M. 1979. Kilamuwa and the Foreign Kings. *Welt des Orients* 10:6–22.

———. 1986. Review of Lemaire and Durand 1984. *Revue d'Assyriologie* 80:88–93.

Finley, M. 1985. *Ancient History. Evidence and Models.* New York: Viking.

Fishbane, M. 1985. *Biblical Interpretation in Ancient Israel.* Oxford: Clarendon.

Forsyth, N. 1987. *The Old Enemy: Satan and the Combat Myth.* Princeton, N.J.: Princeton University Press.

Freedman, D. N., ed. 1992. *The Anchor Bible Dictionary,* 5 vols. New York: Doubleday.

Garbini, G. 1969. L'iscrizione di Siloe e gli "Annali dei re di Giuda." *Annali dell'Istituto orientale di Napoli* 19:261–63.

———. 1988. *History and Ideology in Ancient Israel.* New York: Crossroad.

Garrone, D., and F. Israel, eds. 1991. *Storia e tradizioni di Israele. Scritte in onore di J. Alberto Soggin.* Brescia: Paideia.

Gibson, J.C.L. 1975. *Textbook of Syrian Semitic Inscriptions.* Vol. 1, *Aramaic Inscriptions.* Oxford: Clarendon Press.

———. 1982. *Textbook of Syrian Semitic Inscriptions.* Vol. 3, *Phoenician Inscriptions.* Oxford: Clarendon Press.

Gill, D. 1991. Subterranean Waterworks of Biblical Jerusalem: Adaptation of a Karst System. *Science* 254:1467–71.

———. 1994. How They Met. *Biblical Archaeology Review* 20:20–33, 64.

Glassner, J.-J. 1993. *Chroniques Mésopotamiennes.* Paris: Les Belles Lettres.

Gonçalves, F. J. 1986. *L'expédition de Sennachérib en Palestine dans la littérature hébraïque ancienne.* Etudes Bibliques, n.s. 7. Paris: Gabalda.

Grayson, A. K. 1975. *Assyrian and Babylonian Chronicles.* Texts From Cuneiform Sources 5. Locust Valley, N.Y.: Augustin.

———. 1976. *Assyrian Royal Inscriptions. Part 2: Records of the Ancient Near East.* Vol. 2. Wiesbaden: Harrassowitz.

———. 1987. *Assyrian Rulers of the Third and Second Millennia B.C. (to 1115 B.C.). The Royal Inscriptions of Mesopotamia: Assyrian Periods 1.* Toronto: University of Toronto Press.

Greenberg, M. 1983. *Biblical Prose Prayer as a Window to the Popular Religion of Ancient Israel.* Berkeley: University of California Press.

Greenfield, J. C. 1969. The Zakir Inscription and the *Danklied.* In *Proceedings of the Fifth World Congress of Jewish Studies,* 174–91. Jerusalem: World Union of Jewish Studies.

———. 1991. Doves' Dung and the Price of Food: The Topoi of II Kings 6:24–7:2. In Garrone and Israel, 121–26.

Greenstein, E.L., and D. Marcus. 1976. The Akkadian Inscription of Idrimi. *Journal of the Ancient Near Eastern Society of Columbia University* 8:59–96.

Gressman, H. 1907. Das salomonische Urteil. *Deutsche Rundschau* 130:212–28.

Gunkel, H. 1921. *Das Märchen im Alten Testament.* Religionsgeschichtliche Volksbücher 2. Tübingen: Mohr. *The Folktale in the Old Testament.* Sheffield: Almond, 1987.

Gunn, D. M. 1978. *The Story of King David: Genre and Interpretation.* Journal for the Study of the Old Testament Supplement Series 6. Sheffield: JSOT.

Gunn, D. M., and D. N. Fewell. 1993. *Narrative in the Hebrew Bible.* Oxford: Oxford University Press.

Güterbock, H. G. 1938. Die historische Tradition bei Babyloniern und Hethitern. *Zeitschrift für Assyriologie* 44:93–149.

Guthe, H. 1882. Die Siloahinschrift. *Zeitschrift der deutschen morgenländischen Gesellschaft* 36:725–50.

Hagan, H. 1979. Deception as Motif and Theme in 2 Sm 9–20; 1 Kgs 1–2. *Biblica* 60: 301–26.

Halverson, J. 1992. Goody and the Implosion of the Literacy Thesis. *Man* n.s. 27: 301–17.

Hardmeier, C. 1990. *Prophetie im Streit vor dem Untergang Judas.* Beiheft zur Zeitschrift für die alttestamentliche Wissenschaft 187. Berlin: de Gruyter.

Hawkins, J. D. 1982. The Neo-Hittite States in Syria and Anatolia. In *The Cambridge Ancient History,* ed. 2. Vol. 3, Part 1, ed. J. Boardman et al., 372–441. Cambridge: Cambridge University Press.

Hecker, K., and W. Sommerfeld, eds. 1986. *Keilschriftliche Literaturen.* Berlin: Reimer.

Held, M. 1961. A Faithful Lover in an Old Babylonian Dialogue. *Journal of Cuneiform Studies* 15:1–26.

Hertzberg, H. W. 1964. *I and II Samuel.* Philadelphia: Westminster.

Hillers, D. R. 1992. *Lamentations,* ed. 2. The Anchor Bible. New York: Doubleday.

Hobbs, T. R. 1989. *A Time of War: A Study of Warfare in the Old Testament.* Wilmington, Del.: Glazier.

Hocherman, Y. 1990–91. Does the Concept of Bribery Have a Positive Side? *Beth Mikra* 36:220–22 (Hebrew).

Hoftijzer, J. 1970. David and the Tekoite Woman. *Vetus Testamentum* 20:419–44.

———. 1986. A Grammatical Note on the Yavne-Yam Ostracon. In *Tradition and Re-Interpretation in Jewish and Early Christian Literature: Essays in Honour of Jürgen C. H. Lebram,* edited by J. W. van Henten, et al., 1–6. Leiden: Brill.

Hoftijzer, J., and K. Jongeling. 1995. *Dictionary of the North-West Semitic Inscriptions.* Handbuch der Orientalistik, Abt. 1, Bd. 21, 2 vols. Leiden: Brill.

Hoftijzer, J., and G. van der Kooij. 1976. *Aramaic Texts from Deir ʿAlla.* Leiden: Brill.

———. 1991. *The Balaam Text from Deir ʿAlla Revisited.* Leiden: Brill.

Hurowitz, V. A. 1992. *I Have Built You an Exalted House: Temple Building in the Bible in the Light of Mesopotamian and North-West Semitic Writings.* Sheffield: JSOT.

———. 1994. Joseph's Enslavement of the Egyptians (Genesis 47:13–26) in Light of Famine Texts from Mesopotamia. *Revue Biblique* 101:355–62.

Ikeda, Y. 1993. Once Again *KTK* in the Sefire Inscriptions. *Eretz Israel* 24:104*–108*.

Irvine, S. A. 1990. *Isaiah, Ahaz, and the Syro-Ephraimitic Crisis.* Society of Biblical Literature Dissertation Series 123. Atlanta: Scholars Press.

———. 1994. The Southern Border of Syria Reconstructed. *Catholic Biblical Quarterly* 56:21–41.

Israel, F. 1984. Classificazione tipologica delle iscrizioni ebraiche antiche. *Rivista Biblica* 32:85–110.

Jamieson-Drake, D. W. 1991. *Scribes and Schools in Monarchic Judah: A Socio-Archeological Approach.* Social World of Biblical Antiquity 9; Journal for the Study of the Old Testament Supplement Series 109. Sheffield: Almond.

Janzen, J. G. 1986. Rivers in the Desert of Abraham and Sarah and Zion (Isaiah 51:1–3). *Hebrew Annual Review* 10:139–55.

Jones, G. H. 1984. *1 and 2 Kings.* 2 vols. New Century Bible Commentary. Grand Rapids: Eerdmans.

Joüon, P. 1928. Notes Philologiques sur le Text Hébreu de 2 Samuel. *Biblica* 9:302–15.

Joüon, P., and T. Muraoka. 1991. *A Grammar of Biblical Hebrew,* 2 vols. Rome: Pontifical Biblical Institute.

Kalluveettil, P. 1982. *Declaration and Covenant: A Comprehensive Review of Covenant Formulae from the Old Testament and the Ancient Near East.* Analecta Biblica 88. Rome: Biblical Institute Press.

Kempinski, A. 1983. *Syrien und Palästina (Kanaan) in der letzten Phase der Mittelbronze IIb-Zeit (1650–1570 V. Chr.).* Ägypten und Altes Testament 4. Wiesbaden: Harrassowitz.

Knauf, E. A., A. de Pury, and T. Römer. 1994. **BaytDawīd ou *BaytDōd? Biblische Notizen* 72:60–69.

Knoppers, G. N. 1993. *Two Nations Under God: The Deuteronomistic History of Solomon and the Dual Monarchies.* Vol. 1. Harvard Semitic Monographs 52. Atlanta: Scholars Press.

———. 1994. Jehoshaphat's Judiciary and "the Scroll of YHWH's Torah." *Journal of Biblical Literature* 113:59–80.

Konkel, A. H. 1993. The Sources of the Story of Hezekiah in the Book of Isaiah. *Vetus Testamentum* 43:462–82.

Kuyt, A. and J. W. Weselius 1991. The Yavne-Yam Ostracon: An Exercise in Classical Hebrew Prose? *Bibliotheca Orientalis* 48:726–35.

Lasine, S. 1984. Melodrama as Parable: the Story of the Poor Man's Ewe-Lamb and the Unmasking of David's Topsy-Turvy Emotions. *Hebrew Annual Review* 8:101–24.

———. 1991. Jehoram and the Cannibal Mothers (2 Kings 6.24–33): Solomon's Judgment in an Inverted World. *Journal for the Study of the Old Testament* 50:27–53.

Leibowitz, E., and G. Leibowitz. 1989–90. Solomon's Judgment. *Beth Mikra* 35:242–44 (Hebrew).

Lemaire, A. 1987. Notes d'épigraphie nord-ouest sémitique. *Syria* 64:205–16.

———. 1991. La stèle de Mésha et l'histoire de l'ancien Israël. In Garrone and Israel, 143–69.

———. 1992. Review of Jamieson-Drake 1991. *Journal of the American Oriental Society* 112:707–8.

———. 1994a. "House of David" Restored in Moabite Inscription. *Biblical Archaeology Review* 20:30–37.

———. 1994b. La dynastie davidique *(byt dwd)* dans deux inscriptions ouest-sémitiques du IXe s. av. J.-C. *Studi Epigrafici e Linguistici* 11:17–19.

Lemaire, A., and J.-M. Durand. 1984. *Les inscriptions araméennes de Sfiré et l'Assyrie de Shamshi-Ilu.* Geneva-Paris: Librairie Droz.

Leslau, W. 1991. *Comparative Dictionary of Geʿez (Classical Ethiopic).* Wiesbaden: Harrassowitz.

Levenson, J. D. 1978. 1 Samuel 25 as Literature and as History. *Catholic Biblical Quarterly* 40:11–28.

Levi Della Vida, G. 1968. The Shiloaḥ Inscription Reconsidered. In *In Memoriam Paul Kahle,* edited by M. Black and G. Fohrer, 162–66. Beihefte zur Zeitschrift der alttestamentliche Wissenschaft 103. Berlin: Töpelmann.

Levine, L. D. 1983. Preliminary Remarks on the Historical Inscriptions of Sennacherib. In Tadmor and Weinfeld, 58–75.

Levinson, B. M. 1991. The Right Chorale: From the Poetics to the Hermeneutics of the Hebrew Bible. In *"Not in Heaven": Coherence and Complexity in Biblical Narrative,* ed. J. P. Rosenblatt and J. C. Sitterson, 129–53. Bloomington: Indiana University Press.

Lewis, I. M. 1986. *Religion and Context: Cults and Charisma.* Cambridge: Cambridge University Press.

Lewis, T. J. 1991. The Ancestral Estate (נַחֲלָה) in 2 Samuel 14:16. *Journal of Biblical Literature* 110:597–612.

Lichtheim, M. 1973–80. *Ancient Egyptian Literature. A Book of Readings,* 3 vols. Berkeley: University of California Press.

Lindenberger, J. M. 1983. *The Aramaic Proverbs of Ahiqar.* Baltimore: Johns Hopkins University Press.

———. 1985. Ahiqar (Seventh to Sixth Century B.C.). In *The Old Testament Pseudepigrapha,* edited by J. H. Charlesworth. 2:479–507. Garden City, N.Y.: Doubleday.

Lingen, A. van der. 1992. *BWˀ-YṢˀ* ("to Go Out and to Come In") as a Military Term. *Vetus Testamentum* 42:59–66.

Lipiński, E. 1975. *Studies in Aramaic Inscriptions and Onomastics.* Orientalia Lovanensia Analecta 1. Leuven/Louvain: Leuven University Press.

Liverani, M. 1972. Partire sul carro, per il deserto. *Annali del Istituto orientali di Napoli* 32 (n.s. 22):403–15.

———. 1974. L'histoire de Joas. *Vetus Testamentum* 24:438–53.

———. 1990. *Prestige and Interest: International Relations in the Near East ca. 1600–1100* B.C. History of the Ancient Near East Studies 1. Padua: Sargon.

———. 1991. Kilamuwa 7–8 e II Re 7. In Garrone and Israel, 177–83.

Long, B. 1984. *1 Kings with an Introduction to Historical Literature.* The Forms of Old Testament Literature 9. Grand Rapids; Eerdmans.

———. 1987. Framing Repetitions in Biblical Historiography. *Journal of Biblical Literature* 106:385–99.

———. 1991. *2 Kings.* The Forms of Old Testament Literature 10. Grand Rapids: Eerdmans.

Luschan, F. von. 1893. Fünf Bildwerke aus Gerdschin. In *Ausgrabungen in Sendschirli 1,* 44–54. Mittheilungen aus den orientalischen Sammlungen der königlichen Museen zu Berlin 11. Berlin: Spemann.

———. 1911. Bildwerke und Inschriften. In *Ausgrabungen in Sendschirli 4,* 325–80. Mittheilungen aus den orientalischen Sammlungen der königlichen Museen zu Berlin 14. Berlin: Reimer.

Lyons, J. 1977. *Semantics,* 2 vols. Cambridge: Cambridge University Press.

Margalit, B. 1986. Why King Mesha Sacrificed His Oldest Son. *Biblical Archaeology Review* 12/6:62–63.

———. 1994. Studies in NWSemitic Inscriptions. *Ugarit-Forschungen* 26:271–315.

Mazar, A. 1990. *Archaeology of the Land of the Bible 10,000–586 B.C.E.* New York: Doubleday.

McCarter, P. K. 1984. *II Samuel: A New Translation with Introduction, Notes and Commentary.* Anchor Bible 9. New York: Doubleday.

McCarthy, D. J. 1973. 2 Kings 13,4–6. *Biblica* 54:409–10.

McKenzie, S. L. 1991. *The Trouble with Kings. The Composition of the Book of Kings in the Deuteronomistic History.* Supplements to Vetus Testamentum 42. Leiden: Brill.

———. 1992. Deuteronomistic History. In Freedman, 2:160–68.

Meier, S. A. 1991. The King as Warrior in Samuel-Kings. *Hebrew Annual Review* 13:63–76.

———. 1992. *Speaking of Speaking: Marking Direct Discourse in the Hebrew Bible.* Vetus Testamentum Supplement 46. Leiden: Brill.

Millard, A. R. 1978. Epigraphic Notes, Aramaic and Hebrew. *Palestine Exploration Quarterly* 110:23–26.

———. 1985. An Assessment of the Evidence for Writing in Ancient Israel. In *Biblical Archaeology Today. Proceedings of the International Congress on Biblical Archaeology, Jerusalem, April 1984,* 301–12. Jerusalem: Israel Exploration Society.

———. 1990. The Homeland of Zakkur. *Semitica* 39:47–52.

Miller, J. H. 1990. Narrative. In *Critical Terms for Literary Study,* ed. F. Lentricchia and T. McLaughlin, 66–79. Chicago: University of Chicago Press.

Miller, M. 1974. The Moabite Stone as a Memorial Stela. *Palestine Exploration Quarterly* 106:9–18.

Miller, P. D. 1969. A Note on the Meša' Inscription. *Orientalia* 38:461–64.

———. 1988. Prayer and Sacrifice in Ugarit and Israel. In *Text and Context. Old Testament and Semitic Studies for F. C. Fensham,* ed. W. Classen, 139–55. Sheffield: JSOT.

Montgomery, J. A. 1951. *A Critical and Exegetical Commentary on the Books of Kings,* ed. H. S. Gehman. International Critical Commentary. Edinburgh: T & T Clark.

Moor, J. C. de, ed. 1995. *Synchronic or Diachronic? A Debate on Method in Old Testament Exegesis.* Oudtestamentische Studiën 34. Leiden: Brill.

———. 1988. Narrative Poetry in Canaan. *Ugarit-Forschungen* 20:149–71.

Müller, H.-P. 1994. König Mesha' von Moab und der Gott der Geschichte. *Ugarit-Forschungen* 26:373–95.

Na'aman, N. 1991. Forced Participation in Alliances in the Course of the Assyrian Campaigns to the West. In Cogan and Eph'al, 80–98.

———. 1995. The Deuteronomist and Voluntary Servitude to Foreign Powers. *Journal for the Study of the Old Testament* 65:37–53.

Naveh, J. 1960. A Hebrew Letter from the Seventh Century B.C. *Israel Exploration Journal* 10:129–39.

———. 1968. A Palaeographic Note on the Distribution of the Hebrew Script. *Harvard Theological Review* 61:68–74.

———. 1982. *Early History of the Alphabet. An Introduction to West Semitic Epigraphy and Palaeography.* Jerusalem: Magnes Press; Leiden: Brill.

Nelson, R. D. 1986. The Altar of Ahaz: A Revisionist View. *Hebrew Annual Review* 10:267–76.

———. 1987. *First and Second Kings.* Interpretation. Atlanta: John Knox.

Niccacci, A. 1994. The Stele of Mesha and the Bible: Verbal System and Narrativity. *Orientalia* 63:226–48.

Nicol, G. G. 1982. The Wisdom of Joab and the Wise Woman of Tekoa. *Studia Theologica* 36:97–104.

Niditch, S. 1996. *Oral World and Written Word. Ancient Israelite Literature.* Louisville: Westminster/John Knox.

Noth, M. 1987. *The Chronicler's History.* Translated by H. G. M. Williamson. Journal for the Study of the Old Testament Supplement Series 50. Sheffield: JSOT.

Nougayrol, J. 1956. *Le Palais Royale d'Ugarit IV: Textes Accadiens des Archives Sud.* Mission de Ras Shamra 9. Paris: Imprimerie Nationale.

O'Connor, M. 1977. The Rhetoric of the Kilamuwa Inscription. *Bulletin of the American Schools of Oriental Research* 226:15–30.

Oppenheim, A. L. 1955. "Siege-Documents" from Nippur. *Iraq* 17:69–89.

Pardee, D. 1978. The Judicial Plea from Meṣad Ḥashavyahu (Yavneh-Yam): A New Philological Study. *Maarav* 1/1:33–66.

———. 1982. *Handbook of Ancient Hebrew Letters.* Society of Biblical Literature Sources for Biblical Study 15. Chico, Calif.: Scholars Press.

Parker, S. B. 1989. *The Pre-Biblical Narrative Tradition: Essays on the Ugaritic Poems* Keret and Aqhat. Society of Biblical Literature Resources for Biblical Study 24. Atlanta: Scholars Press.

———. 1994. Siloam Inscription Memorializes Engineering Achievement. *Biblical Archaeology Review* 20:36–38.

———. 1995a. Council סוד. In van der Toorn, Becking, and van der Hoorst, 391–98.

———. 1995b. Sons of (the) God(s) בני עליון/אלים/אלים/(ה)אלהים. In van der Toorn, Becking, and van der Hoorst, 1499–1510.

————. 1995c. The Beginning of the Reign of God: Psalm 82 as Myth and Liturgy. *Revue Biblique* 102:532–59.

————. 1996. Appeals for Military Intervention: Stories from Zinjirli and the Bible. *Biblical Archaeologist* 59:213–24.

Parpola, S., and K. Watanabe, 1988. *Neo-Assyrian Treaties and Loyalty Oaths.* State Archives of Assyria, vol. 2. Helsinki: Helsinki University Press.

Piepkorn, A. C. 1933. *Historical Prism Inscriptions of Ashurbanipal.* Assyriological Studies 5. Chicago: University of Chicago Press.

Pitard, W. T. 1987. *Ancient Damascus: A Historical Study of the Syrian City-State from Earliest Times until its Fall to the Assyrians in 732* B.C.E. Winona Lake, Ind.: Eisenbrauns, 1987.

Pognon, H. 1907. *Inscriptions de la Syrie, de la Mésopotamie et de la Région de Mossoul.* Paris: Imprimerie Nationale.

Polanyi, L. 1982. Literary Complexity and Everyday Storytelling. In *Spoken and Written Languages: Exploring Orality and Literacy,* ed. D. Tannen, 155–70. Advances in Discourse Processes 9. Norwood, N.J.: Ablex.

Porten, B., and A. Yardeni. 1986. *Textbook of Aramaic Documents from Ancient Egypt:* Vol. 1, *Letters.* Jerusalem: Bezalel Porten.

————. 1993. *Textbook of Aramaic Documents from Ancient Egypt:* Vol. 3, *Literature, Accounts, Lists.* Jerusalem: The Hebrew University of Jerusalem, Department of the History of the Jewish People.

Prince, G. 1987. *A Dictionary of Narratology.* Lincoln: University of Nebraska Press.

Puech, E. 1974. L'Inscription du Tunnel de Siloé. *Revue Biblique* 81:196–214.

————. 1994. La stèle araméenne de Dan: Bar Hadad II et la coalition des Omrides et de la maison de David. *Revue Biblique* 101:215–41.

Reade, J. 1975. Sources for Sennacherib: The Prisms. *Journal of Cuneiform Studies* 27:189–96.

Redford, D. B. 1992. *Egypt, Canaan, and Israel in Ancient Times.* Princeton: Princeton University Press.

Reiner, E. 1985. *Your Thwarts in Pieces, Your Mooring Rope Cut: Poetry from Babylonia and Assyria.* Ann Arbor: University of Michigan.

Renz, J. 1995. *Die Althebräischen Inschriften. Teil I. Text und Kommentar.* Handbuch der althebräischen Epigraphik (3 vols.), Vol. 1. Darmstadt: Wissenschaftliche Buchgesellschaft.

Rogerson, J. 1995. Synchrony and Diachrony in the Work of De Wette and Its Importance for Today. In de Moor, 145–58.

Ross, J. F. 1970. Prophecy in Hamath, Israel and Mari. *Harvard Theological Review* 63:1–28.

Roth, W. 1977. You Are the Man! Structural Interaction in 2 Samuel 10–12. *Semeia* 8:1–13.

Rudolph, W. 1951. Zum Text der Königsbücher. *Zeitschrift für die alttestamentliche Wissenschaft* 63:201–15.

Sawyer, J.F.A. 1984. Biblical Alternatives to Monotheism. *Theology* 87:172–80.

Schmitt, H.-C. 1972. *Elisa. Traditionsgeschichtliche Untersuchungen zur vorklassischen nordisraelitischen Prophetie.* Gütersloh: Gütersloher Verlagshaus.

Schweizer, H. 1974. *Elischa in den Kriegen.* Studien zum Alten und Neuen Testament 37. München: Kösel.

Segert, S. 1961. Die Sprache der Moabitischen Königsinschrift. *Archiv Orientální* 29:197–267.

Seitz, C. R. 1991. *Zion's Final Destiny: The Development of the Book of Isaiah: A Reassessment of Isaiah 36–39.* Minneapolis: Fortress.

Shiloh, Y. 1980. The Population of Iron Age Palestine in the Light of a Sample Analysis of Urban Plans, Areas, and Population Density. *Bulletin of the American Schools of Oriental Research* 239:25–35.

———. 1986. A Group of Hebrew Bullae from the City of David. *Israel Exploration Journal* 36:16–38.

———. 1987. Underground Water Systems in Eretz-Israel in the Iron Age. In *Archaeology and Biblical Interpretation. Essays in Memory of D. Glenn Rose,* edited by L. G. Perdue, L. E. Toombs, and G. L. Johnson, 203–44. Atlanta: John Knox.

Shiloh, Y., and D. Tarler. 1986. Bullae from the City of David: A Hoard of Seal Impressions from the Israelite period. *Biblical Archaeologist* 49:196–209.

Simon, U. 1967. The Poor Man's Ewe-Lamb. An Example of a Juridical Parable. *Biblica* 48:207–42.

Simpson, W. K., ed. 1973. *The Literature of Ancient Egypt. An Anthology of Stories, Instructions, and Poetry,* ed. 2. New Haven: Yale University Press.

Smelik, K.A.D. 1986. Distortion of Old Testament Prophecy. The Purpose of Isaiah xxxvi and xxxvii. In *Crises and Perspectives,* 70–93. Oudtestamentische Studiën 24. Leiden: Brill.

———. 1990. The Literary Structure of King Mesha's Inscription. *Journal for the Study of the Old Testament* 46:21–30.

———. 1992a. *Converting the Past. Studies in Ancient Israelite and Moabite Historiography.* Oudtestamentische Studiën 28. Leiden: Brill.

———. 1992b. The Literary Structure of the Yavneh-Yam Ostracon. *Israel Exploration Journal* 42:55–61.

Sperling, S. D. 1988. KAI 24 Re-examined. *Ugarit-Forschungen* 20:323–37.

Stager, L. E. 1985. The Archaeology of the Family in Ancient Israel. *Bulletin of the American Schools of Oriental Research* 260:1–35.

Stern, P. D. 1990. The *ḥerem* in 1 Kgs 20,42 as an Exegetical Problem. *Biblica* 71:43–47.

———. 1991. *The Biblical ḤEREM: A Window on Israel's Religious Experience.* Brown Judaic Studies 211. Atlanta: Scholars Press.

———. 1993. Of Kings and Moabites: History and Theology in 2 Kings 3 and the Mesha Inscription. *Hebrew Union College Annual* 64:1–14.

Sternberg, M. 1985. *The Poetics of Biblical Narrative. Ideological Literature and the Drama of Reading.* Bloomington: Indiana University Press.

Stoebe, H. J. 1994. *Das zweite Buch Samuelis.* Kommentar zum Alten Testament 8/2. Gütersloh: Gütersloher Verlagshaus.

Tadmor, H. 1983. Autobiographical Apology in the Royal Assyrian Literature. In Tadmor and Weinfeld, 36–57.

———. 1994. *The Inscriptions of Tiglath-Pileser III King of Assyria. Critical Edition, with Introduction, Translations and Commentary.* Jerusalem: Israel Academy of Sciences.

Tadmor, H., and M. Cogan. 1979. Ahaz and Tiglath-Pileser in the Book of Kings: Historiographic Considerations. *Biblica* 60:491–508.

Tadmor, H., and M. Weinfeld, eds. 1983. *History, Historiography and Interpretation: Studies in Biblical and Cuneiform Literatures.* Jerusalem: Magnes.

Tawil, H. 1974. Some Literary Elements in the Opening Sections of the Hadad, Zakir, and the Nerab II Inscriptions in the Light of East and West Semitic Royal Inscriptions. *Orientalia* 43:40–65.

Thompson, T. L. 1992. *Early History of the Israelite People from the Written and Archaeological Sources.* Leiden: Brill.

———. 1995. Dissonance and Disconnections: Notes on the *bytdwd* and *hmlk.hdd* Fragments from Tel Dan. *Scandinavian Journal of the Old Testament* 9:236–40.

Timm, S. 1982. *Die Dynastie Omri: Quellen und Untersuchungen zur Geschichte Israels im 9. Jahrhundert vor Christus.* Forschungen zur Religion und Literatur des Alten und Neuen Testaments 124. Göttingen: Vandenhoeck & Ruprecht.

van der Toorn, K. 1987. L'oracle de victoire comme expression prophétique au proche-orient ancien. *Revue Biblique* 94:63–97.

van der Toorn, K., B. Becking, and P. W. van der Hoorst, eds. 1995. *Dictionary of Deities and Demons in the Bible.* Leiden: Brill.

Tov, E. 1985. The Composition of 1 Samuel 16–18 in the Light of the Septuagint Version. In *Empirical Models for Biblical Criticism,* ed. J. H. Tigay, 97–130. Philadelphia: University of Pennsylvania Press.

———. 1992. *Textual Criticism of the Hebrew Bible.* Minneapolis: Fortress: Assen: Van Gorcum.

Tropper, J. 1993. *Die Inschriften von Zincirli: Neue Edition und vergleichende Grammatik des phönizischen, sam'alischen und aramäischen Textkorpus.* Abhandlungen zur Literatur Alt-Syrien-Palästinas 6. Münster: UGARIT-Verlag.

———. 1994. "Sie Knurrten wie Hunde" Psalm 59,16, Kilamuwa:10 und die Semantik der Wurzel *lṇn. Zeitschrift für die alttestamentliche Wissenschaft* 106:87–95.

Van Seters, J. 1983. *In Search of History: Historiography in the Ancient World and the Origins of Biblical History.* New Haven: Yale University Press.

———. 1990. Joshua's Campaign of Canaan and Near Eastern Historiography. *Scandinavian Journal of the Old Testament* 2:1–12.

de Vaux, R. 1961. *Ancient Israel.* New York: McGraw Hill.

Vogt, E. 1986. *Der Aufstand Hiskias und die Belagerung Jerusalems 701 v. Chr.* Analecta Biblica 106. Rome: Pontifical Biblical Institute.

Warner, S. 1980. The Alphabet: An Innovation and Its Diffusion. *Vetus Testamentum* 30:81–90.

Weinfeld, M. 1972. *Deuteronomy and the Deuteronomic School.* Oxford: Oxford University Press.

———. 1988. Initiation of Political Friendship in Ebla and Its Later Developments. In *Wirtschaft und Gesellschaft von Ebla,* edited by H. Waetzoldt and H. Hauptmann, 345–48. Heidelberger Studien zum Alten Orient 2. Heidelberg: Heidelberger Orientverlag.

Weippert, H., and M. Weippert. 1989. Zwei Frauen vor dem Königsgericht: Einzelfragen der Erzählung vom "Salomonischen Urteil." In *Door Het Oog van de Profeten: Exegetische studies aangeboden aan prof. dr. C. van Leeuwen,* edited by B. Becking, J. van Dorp, and A. van der Kooij, 133–60. The Hague: CIP Gegevens Koninklijke Bibliotheek.

Welten, P. 1973. *Geschichte und Geschichtsdarstellung in den Chronikbüchern.* Wissenschaftliche Monographien zum Alten und Neuen Testament 42. Neukirchen: Neukirchener Verlag.

Wenning, R. 1989. Mesad Hasavyahu: Ein Stutzpunkt des Jojakim? In *Vom Sinai zum Horeb: Stationen alttestamentlicher Glaubensgeschichte,* edited by F.-L. Hossfeld, 169–96. Würzburg: Echter.

Wenning, R., and E. Zenger. 1982. Die verschiedenen Systeme des Wassernutzung im südlichen Jerusalem und die Bezugnahme darauf in biblischen Texten. *Ugarit-Forschungen* 14:279–94.

Westbrook, R. 1988. *Studies in Biblical and Cuneiform Law.* Cahiers de la Revue Biblique 26. Paris: Gabalda.

Whitt, W. 1995. The Story of the Semitic Alphabet. In *Civilizations of the Ancient Near East,* edited by J. M. Sasson, vol. 2, 2379–97. New York: Scribner's.

Wildberger, H. 1972. *Jesaja I*. Biblischer Kommentar: Altes Testament 10/1. Neukirchen-Vluyn: Neukirchener Verlag.

———. 1982. *Jesaja III*. Biblischer Kommentar: Altes Testament 10/3. Neukirchen-Vluyn: Neukirchener Verlag.

van Wolde, E. 1995. Who Guides Whom? Embeddedness and Perspective in Biblical Hebrew and in 1 Kings 3:16–28. *Journal of Biblical Literature* 114:623–42.

Würthwein, E. 1977. *Das Erste Buch der Könige: Kapitel 1–16*. Das Alte Testament Deutsch 11,1. Göttingen: Vandenhoeck und Ruprecht.

———. 1984. *Die Bücher der Könige: 1. Könige 17–2. Könige 25*. Das Alte Testament Deutsch 11, 2. Göttingen: Vandenhoeck und Ruprecht.

Young, I. 1990. The Language of the Judicial Plea from Mesad Hashavyahu. *Palestine Exploration Quarterly* 122:56–58.

Younger, K. L. 1994. The Siloam Tunnel Inscription: An Integrated Reading. *Ugarit-Forschungen* 26:543–56.

Zevit, Z. 1990. Phoenician *nbš/npš* and Its Hebrew Semantic Equivalents. *Maarav* 5–6 (Segert Festschrift): 337–44.

Index of Ancient Sources

General Index